Memoir and Letters of Francis W. Newman

Giberne Sieveking

Table of Contents

Table of Contents

Memoir and Letters of Francis W. Newman

Giberne Sieveking

MEMOIR AND LETTERS OF FRANCIS W. NEWMAN

[Illustration: FROM A DAGUERREOTYPE OF 1851. PHOTO BY JOHN DAVIES, WESTON–SUPER–MARE Frontispiece]

MEMOIR AND LETTERS OF FRANCIS W. NEWMAN

BY I. GIBERNE SIEVEKING

outos ge axios estin epainesthai ostis an tois hetairois os teleion ti on protithae to eu neoterizein taen ton pollon katastasin

THIS BOOK IS DEDICATED TO MY MOTHER

TO THE READER WHO UNDERSTANDS

MY DEAR READER,

Rightly understood, the two points of view, as regards Religion, of the brothers, Cardinal Newman and Francis Newman, which most separated them, would, together, have approached the realization of a great conception.

For the Cardinal, Authority was the *sine qua non* without which there could be no real faith. Authority was the pilot, without whose steering he could not feel secure in his personal ship. But with Authority at the helm, his fears dispersed, his doubts removed.

> "I was not ever thus.....
> I loved to choose and see my path, but now
> Lead Thou me on!"

Over Francis Newman, dogma and the authority of the Church had no sway. He dimly discerned a religion which should move forward with men's advance in knowledge. He imagined an unformalized inward revelation which should reveal new truths to those who passionately desired Truth above all things. And when all is said, the union of Authority given in the past, with the very real mental development which makes for spiritual progress in the present, is not antagonistic to a wise, strong breadth of view in the conception of a perfect Church.

But in both points of view, carried to extremes, there are grave perils to the man who thinks. And I find it impossible to avoid saying here that Francis Newman did not realize this risk when he refused to "ask for the old paths," and determined to "see and choose his path" alone and unaided. We know what the endeavour to found a new church in Syria ended in. We know how, later, he wrote, held back by no reverence for revealed religion, no reverence for other men's belief in it. Many of his writings therefore are painful reading. Though from very early boyhood he had been really a keen seeker after true religion, an earnest student of the Holy Scriptures, and a deep thinker, yet, very soon after he had reached young manhood, it began to be realized by all who knew him that he was very evidently breaking away from all definite dogmatic faith. He was bent, so to speak, on inventing a new religion for himself.

Gradually every year made the spiritual breach wider between him and those who held the Christian Faith. Soon he did not hesitate to say out, in very unguarded language, what he really thought of doctrines which he knew were precious to them. Sometimes to−day, indeed, in reading his books, one comes across some statement in letter, article, or lecture flung out almost venomously; and one steps back mentally as if a spiritual hiss had whipped the air from some inimical sentence which had suddenly lifted its heretical head from amongst an otherwise quiet group of words.

At the end of life it is said that he showed signs of some return to the early faith of his boyhood. That he said, just before his death, to Rev. Temperley Grey, who was visiting him in his last illness, "I feel Paul is less and less to me; and Christ is more and more."

And those who knew that side of him which was splendid in its untiring effort for the betterment of mankind—for the righting of wrongs to women, and others unable to achieve it for themselves—cannot but hope that the faith of earlier days was his once more, before he passed into the silence that lies—as far as we are concerned in this world—at the back of Death.

I remember being told once, that of Stanley it was said by someone who knew him well, that she had always felt that "he believed more than he knew he did."

And when one thinks how Francis Newman looked up in faith—even though it was an absolutely undogmatic, formless faith—to a God who watched over mankind, one may hope that he too "believed more than he knew he did."

This life is only a short chapter in our existence. Personality is in its essence immortal, though not unchanging in its presentment. Some of us have many "phases of faith" even in this short existence. Some of us, like St. Paul, only two. The first, fiery in its denunciations, and persecutions and uncompromising attitude towards all who differed from him as regards the Faith which afterwards, "when the scales had fallen from his eyes," he was to champion. The second, just as splendid in its enthusiasm for the doctrine he had formerly abused. Just as passionate in righting the wrongs of the people, as once in his first phase of faith he had been in enforcing persecution and injustice upon them. By now, Newman may have gained *his* second sight. Whatever was the shortsightedness of Francis Newman's spiritual focus, there can be no manner of doubt that *he* was an earnest seeker after Truth, though his methods of search were sorely to be regretted, in so far as doctrinal theory was concerned, as in his judgments on his brother's career.

According to his lights he lived his life. It was a life spent always in untiring, unselfish effort for the good of his fellows. He was always in the forefront of Social Reform, of social high principle and justice. He was, at any rate, one with St. Paul—that champion of Christian Socialism —in his attitude towards that larger half of mankind whose wrongs need righting. He, too, practically said by his life, "Who is weak, and *I* am not weak? Who is afflicted, and I *burn* not?" to avenge the injustice.

To–day, if more of Francis Newman's social views were voiced again, England might take a glad step forward. For, undoubtedly, he *had* a message to deliver. And, equally undoubtedly, he delivered it to his generation.

This message of Social Reform sounded in men's ears fifty years ago.

In his memoir it sounds again to–day.

My very hearty thanks are due to the following persons who have most kindly helped me in this "Memoir," by lending me letters and photographs; by writing reminiscences, and giving information, etc.: Sir John Kennaway, Bart., Sir Alfred Wills, Sir Edward Fry, Mr. William de Morgan, Father Bacchus, Mr. Talfourd Ely, Mr. Winterbotham, the present Rector of Worton, Mr. Norris Mathews, Mr. George Hare Leonard, Mr. George Pearson, Miss Humphreys, Miss Nicholson, Mrs. Heather (*nee* Wilson), Miss Bruce, Miss Toulmin Smith, Miss Gertrude Martineau, Miss Elizabeth Pearson, Mrs. Georgina Bainsmith, sculptor, Rev. Thomas Smith, Mrs. Kingsley Tarpey, Dr. Makalua, and many others.

I. GIBERNE SIEVEKING. 1 EXMOUTH PLACE, HASTINGS.

MEMOIR AND LETTERS OF FRANCIS W. NEWMAN

CHAPTER I. HIS ANCESTORS

Of all the influences which have most to do in the making of an individual, heredity is perhaps the greatest. It is the crucible in which the gold and dross of many generations of his ancestors are melted down and remixed in the man, who is, indeed, "a part of all" from whom he claims descent.

There is no more engrossing study than to trace back through many a century of ancestors, the various—often conflicting—elements which go to make up the character of someone whose life (without the clue given by the history of his forbears) is often a strange contradiction. Unable to understand some disability which spoils an otherwise fine personality, one looks back and there is the explanation. One's finger rests on the *raison d'etre* of this disability. Long since it had its birth, its inauguration, in the squeeze, so to speak, into that strange crucible, of the taint, the essence, of some ancestor's moral lapses, or of the effect of his moral, mental, or physical ill–health.

Dr. Maudsley says very definitely that the faults, the disabilities, of men and women of to–day, are sometimes an undesirable inheritance. "Mental derangement in one generation is sometimes the cause of an innate deficiency, or absence of the moral sense in the succeeding generation."

I remember once hearing a London doctor strongly emphasize the need for every family to keep a careful, conscientious family record book, which from generation to generation should act as a *vade mecum* —showing what failings must be fought at all costs, and what connections avoided, if we would not perpetuate disease. Such a thing, if done universally, might check many national evils in our midst to–day.

But even with no definite aim of this kind, the study of a long chain of ancestors of some great man cannot fail to be of special interest. And those of the subject of this memoir contain among their number many honourable names—names of those who have done real and unforgettable service to their country.

    * * * * *

Francis Newman's father, John Newman, is said to have belonged to a family of small landed proprietors in Cambridgeshire, who originally came from Holland—the name having been formerly spelt "Newmann." Thus it will be seen, as I shall shortly show, that Francis Newman had Dutch blood in his veins, both on his father's and mother's side.

[Illustration: JOHN NEWMAN FATHER OF CARDINAL NEWMAN AND FRANCIS NEWMAN FROM AN OLD PORTRAIT. BY KIND PERMISSION OF MR. J. R. MOZLEY]

John Newman was the only son of John Newman of Lombard Street, London, and of Elizabeth Good, his wife. The arms granted the family on 15th Feb., 1663–4, were *Or, fers dancettee between 3 hearts gules*. John Newman, the father of Francis Newman, was partner in the banking house of Ramsbottom, Newman and Co. He married Jemima Fourdrinier, 29th Oct., 1799, at St. Mary's, Lambeth. [Footnote: She died at Littlemore, Oxon, at the age of sixty–two.] In the portrait of him, which is shown in this memoir, there is a strong resemblance to his son Francis.

By this marriage there were seven children. John Henry (the future Cardinal), was the eldest. He was born 21st Feb., 1801. Charles Robert was the second son; and Francis William, the third son, was born 27th June, 1805. Harriette Elizabeth was the eldest daughter, Jemima Charlotte the second, and Mary Sophia, who was born in 1809, only lived to the age of nineteen.

Francis Newman's ancestry, on his mother's side, is proved to have reached back as far as 1575; of this one can be reasonably certain. It was then, that Henri Fourdrinier was born at Caen, in Normandy. He was made Admiral of France in later life, and crested Viscount. ARMS: *per bend argent and sable, two anchors, the upper one reversed, counterchanged.* His son was also Henri Fourdrinier. Indeed, the name "Henri" seemed like some rare jewel which was bequeathed from father to son in never–failing regularity, for there was always a "Henri" among the Fourdriniers from 1575 until 1766.

It was during the lifetime of this Henri Fourdrinier, the son of Admiral Fourdrinier, that the family fled from France to Groningen, in Holland. In all probability this flitting took place during those endless civil wars which disturbed France at that time. Possibly at the time when the heavy taxes imposed on the people made it almost impossible to live. The "Fronde" was ravaging the country too, in 1648, and for four years later. Of course it is possible that he did not leave France until 1685, when the Revocation of the Edict of Nantes took place. But at whatever date he actually went, his reasons for going were certainly no small ones. For more than a hundred years the Huguenots—and the Fourdriniers were noted Huguenots—had found France more and more an impossible country to live in. Persecutions, massacres, torturings pursued them relentlessly. Thousands of French Huguenots emigrated to England, Holland, and Germany. And great was the loss which their emigration caused to France. For they were the most intelligent and hardworking part of the French population, so that when Louis XIV drove them away, he found out, only too surely, the truth of the old proverb, that "Curses come home to roost." Trade slowly but surely forsook France. The emigrants taught their arts and manufactures to the countries where they had taken refuge; and gradually trade guided its ships in their direction, and changed their course from France to Holland and Germany.

The next entry [Footnote: I quote from a copy I had made from *Miscellanea Genealogica et Heraldica*, N.S. III, 385.—*Pedigree of Fourdrinier and Grolleau*, by Rev. Dr. Lee, Vicar of All Saints, Lambeth.] is dated from Groningen, and concerns the birth of Paul Fourdrinier, 20th Dec., 1698. Now in the *Dict. Nat. Biography* there occurs the name of Peter Fourdrinier, of whom no mention at all is made in the *Miscellanea Genealogica et Heraldica*, amongst the record of the other Fourdriniers. It is therefore not very clear to what branch of the family he belonged. But as far as I can make out, he and Paul Fourdrinier seem to have come to England about 1720. Certainly, in October, 1721, the latter's marriage with Susanna Grolleau took place, as far as one can discover, in or near Wandsworth. Susanna Grolleau died in 1766, and was buried at Wandsworth. Here, I think, a few words with regard to the Grolleau family seem to be called for.

Louis Grolleau, early in the seventeenth century, lived at Caen; and later emigrated to Groningen. To me, everything seems to point to the fact that the Fourdriniers and Grolleaus were in some way connected, either in friendship or relationship. First, we find them resident at Caen: later, at Groningen; and then again, later on still, members of both families marry at Wandsworth, and there both Paul Fourdrinier's wife and her sister, who married the son of a Captain Lloyd, are buried.

This Peter Fourdrinier mentioned by the *Dict. Nat. Biography* seems to have been pupil to Bernard Picart, at Amsterdam, for six years. By profession he was an engraver of portraits and book illustrations. I believe there are portraits extant engraved by him of Cardinal Wolsey and Bishop Tonstall, amongst others. There is certainly an engraving of his called *The Four Ages of Man*, after Laucret.

Some authorities believe him to have been identical with the Pierre Fourdrinier who married, in 1689, Marthe Theroude. But if this was the case, then he was not the Peter Fourdrinier who accompanied Paul to England in 1720. Other authorities, again, attribute the engravings I have just mentioned as having been the work of Paul Fourdrinier. At any rate, it is certain that Paul Fourdrinier belonged to the parish of St. Martin's–in–the–Fields. He died in February, 1758, and was buried at Wandsworth.

His son Henry—by now the English spelling of the name is adopted—was born February, 1730. He married Jemima White, and died in 1799. Apparently now for the first time the interest in the town of Wandsworth ceased, for the records show that both Henry and his wife were buried in St. Mary Woolnoth. And now we come to the direct ancestors of Francis Newman, for Henry Fourdrinier and Jemima White, his wife, were the parents of Jemima, who married at St. Mary's, Lambeth, in 1799, John Newman of the firm of Ramsbottom, Newman &Co., and gave birth in 1801 to John Henry, the future Cardinal, and in 1805 to the subject of this memoir, Francis William.

* * * * *

In *Civil Architecture*, by Chambers, it is mentioned that the plates were engraved by "old Rooker, old Fourdrinier, and others," thus seeming to imply that there was more than one Fourdrinier then in England.

Perhaps the most interesting of all the Fourdrinier family was the Henry Fourdrinier, the eldest brother to the mother of Francis Newman. He was born in 1766 at Burston Hall, Staffordshire, and lived until 1854. His father was a paper–maker, and both he and his brother Sealey (born 1747, and married Harriett, daughter of James Pownall, of Wilmslow) gave up their time almost entirely to the invention of paper machinery. This invention was finished in 1807, [Footnote: *Dict. Nat. Biog.* Vol. XX.] and then misfortune fell upon them: the misfortune that so often descends like the "black bat night" upon those who have spent all their money, thought, and labour on the effort to launch their self–designed ship upon the uncertain sea of trade.

The Fourdrinier brothers had spent L60,000 upon this venture, and the immediate result of the finished invention was bankruptcy to the unfortunate inventors. Then, in 1814, the Emperor Alexander of Russia promised to pay them L700 per annum during the space of ten years if he could use two of their paper–making machines. Of this sum they saw not a penny.

In 1840, Parliament voted the sum of L7000 to the Fourdriniers as a tardy recognition of the great service they had rendered their adopted country by their invention. The descendant of these gifted men showed no special taste for invention along the lines taken by his ancestors, it is true; but his brilliant intellect, no doubt, owed many of its qualities to their inventive force and power. Where they made paper and spent their whole energies in inventing machines for making it quicker, Francis Newman wrote on it—used it as a medium for spreading far and wide his own splendid aims and purposes for the betterment of existing social conditions. Before all things, Newman was a Social Reformer. There was no possible doubt that, as far as that question went, he left his country further forward on the road to real progress as regarded conditions of life for her citizens, and higher, broader ideas of her duty to other nations. As far as all these questions went he did not live in vain, for to–day we are learning the wisdom of his views for justice for the oppressed and for "the cause that needs assistance."

He was essentially one of those rare men who *prefer* to be on the weaker side, and whose sword is ever ready for its defence and championship.

CHAPTER II. THE TWO BROTHERS—SCHOOL AND COLLEGE DAYS

Francis William Newman was born at 17 Southampton Street, Bloomsbury Square, on 27th June, 1805. His father was a London banker. Rev. T. Mozley, in his *Reminiscences of Oriel*, says he was partner in the firm of "Ramsbottom, Newman, Ramsbottom &Co., 72 Lombard Street, which appears in the lists of London bankers from 1807 to 1816 inclusive." He tells us that the family of "Newman" (or, as it was originally spelt, "Newmann") was of Dutch extraction. The father of Francis Newman had great schemes for making England "independent of foreign timber by planking all our waste lands."

In 1800 John Newman married Jemima Fourdrinier, and in the year 1801 John Henry, the future Cardinal, was born. The latter and the subject of our memoir were in effect the two sheaves before whom all the rest bowed down. There were four other children: Charles Robert, Harriette Elizabeth, Jemima Charlotte, and Mary Sophia.

[Illustration: SEALE'S COFFEE HOUSE, OXFORD (NOW DEMOLISHED) Done from an old drawing in the year when Francis Newman and John Henry Newman stayed there with Blanco White.]

John Henry and Francis went to a school at Ealing (of which Dr. Nicholas was head–master), then, as Mr. Mozley says, considered the best preparatory school in the country. There were three hundred boys there at that time, but none were so brilliant or showed so much talent as the two Newmans. One after the other they rose to the top of the school. Frank was captain in 1821. There was some talk of removing John Henry after he had spent some years there, but he himself begged to be allowed to remain a little longer. Miss Anne Mozley, in her *Life and Correspondence of John Henry Newman*, quotes Dr. Nicholas as having said, "No boy had run through the school from bottom to top as rapidly as John Newman." He was eight and a half years at Ealing; yet during the whole of that time, it is reported that his school–fellows declared they had hardly ever seen him play in any game, though at that time games did not occupy the prominent place in the curriculum of schools that now they do in our day.

It was not until his last half–year that one of the greatest spiritual influences of his life began. It was one of those seemingly curious chances which sometimes change a man's, or a woman's, whole outlook; and beginning, as it seems at the time, quite casually, quite unconsciously, lead not only the one chiefly concerned, but others, far afield into absolutely new environments.

Quite, as it seems, by chance, the destiny of a lifetime approaches through the conventional door of everyday life—steals up, lays the hand that none can resist on the handle of some door which opens of itself into a new, a wider world. Before one is aware of it, perhaps, one's feet have crossed the threshold into the Land of the New Outlook, and "old things are passed away."

In August, 1816, John Henry Newman found himself at school, in a sense alone, because his special personal friends there had left, and thus he began to be thrown more and more under the influence of the Rev. Walter Mayer (of Pembroke College, Oxford), who was one of the classical masters. Long religious talks with him had a great effect upon his mind, and he himself traces much of his spiritual development to Mr. Mayer's point of view in religion. He was what is known as a "high Calvinist." When school was over for John Henry and Francis Newman, Mr. Mayer's influence was not lost, for both the brothers wrote to him, and stayed with him, when some time later he became curate to the Rev. William Wilson at Worton.

When his brother left school and went straight to Trinity College, Oxford (though only fifteen years of age), Frank remained on at Ealing for a time; and then, when he was seventeen, went up to Oxford to join him, and be with him through the Long Vacations in preparation for entering Worcester College in 1822. [Footnote: They lodged first at

Scale's Coffee House in 1821, then at Palmer's, in Merton Lane, in 1822. Both now are pulled down.] In Anne Mozley's volume there occur several entries regarding this time from J. H. Newman's letters. For instance, on 25th Sept., "Expecting to see Frank. I am in fact expecting to see you all. I shall require you to fill him full of all of you, that when he comes I may squeeze and wring him out as some sponge."

It is necessary, before touching further on the college life of the two famous brothers, to remember that early in life there was a strong spiritual antagonism between them as regarded their points of view— religious, social, political, etc. And this notwithstanding the fact that a very real affection for each other existed in both, which made the inevitable disputes in no sense unfriendly bouts, but only the exercise of two keen wits of very different calibre.

[Illustration: WORCESTER COLLEGE, OXFORD VIEW OF COLLEGE BUILDINGS FROM THE GARDENS]

[Illustration: WORCESTER COLLEGE, OXFORD FRONT QUADRANGLE]

Both had been trained in a home of strict Calvinism. Both had eminently religious tendencies. Both, when the time came for judging for themselves, threw aside the grim tenets which they had been taught as children to believe, and struck into absolutely different paths.

There is a very pathetic incident in their home life, which occurred just before Frank Newman went to college, which reveals to the thoughtful reader a world of information as to what was the attitude of thought in that household.

I quote from J. H. Newman's diary:—

"Sept. 30, 1821. Sunday. After dinner to–day I was suddenly called downstairs to give an opinion whether I thought it a sin to write a letter on Sunday. I found dear F——had refused to copy one. A scene ensued more painful than any I have experienced." And adds, "I have been sadly deficient in ... patience, and filial obedience."

I quote this chiefly to show that at sixteen Francis Newman [Footnote: In later years Francis Newman declared that he had been "converted" in 1816, and again confirmed in religious conviction in 1819, from the influence of the writings of Dr. Doddridge.] was certainly under the Calvinistic influence still, and that he was very dogged in upholding its rules and restrictions. During the last months of the year 1822, the latter read with his brother at Oxford, and from time to time, in his letters home, J. H. Newman mentions him [Footnote: *Letters and Correspondence of J. H. Newman*, by Anne Mozley.] as working and reading in preparation for entering Worcester College.

"Frank ... seems to have much improved.... I am convinced that he knows much of Greek as a language, in fact is a much better Greek scholar than I.... Again, he is a much better mathematician than I am. I mean, he reads more mathematically, as Aristotle would say."

It is necessary here to mention a great blow which fell on the Newman family soon after John Henry Newman had gone to college. His father's bank failed. There was no bankruptcy, and everyone was paid in full, but still it naturally proved a time of great family trial; for though his father took the Alton brewery and tried to make his way in this new line, yet it was not a successful venture. Happily, by this time, J. H. Newman was not only able to maintain himself, but also to help his people. Rev. T. Mozley mentions that in 1823 Newman had been elected to a Fellowship at Oriel, adding that "it was always a comfort to him that he had been able to give his father" (who did not live many years after the bankruptcy), "this good news at a time of great sorrow and embarrassment."

In 1826 Francis Newman took first–class honours in classics and mathematics, and gained a Fellowship in Balliol College. The college authorities described his as one of the best "Double Firsts" ever known. As, however, he felt conscientiously unable to sign the Thirty–nine Articles, he was obliged to resign his Fellowship, and could not take his M.A. degree.

Many a man must have felt in his inmost self that a bona fide signing to *all* of the Articles was a task beyond his mental reach. There are points in numbers 8, 17, 22, 25, for instance, which are difficult indeed to reconcile with the highest ideal of the Christian religion. One looks at the reprinted introduction (1562) which prefaces them, and one sees that *it* was traceable to that irreligious old sensualist, the father of Queen Elizabeth. One sees that it dated back to the time when the Church in this country began to be more especially "by *Law* established," instead of "by Christ established," as was the case in early ages of its formation. One sees, too, that part of the reasons for this preface being

13

set forth was very evidently the reiteration of the kingly assertion that "We are Supreme Governor of the Church of England," although the ostensible reason was because of the "curious and unhappy differences" which seemed, in His Majesty's opinion, to show the wisdom of decisive adjudication with respect to those "fond things vainly invented," for which some of his subjects had so great an affection.

Francis Newman by the time he had reached the age of twenty–five, however, had been finding out, more and more, that he could not receive most of the Church dogmas. While his brother and he had been practically re–adapting to their needs and growing personal convictions the Calvinistic religion (some writers, I am aware, consider that to have been more Puritan than Calvinistic), given them by their mother in their childhood days, John Henry Newman had drawn ever closer to the authority of the Church, while Francis found himself seceding more and more from her, and more and more drifting into undogmatic religion. It will be remembered that there had been originally an idea that he should take Holy Orders. This, however, very soon during his college life he found to be impracticable of attainment, owing to his own pronounced and undogmatic views.

At that time, Cardinal Newman has said, earnest religious feeling among the undergraduates was decidedly rare. Only one in every five could be called religious–minded. So that the influence of these two young men, whose very evident purpose was to attain some measure of spiritual truth, was the more remarkable and powerful among their fellow students.

It was J. H. Newman, indeed, on one occasion who, on remonstrating with those in authority, that the undergraduates should make their communions at certain stated intervals because of the fact that he himself had seen some of them get intoxicated at the college "breakfasts" on the *very* day after the service—was met by the remark that even if such a thing *did* happen, they would rather not know of it!

Not far from Oxford there is a little village called Worton (or W_a_rton, as I see in old papers it used to be spelt), or rather there are two villages—Over Worton and Nether Worton, or Upper Worton and Lower Worton. They lie between Banbury and Woodstock, near Oxford. Mr. Bateman, in his *Life of Bishop Wilson* (1860), says "their united population, consisting of farmers and agricultural labourers, does not exceed two hundred." From one village to the other is a distance of about three–quarters of a mile, or perhaps a little less by the field path. Mr. Bateman says that before Bishop Wilson came, "the church was much neglected, as a sporting curate used to race through the services so as to get through in as little time as possible."

Mr. Wilson revolutionized all this. He was accustomed to preach straight to "his people." He seems, indeed, to have preached too "straight" for some, for after some sermon he had given in an adjoining parish, a lady who had "sat under him" said to her vicar, *Pray* do not let Mr. Wilson preach here again. He alarms me so."

I am indebted to the Rev. W. H. Langhorne, present Rector of Worton, for the following information about the place. He tells me that the church is of the thirteenth or fourteenth century; Early decorated, but so altered by Derick in 1844 "as almost to destroy its identity." The chalice in Over Worton Church has the date 1574 upon it. The rectory is about one hundred years old. The low building attached to it on the left (in the photograph) was added in 1823. The parish of the two Wortons has for years been a family living in the possession of the Wilsons, so an old friend, a relation of Bishop Wilson, tells me. It was at Worton Church that John Newman preached his first sermon, 23rd June, 1825.

Rev. Walter Mayers went as curate, in 1823, to Rev. William Wilson, and took charge of Worton parish. In the following year he met—and later married—my aunt Sarah Giberne. She and her sister had been staying with Rev. and Mrs. William Wilson, and it was there that Mayers first made her acquaintance. Mr. Mayers asked Frank Newman, during the Long Vacation, to come and help him in teaching the pupils who came to read with him at Worton. Newman was then nineteen. He had been four years longer at the Ealing School, under the tuition of Walter Mayers, than his brother, who had gone to Oxford, according to the notion prevalent at that time, at about the age of fifteen or sixteen. Francis Newman says, consequently, "I knew him (Mayers) much better than did my brother.... He allured me to his new curacy, three miles from Deddington, Oxon, to help him in mathematics with his pupils; first 1822, and again in 1823, after his marriage."

It was in connection with this marriage of Mr. Mayers to Sarah Giberne that the two families of Newman and Giberne first became acquainted, and that friendship began which lasted throughout their lives.

Sarah Giberne was the daughter of Mark Giberne, who, in partnership with Mr. George Stainforth, was court wine merchant in 1750. He came of an old French family, descended from the noble Jean de Giberne, Sieur de Gibertene, in the sixteenth century. The family owned two castles in the country of the Cevennes, which were destroyed by the Camisards. In the seventeenth century some of the family came over and settled in England, and it was from this branch of it that Gabriel de Giberne, secretary to Sir Horace Mann, was descended, and from his son Mark—Sarah Giberne—who married Rev. Walter Mayers.

I shall now give extracts from the diary of Mrs. Benjamin Pearson (*nee* Charlotte Elizabeth Giberne), to which I have access through the kindness of my cousin, Mr. George Pearson. It was in the spring of 1823 that Sarah and Charlotte Giberne spent a week with John Whitmore and his wife, Maria, the daughter of their father's partner, Mr. Stainforth (of the firm "Stainforth &Giberne"). Mrs. Pearson mentions that they both helped her and her sisters to a "knowledge of the Scriptures and of the Christian life."

[Illustration: WORTON CHURCH, OXFORDSHIRE FROM AN OLD PRINT BY KIND PERMISSION OF REV. V. H. LANGHORNE]

[Illustration: HOLY TRINITY, WEST END, OVER WORTON, MAY, 1905 BY KIND PERMISSION OF REV. W. H. LANGHORNE, PRESENT RECTOR OF WORTON]

"We were introduced by Maria, Mrs. Whitmore, about June, 1823, to a good clergyman who had lately come to reside at Walthamstow, about two miles from our home" (they were living at Wanstead), "the Rev. William Wilson, who received us into his friendship, and whose preaching we attended with joy and profit for several years.

"It was on Christmas Day of this year, I think, that we first heard the Rev. Walter Mayers preach from Nahum i. 7 a most beautiful experimental discourse which impressed us very much. On making enquiry concerning him, we found that he was Mr. Wilson's curate at Worton, in Oxfordshire, and that he received pupils into his house. Later, their brother, Charles Giberne, was sent for a year to him. This led to Mr. Mayers being invited to dinner at our house. There he formed an attachment to Sarah, to whom he was married the following year, 1824.

"In the midsummer holidays, 1825, I went to pay a visit to Walter and Sarah, and it was then I first made acquaintance with John and Frank Newman. The latter was spending the Long Vacation with Mr. Mayers to assist him in teaching the young men, though he was only nineteen. Among these pupils was Charles Baring, seventeen years old, afterwards Bishop of (the Palatinate see) Durham.

"John Newman walked over from Oxford to breakfast one morning: he was then twenty–four, and a most interesting young man; but him I only saw then once, whereas his brother (Frank) was our daily companion, and took great pains in instructing Sarah (Mrs. Walter Mayers) and myself in Political Economy. His talents and piety attracted my admiration, for I had never seen such young men before. They had both been pupils of Mr. Mayers at a large school at Ealing (in which he was a master), and were considered to be converted in very early life."

Later on is another entry:—

"In the midsummer holidays of 1825" (John Henry Newman was ordained priest on 29th May, 1825), "I went to stay with Walter and Sarah Mayers, and then began my first acquaintance with John Henry Newman and his brother Frank. The former having walked over from Oxford, seventeen miles, to breakfast, and repeating Milman's beautiful hymn from the *Martyr of Antioch*, 'Brother, thou art gone before us.'

"He was just twenty–four, and his brother Frank, who came soon after to assist Walter Mayers with his pupils ... was only twenty, but as bright a specimen of a young Oxford student as I had ever met with. They had both been considered converted in early youth, and so uncommon an event was it to me to meet with Christian young men" (men, that is, whose religion was their motive power, and not only used in the conventional and cold formality then usual in the case of so many families in England), "that my admiration knew no bounds. Of course, I told my sister Maria ... all this, and she was quite prepared to appreciate in like manner, when she went to stay at Worton the following summer."

We come now to the time which, whether for happiness or regret, inevitably enters into the lives of most men on this earth—the time when they first meet "the Woman they Never Forget." It does not follow that they are able to marry her, but it *does* follow that, meet whom they may later, no one will ever oust from her place that first woman in their memories.

Francis Newman was only twenty–one when he first met her.

Memoir and Letters of Francis W. Newman

Maria Rosina Giberne was a beautiful girl, possessing special charm of manner. It was not long after his first meeting with her that Frank Newman fell passionately in love with her. Long talks on scientific and religious subjects passed between them. But though he cared for her, evidently her feeling for him was only that of friendship and interest, for when, later, he asked her to marry him, she refused. He did not, however, take this for an absolutely final decision (as in effect it was), for five or six years later, when he was on his missionary journey to Syria, and he wrote and begged her to give him a different answer, she refused him again.

[Illustration: OVER WORTON RECTORY, OXFORDSHIRE BY KIND PERMISSION OF REV. W. H. LANGHORNE, PRESENT RECTOR OF WORTON]

The extracts that follow are from her diary of the summer at Worton in 1826—the year she first met the Newman brothers. The extracts are taken from an autobiography of hers, which was originally written in French for the nuns of the "Order of the Visitation" convent at Autun, Saone et Loire, to which she went, as professed nun, after her conversion to the Roman Church.

This is Maria Rosina Giberne's description of Worton (to which I have access by the kindness of my cousin):—

"It was a delightful place; far from towns and quite country. There I spent my days as much as possible under the trees, or in the fields sketching the lovely views. My sister had told me that Mr. Francis Newman and a friend were coming to the village to spend the vacation. I did not pay much attention, being preoccupied with this delicious solitude. In a while the two friends appeared, and I enjoyed hearing them talk, having a great respect for learned men, although far from being learned myself. I asked them questions and propounded religious difficulties which troubled me. I was struck with his (Frank Newman's) piety, which had nothing affected about it like the manner of some good people. We often talked whilst I was sketching in the fields, and he explained to me many things in Holy Scripture that I had not understood. Before leaving the village he expressed a wish that I could become acquainted with his sisters.... This idea pleased me much, and on returning home I gave our mother no peace until she gave me permission to invite two of his sisters to spend a fortnight with us.

"They accepted the invitation, and Mrs. Newman brought her three daughters—Harriet, Jemima, and Mary. She left Harriet and Mary with us. I was much taken at once with Mary, who was nice–looking, unaffected, and only seventeen years of age. I was resolved to make friends with them, otherwise should not have been greatly attracted by Harriet who had a way I could not understand, and who embarrassed me greatly by her knowledge of religious matters, because I had thought that I might be able to lead *them* to the good way, [Footnote: In some notes she expressly says this was Frank Newman's suggestion primarily.] and behold, they seemed to know all beforehand, and often showed me that I was mistaken in my explanations.... I remember the first thing I opposed with all my might was the idea of a visible Church, and it was not till long afterwards, when I was staying with their mother in the country, that I took up this idea. It was, I think, in the winter of 1827 that I embraced this doctrine.

"Then in the summer the Newman family stayed some months at Brighton. After John Newman's death the family had no settled home, but moved from place to place. It happened that one of Maria Rosina's married sisters was also at Brighton, and consequently it naturally followed that the two families of Newman and Giberne met often.

"Naturally we called now and then to see Mrs. Newman, who invited us one day to spend the afternoon and evening, and then, for the first time, I became acquainted with Mr. Newman, now Father Newman. It was a great pleasure, for I had heard so much about him, and I enjoyed seeing him though he spoke very little to me, and paid me no compliments or special attentions like most young men of our acquaintance, who neglected the ladies of their families. The delicate and repeated attention of Mr. Newman to his mother and sisters therefore aroused my admiration and respect."

[Illustration: SKETCH OF NEWMAN FAMILY BY MARIA ROSINA GIBERNE BY KIND PERMISSION OF MR. J. R. MOZLEY. As one faces the picture, John Henry is sitting on Mrs. Newman's right; Francis William to her left; Harriet to the right of John; Jemima below her mother.]

To my mind there speaks, in this last sentence, something unusual too as regards the writer, who, accustomed to the "compliments and special attentions" which other young men paid her, could yet appreciate and admire these delicate thoughtfulnesses which *this* young man, who saw so much further into the inner heart and meaning of things, loved to show to his own mother and sisters instead of to other people's sisters, as was and is the ordinary way of most young men.

In some other MSS. by Maria Rosina, sent me from the Oratory, Birmingham, [Footnote: By the kindness of Father Bacchus.] there is a rather different account, in which there is mention of Frank Newman having even then shown a great tendency to free thought.

She adds: "I had not a suspicion that there was any danger of his getting to care for me, for, firstly, he was two years younger than I was; and, secondly, because I myself was occupied almost altogether with the thought of how to rid myself of the narrow religion which was becoming every day more unbearable, and also because I had no other thought for him than for Robert." (Robert Murcott was a young man belonging to a family with whom her people were intimate, and who had always wished to marry her. He went out to India, and when he died left her all his money.)

In years to come, a great and lasting friendship began between her and Cardinal Newman—a friendship which lasted unbroken to the end. When he went to Rome for the red hat, he was too ill to call and see her at Autun on his way home, but he had previously been to see her there.

The picture of the Newman family given here was drawn in chalks by her when she was a girl at a little cottage at Horspath (near Nuneham, in 1829), at which the Newmans were staying. It had been offered them by Mr. Dornford, Fellow, tutor, and proctor of Oriel, and afterwards rector of Plymtree.

In the book, to which allusion has before been made, by Rev. Thomas Mozley, there is a description of Maria Rosina in later life. He says she was "tall, strong of build, majestic, with aquiline nose, well–formed mouth, dark penetrating eyes, and a luxuriance of glossy black hair. She would command attention anywhere.... She was very early the warmest and most appreciative of Newman's" (John Henry Newman's) "admirers.... Her great power lay in the portraits she did in chalks.... Besides many portraits of Newman himself ... she drew a portrait of old Mr. Wilberforce...."

The portrait of Maria Rosina in this volume was painted by herself in the spring of 1827, to send to her eldest brother, George Giberne (at Dhoolia, Candeish), afterwards Judge in the Bombay Presidency (East India Co.). On the back of it her brother had written in pencil:—

> "Yes, here's a silent, thoughtful thing, and yet
> Her soft blue eye beams Eloquence: her lips
> Oh! who could teach his spirit to forget
> Their deep expressiveness, that far eclipse
> All that kind nature to this world hath given,
> All we can see of Earth, or guess of Heaven."

[Illustration: MARIA ROSINA GIBERNE FROM A PAINTING BY HERSELF]

At this time she had taken many portraits of her friends, and I have, in my own possession, one of Miss Wigram, and one, in a riding–hat, of her sister Emily, both done in chalks, as is her picture of herself sent to her brother. Later on she went to Rome, where for twenty years she studied art and copied pictures "for the use," Mr. Mozley says, "of English chapels." Years after, when my aunt was in the convent of the Order of Visitation at Autun, she wrote an interesting letter to Cardinal Newman, which is given by Miss Anne Mozley in her *Letters and Correspondence of John Henry Newman* alluding to the old days when their friendship, which had never wavered during all the years which had gone by, was but just beginning:—

"I do not want to talk of myself. I want to tell you of my entire sympathy with you in what you say and feel about the anniversary of dear Mary's" (the Cardinal's youngest sister) "death." (She died 5th Jan., 1828.) "This season never comes round without my repassing in my heart of hearts all the circumstances of those few days—my first visit to your dear family.... Who could ever have been acquainted with the soul and heart that lent their expression to that face, and not love her? My sister Fanny and I arrived at your house on 3rd January, and sweet Mary, who had drawn figures under my advice when she was staying with us at Wanstead, leant over me at a table in the drawing–room, and in that sweet voice said, 'I am so glad you are come; I hope you will help me in my drawing.'"

The next day she was taken ill at dinner, and on the ensuing evening— dead.

She goes on to say: "Do you recollect that you and I are the only survivors of that event?"

But to go back to the end of the college life of the subject of this memoir. In the year 1828, Frank Newman was working amongst the poor at Littlemore, near Oxford. His brother [Footnote: *Reminiscences of Oriel*, by Rev. T. Mozley.] at that time was vicar of S. Mary's, the University Church, and as the hamlet of Littlemore had then no church, [Footnote: A church was built there later by Newman. In Ingram's *Memorials of Oxford*, 1838, it is said that in former days Littlemore was beautifully wooded, and that in Saxon times there was a convent (of which there still remain some ruins) which was called by the Saxon name of the "Mynchery," and which belonged to the nuns of the Benedictine Order, and the church which Alfred built on the site of the University Church of to-day, was known as early as the Conquest as "Our Lady of Littlemore."] he attended to the spiritual needs of the people there. Indeed, he considered it his duty to go there every day; and Francis worked also constantly with him in teaching the villagers. Some little time later, his mother and sisters came to live at Horspath, in Iffley village, close to Oxford. They, too, assisted in parochial matters, taught in the schools, visited the sick, and generally helped the brothers.

By this time John Henry Newman's sermons were attracting great attention in Oxford, and whenever he preached his University sermons, he had a crowded congregation of undergraduates. The college authorities, however, did not approve of his popularity with the undergraduates, and in Canon Carter's *Life and Letters of Archdeacon Hutchings*, there is a note showing this:—"I went to Christ Church in 1827.... Newman was at Oriel, and for the last two years of my time Vicar of S. Mary's. But it was the object of the college authorities to prevent our going to hear him preach, and the chapel services were so arranged as to make it impossible."

In 1829 Dr. Pusey was Professor of Hebrew and Canon of Christ Church, and as he had been for some years the close friend of Frank Newman's brothers, it was inevitable that the former should see a great deal of him at that time. He was delighted with Pusey's first books; but it was for the "pietism and rationalism" which he found in them, more than for any hint of the spirit of Churchmanship which distinguished his other works so much. J. H. Newman had been a tutor at Oriel College since 1826. Oriel College, Rev. Thomas Mozley tells us, was then "held to be in the very front of academic progress ... with a Provost" (Edward Hawkins) "who owed his election largely to Newman." Newman, Robert Wilberforce, and Froude were close friends. Dr. Hawkins had a strong influence over John Newman. Indeed, he had won love and respect from almost everyone; "he spoke incisively, and what he said remained in the memory"—so much a part of his own strong convictions and thought did it seem to be.

Yet Francis Newman was as convincing in his *writings*, at any rate, as his better–known brother, who, as some thought, "overshadowed" him in the eyes of the world to a large extent. A friend of mine, writing to me a short time since, said that a statement had been made recently, by some one entitled to judge of the matter, that Francis was the "greater of the two brothers."

Be this as it may, certainly both were pioneers "in a world movement of reconstruction." Both were prophets in a sense. Both were mental Samsons— giants among the crowd of those who never see a yard beyond their own narrow scope of vision. Both were inspired movers of the crusade of purity, of new and original points of view, and of reformation in the old.

It is true neither could work with the other shoulder to shoulder. *But they worked.* And it is possible to have a great brotherly affection notwithstanding strong antagonism of views which render combined work impossible.

CHAPTER III. HIS MISSIONARY JOURNEY TO THE EAST

In 1826 Francis Newman gained, as it is said, with no special effort, one of the best Double Firsts in classics and mathematics ever known. He had a Fellowship in Balliol College, was Emeritus Professor later, and considered to be one of the most promising, brilliant men at his University. Many thought his intellect superior to that of his better–known brother. Many thought also, later on, that, as I have said, all his life he was more or less overshadowed by the fame of that elder brother.

Francis Newman never took his M.A. degree, and for this reason: he felt he could not conscientiously sign the Thirty–nine Articles, in which all had to profess belief. He could not reconcile this signing with his inner convictions. Rather than do violence to them he preferred being without the degree. No one could say of him that all his life long he did else than bear his convictions boldly emblazoned on his shield. There could never be any doubt of what he thought. He could not beat about the bush in his beliefs—he would not keep them secret—he did not care for unpopularity in the least. His great aim was to fight—at whatever odds— for whatever he felt by dogged conviction. He was often wrong; but never cowardly, never philandering, never vacillating. "I am anti–everything," as he said humorously of himself. And so he was. He *was*, in a sense, "anti–everything," and though, sometimes through the training of previous environments, sometimes through other reasons, he was "anti" things that were right and of good report, he was never against social reform—never against "the cause that needs assistance"; never against the oppressed wherever and whenever they crossed his path. Newman thus gave up his Balliol Fellowship, and with it—more or less—his chances of a brilliant worldly career.

Briefly stated, these are the chief events of the years that followed the taking of the Double First at Oxford. In 1827 he met Maria Rosina Giberne, who was to strongly influence his life for the next six years. In 1828 he was working with his brother at Littlemore; in 1829, I imagine, he met and felt strongly in sympathy with some of those with whom, later, the missionary journey to Syria was planned—Lord Congleton, Mr. Groves, Dr. Cronin, and others.

People have said that Newman gave up all worldly hopes of fame for the sake of this missionary venture. It may be that that is true in part. But, for myself, I cannot help seeing too that there may very well have been other powerful reasons which also influenced him in the matter. It was about this time that he asked my aunt, Maria Rosina Giberne, to whom he was passionately attached, to marry him, and was refused. I think it very probable that this may have been a strong reason why he wished to break up the old life and go for change abroad.

Originally there had been some idea that Francis Newman should take Holy Orders, as well as his brother. This is evidenced by a poem by the latter. Later, contrary tides swung the former from the mooring of the Anglican Church. He could not sign her Thirty–nine Articles; he could not agree with many of her doctrines. He drifted more and more away from her. Then he fell in with Lord Congleton (then Mr. Parnell) and Mr. A. N. Groves— both deeply religious men, though neither of them Churchmen.

Lord Congleton [Footnote: *Memoir of Lord Congleton*, by Henry Groves.] had been given no definite religious training in his youth, though his mother taught him to say daily prayers. Then, when a young man, he felt a deep dissatisfaction with this vague religious teaching he had received, and he began to read more and more in the New Testament, until at length he became a Christian by sheer conviction. He felt his

24

conversion as a revelation.

Mr. Groves, who was a well–known dentist in Devonshire, felt about the same time a great stirring towards missionary work. He offered his services to the Church Missionary Society. He often stayed in Dublin with Lord Congleton. In 1828, when they were walking together, one of those strange mystical approaches of soul to kindred soul took place.

"This, I doubt not, is the mind of God concerning us, that we should come together not waiting on any pulpit or minister, but trusting that the Lord would edify us together by ministering as He pleased." Lord Congleton adds: "At the moment he spoke these words I was assured my soul had got the right idea, and that moment (I remember it as if it were but yesterday) was the birth–place of my mind as a 'brother.'"

He mentions here Edward Cronin (who in 1830 formed one of the missionary party with which Frank Newman was associated), at that time an Independent, "but his mind was at the same time under a like influence, as I may say of us all."

[Illustration: PHOTO OF LORD CONGLETON (LEADER OF SYRIAN MISSIONARY JOURNEY) FROM HIS "LIFE" BY GROVES]

I should perhaps say here (I have the information from the *Memoir of Lord Congleton* before mentioned), that the special truths by which Lord Congleton, Mr. Groves, and Dr. Cronin were led then, were: "The oneness of the Church of God, involving a fellowship large enough to embrace all saints, and narrow enough to exclude the world. The completeness and sufficiency of the written Word in all matters of faith, and preeminently in things affecting our Church life and walk—the speedy pre–millennial advent of the Lord Jesus."

All three of the men just named had made surrender of all that the world had to offer them, Lord Congleton giving the whole of his fortune to missionary work. It was he who provided most of the things needed for the journey.

In 1830 (September) the following party left Dublin:—Lord Congleton (whom in future it will be simpler to call by his family name of Mr. Parnell, as Newman thus mentions him in his diary, the *Personal Narrative*, which he kept throughout this journey to the East);

Mr. Cronin; his mother Mrs. Cronin, and her daughter Nancy Cronin (to whom Lord Congleton was engaged); and Francis Newman. There was also a Mr. Hamilton, but later on he found the work not suited to him, and returned to England. [Footnote: Mr. Groves had already gone as a missionary to Bagdad in 1829, and they were to join him later.]

Mr. Henry Groves says in the *Memoir* that the travellers started with an enormous quantity of luggage. They had practically a small library of books, a lithographic press in two heavy boxes (for printing tracts, etc.), and a large medicine chest, which was Mr. Cronin's property (he was a doctor). When one thinks how the more one travels, even in these travelling–made–easy days, the more one wishes to abridge one's requirements and whittle down one's wants, it is not difficult to understand that in 1830 the difficulties of the rough travelling were largely increased by these foods for the mind and for the stomach which travelled in the wake of the little party, nor how they were hampered by these conditions.

I now quote from Francis Newman's *Personal Narrative* (published 1856), which is one of the most interesting of travel books, and very graphically written in the form of letters to his friends at home. [Footnote: Newman and Lord Congleton were both at this time about twenty–three years of age.]

"River Garonne, At Anchor in Steamboat, *23rd Sept.*, 1830.

"We sailed finely on Saturday from Dublin, while sheltered by the Irish coast; but in the evening we tasted the Atlantic with a south–wester, which proved a bitter dose. For nearly fifty hours we tossed, with very slow progress, until all our bones were bruised, etc., etc.... I have never seen anything like the sea on the French coast.

"The Bay of Biscay fulfilled all its proverbial roughness: the whole sea was dells and knolls. It was terrible to see the pilot jump aboard while his boat was alternately tossed above our deck; he was caught by the sailors in their arms.... The custom–house officers have detained the ship so long that we are left here by the tide.... The officers were very civil. They were all amazed at the number of our packages" (as well they might be!)... "The prospect of our porterages is frightful. Think of us at the top of a hotel and an army of porters carrying up the height of three stories many hundredweights of trunks, chests, hampers, bags, baskets, to stow into our bedrooms *for the night!* And this misery is to be repeated everywhere....

"I talk French clumsily, yet get on somehow.... My French having been chiefly mathematical, I do not know the names of many common things...."

At Toulouse in October:—"I am already a Frenchman. If you doubt it, learn that I take wine or raisins for breakfast, and never speak to a peasant without raising my hat.... This *vin ordinaire* is not 'bad,' in the sense of intoxicating, but in another way. However, if it supplies the place of tea, it is vain to rail at it."

The next entry is while they were staying at Marseilles on 13th October, and concerns the cheapness of the provisions.

"All provisions appear within reach of the poorest. I have been in some very low eating–houses here, and perceive apparently poor people breakfast on meat. Nothing seems dear but milk and butter; we get none but goats' milk here.... The finest purple grapes are here 1d. or 3/4d. a pound, and as much bread as I can eat for 1–1/2d.... I had a provoking accident at Beziers. On our leaving the barge, the carman drove off without securing our boxes—he was in a violent passion against some girl porters (a domestic institution of Beziers).... I roared out, 'Arretez! Arriere! Vous n'avez pas attache la corde!' But in vain; and in an instant down came from the very top the little medicine chest given me by M——. It fell on its corner, which saved the glass bottles; but every dovetailing is broken, the hinges wrenched off, the panels split."

Of course the travelling is chiefly by diligence and canal boat, and for English ladies very often terribly rough and trying. But Mrs. and Miss Cronin had resolved to face discomforts, etc., equally with their companions, and would have no little ameliorations in the way of comforts for themselves.

One great danger, too, occurred, from which they were only rescued by the promptitude of Newman and Mr. Parnell (as throughout the diary Newman alludes to Lord Congleton). Once, in travelling by canal near Marseilles, Newman found the level of the canal–boat was "dangerously high, from the arches. Once we had a narrow escape. There was a sudden cry of '*A bas!*' We turned and saw we were rapidly nearing an arch which would knock off our heads. The horses kept at a short canter. Old Mrs. C. was sitting quietly on deck, wholly absorbed, and never dreaming that the sailors could be calling to her. Miss C. was sitting on a box, fast asleep. Several of us rushed at once towards them, and pulled them off their seats on to the deck. Literally they fell upon me in a heap, and we just passed safe under the arch. Mrs. C.'s bonnet and my hat got smashed."

Here comes a touch of what later on in life was to be the subject of his keenest thought—the subject of statesmanship, the chief aim of which should be *the people:* how to make the land sufficient for the people, how to make the people sufficient for the land—a counsel of perfection far removed from the party spirit of politicians, who then, as now, did not recognize that principles and a sacred sense of responsibility for their country should be their motive power.

"We are delayed here" (Marseilles) "for a ship. We are likely to go to Cyprus. The vintage was going while we were *en route* hither. I was interested to see men walking bare–legged, stained purple nearly to the knee, *with treading the wine vat.* I then understood the Scripture metaphor.... The men seemed to have been wading in blood.... I should deprecate a whole district being dependent for its livelihood on the sale of wine.... for as *some* seasons are sure to be fatal to the crop, the failure, when it comes, is universal.... To make each component part—I mean each *local* part—of society self–supporting, and self–relieving even in times of calamity, ought, I think, to be the aim of every statesman."

As regards sight–seeing for sight–seeing's sake, it was *nil*. And for a reason which seemed not to allow for any of the travellers having discretion, "We make it a tacit rule never to go ten yards to see anything; for if once we became sight–seers it is impossible to draw the line. So in fact I see nothing but what I cannot help seeing."

The next diary–tic letter is not until 14th January of the next year (1831), when the party had arrived at Aleppo.

Frank Newman had been studying Greek and talking it with a master, and during the voyage from Marseilles landed for three days at Larnica. On the ship was an old Greek, and he used to go and talk with him to practise his Greek.

"You may be amused to hear his judgment of my Greek dialect; he called it 'very beautiful and very funny'; that is, no doubt, because I am apt to mix up too much of the old Greek, which seems grandiloquent on trifling subjects....

"Walking in the street at Larnica, I met a person whom I did not know, who, to my extreme surprise, fell on my neck and kissed both cheeks quite affectionately, I had not recognized my dirty acquaintance in this clean, well–dressed gentleman, probably fresh from the bath."

Many were the difficulties Newman and his friends had to encounter in hiring a vessel to sail to Ladakia [Footnote: Laodicea of Syria.] on the opposite coast. At last a bargain was struck with a Turkish ship for five pounds. But the ship had battled already against the contretemps of too many voyages. She could no longer beat against the wind as once she used to do. Four times they set sail, and four times had to put back again into port. The captain had only an old French map "marked with crosses at certain places, the cross meaning *porto*, as the captain explained." He needed help, however, from his passengers to be quite sure which was which! In this ship they lived with discomfort for a whole month. Still, all of the friends kept well. The distance from Ladakia to Aleppo is about 120 English miles. And this journey added to discomfort, hardship, and to hardship—lack of food for the mission party. It necessitated travelling three miles into the hills, and when a lofty bleak plain was reached, the muleteers made it clear that they were to spend the night there.

"We heaped our rudest boxes to make a wall, and on the lee side prepared a sleeping–place, stretching over it some oilskins.... We had a small supply of food in baskets.... All night the rain fell in torrents.... Our whole floor was swamped; we had to sit on carpet bags and let them get wet. Clothes, bedding, bags, baskets, were drenched, and we had to mount in the morning in the midst of rain.... The roads were river–beds.... After riding eleven hours without dismounting (the beasts never leave their walking pace).... We had fasted the whole day, yet none of us suffered; not even old Mrs. Cronin, for whom I greatly feared."

I should add here that Francis Newman was strongly in favour of women riding astride instead of on the Early–Victorian side–saddle, which necessitates a woman riding in an artificial, twisted position. Still, at the period at which he is writing, Early–Victorian ideas about the fitness of things were so much *de rigueur* that Mrs. Cronin, when forced to ride astride, was terribly disturbed.

"'Ach, Edward,' said she to her son, 'I expected they would persecute and murdher us, but I never thought to ride across a mule!'... Three times did her mule come down with her, poor lady, and all three in dangerous places.

"None of the rest suffered so many falls, nor, I think, any of the laden beasts. Her son was in terrible distress at every fall, for he was carrying his infant in his arms ... and he could not put the child down in the mud without danger to it."

Indeed, it must have been a very distressful journey for all, and not least for the poor little infant missionary! People may wonder what was the necessity of taking this last at all. [Footnote: Dr. Cronin and his wife were both engaged to come out to Mr. Groves. Then she died, and as he felt bound to fulfil his promise and did not like to leave the baby, he brought it too.] An old clergyman, however, once said to me, "I would rather take an infant in arms with me, than go all by myself on a journey abroad."

At last Aleppo was reached. In his letter, on 10th February to his mother, Newman says how long their stay there would be is quite uncertain. He "is taking daily lessons in Arabic, and speaking French."

"I am afraid you will not think the better of me when I tell you that I am become a smoker; and this though I had so great a dislike to it in England. I do not mean that I am always smoking—certainly not; but I have bought two pipes and amber mouthpieces, and all the apparatus; which shows that I am in earnest. When a man in college smoked cigars in his room, and we (the Balliol fellows) generally condemned it, I remember, in reply to my remark that a man who smoked made himself a nuisance, one of them said, 'It would not do to generalize; for in Germany the man who *objects* to smoking is the nuisance.' ... If anyone calls on me I must offer him a pipe and smoke one myself; and, conversely, when I call on anyone, I must not refuse the pipe.... The pipe fills up gaps of time, and 'breaks the ice' like an Englishman's remarks on the weather....

"Now I am in for it, I will make you perfect in the theory of smoking. We have here three sorts of pipes, of which I use but one, viz. the long straight pipe. It is generally a cherry stick, and reaches from the mouth to the ground as you sit on a low sofa. The bowl is supported in a tin frame on the ground to catch the ashes; and you smoke in it *tootoon*, which means common dry tobacco.... Ladies, as far as I know, do not smoke the straight pipe, though I have seen Mussulman females, evidently of humble rank, with the long pipe and its smoking bowl protruding from under their long veil as they walked. The second sort is called *Nargili* ... some pronounce it Narjili.... Nargili means a cocoa–nut, which is used in this apparatus to hold the water through which the smoke passes. Vertically out of the cocoa–nut rises a pipe which ends in a long bowl holding the *Tambac*, which is a second species of tobacco having broadish yellow leaves worked up with wet. It needs a piece of red–hot coal laid upon it, and left there, to kindle it. Slanting out of the cocoa–nut proceeds upwards a second tube, a mere cane, which ends in the smoker's mouth. He grasps the vertical tube in his left fist, and, if sitting, rests the cocoa–nut on his knee. This is the way my hostess smokes—an elegant Levantine lady.... I cannot smoke through water; I find it demands too much work for my lungs. The third sort is the *Hooka*, a word which, I believe, means the very long flexible tube which is here substituted for the cane, while a glass vessel, standing on the ground, does duty for the cocoa–nut. The principle of the smoking ... are the same as in the Nargili.... Unless it be overdone, I think the exercise from early youth must enlarge the capacity and power of the lungs.... When people have not a second pipe to offer you, they hand the pipe from their own mouth, and to wipe the mouthpiece before you suck it would be an insult."

Newman says that the Turks are supposed to have a great tenderness for animals. There is a popular saying, which he quotes, "A Turk cares more for the life of a cat than of a man." The following curious scene was witnessed by him in a town on his way to Aleppo:—

"A goat was to be killed, and we had some chance of a bit if one of us would seize a part of the animal before it was dead. *There* stood the victim and its priest.

"In front was a row of cats, sitting up with all the gravity of Egyptian gods, or like the regiment of cats which were the van of Cambyses against Egypt. On the other side a regiment of dogs. When the scarlet flood spouted on to the ground the dogs took their portion of it. I know not what etiquette or what hint from the sacrificer suddenly dispersed them: then the cats came in due order and took *their* portion.... Peace was wonderfully kept between dogs and cats; but when it came to dividing the offal, the cats had plenty of screaming, and, I rather think, some fighting. The number of these wild cats here is a real nuisance."

In May we get another insight into the carrying out of Newman's precept to himself, always to "live in Rome as the Romans."

"I believe you know it was always our idea that we must put on native habits wherever we went, so far at least as to encounter no needless friction. I had not then considered how seriously such change may after a time affect one's own character, and the thought sometimes crosses the mind anxiously.

"We smoke. Well. I say to myself, 'I must try not to be wedded to this practice: I hope to leave it off the moment it proves inexpedient.'.... I have taken to the Syrian gown and slippers; to walk actively in these is arduous and, I suppose, very singular. Here is a question: May not my bodily habit change with it? and may not that affect my mind?... The gown is ridiculously feminine, beyond what I had been aware; not merely in length and amplitude, but above the girdle it is puffed out into two *bosoms*, which are used as pockets" (no doubt the *sinus* of the Romans). "... Some things which in company we do as seldom as possible, such as to blow the nose, or (worse still) to spit, seem to be utterly forbidden here.... The natives are reserved in the use of a pocket–handkerchief as the most fastidious English lady.... I believe Xenophon praises the Persians for never spitting in company." (Would that our own working classes could, in this respect, be more Persian in their habits!) "Are not all Eastern manners probably a plant of very ancient growth?" Then, on religion: "I did not understand till lately how unintelligible to people here is a religion which is not external and almost obtrusive. We are certainly thought much better of, because, two of our party having pretty good voices, we commonly sing praises in daily worship.... To pray standing, or, as I should rather say, lying flat, at the corners of the streets is not ostentation here: for so many do it that it has no pre–eminence.... I always looked to see a missionary church formed in these countries; but I did not foresee what I now discern, that it would not be recognized as Christians at all, but be esteemed a mere Anglicism, not by papists merely, but by Moslems too. I do not know, after all, whether that could be ever a *permanent* obstacle. I believe not; for it is not the name, but the goodness of Christianity that must prevail. However, the now current idea here is, that the English are very good men, but have *no* religion—which means, as I said, no exterior; and in so far *our* exterior inspires something of respect.... I had resolved to read the Koran through—not in the original, but in a translation—that I might get some insight into the Mussulman mind.... But I confess to you I have broken sheer down in the attempt, ... the book makes no impression on my mind. I cannot find where I left off when I recur to it. That so tedious and shallow a work can meet such praises gives me a lower and lower idea of the power of mind in these nations. I now think that the Arabs are captivated by the tinkle and epigrammatic point of an old and sacred dialect, while Turks and Persians take its literary beauty as a religious fact to be believed, not to be felt. How wonderful is the power of tradition!"

In July, Newman and his party were still at Aleppo. By now they had become well accustomed to the native foods, but had at last come to the conclusion that the meat (mutton) was certainly not good; unfortunately it formed a large proportion of the stews. One dish consisted of rice, dressed with butter and salt This is called "Pilau" (pronounced "ow"), and apparently is the same as that common in Russia to–day, which is *delicious*.

"This pilau is, fundamentally, rice dressed with butter and salt: the rice is thrown into boiling water, and is boiled for twenty minutes only. This is the highest luxury of the Bedouins. We saw a company of them dine on it. They scraped the hot outside of the rice with the tips of their fingers, squeezed it into a ball in their hand, and shot the ball into their mouth. The dexterity of this, so as not to burn their fingers, miss their mouths, nor drop about their garments, is astonishing.... Carrots with lemon or sour milk make delicious fritters...."

It was during this month that the news came to them from Bagdad that Mr. Groves (who, it will be remembered, had been there for some time, expecting them later to join him) had just lost his wife from plague; that she had been the only one who had caught the disease. Newman himself, about this time, had a sharp attack of fever. Dr. Cronin was much alarmed about him; indeed, he believed him to be dying, and leeched his temples and bled his right arm. Then he tried calomel, and he said that he had resolved on opening his temporal artery if his pulse had kept as rapid as at first it was.

[Illustration: DR. CRONIN ONE OF THOSE WHO WENT TO SYRIA WITH FRANCIS NEWMAN IN 1830 BY KIND PERMISSION OF MRS. CRONIN PHOTO BY MESSRS. WEBSTER, CLAPHAM COMMON]

In Aleppo, he tells us in one of his letters home, "madmen are looked on as sacred characters... there are no madhouses in the land.... Certainly in England the results of turning all the mad loose would be awful.

"But when one sees the entire satisfaction there is here with so ugly and revolting a state of things, and the inability people have to conceive the inconvenience of it... I am driven to speculate.... Is insanity excessively rare here, so that outrages, if they do occur, are naturally very few? or is the insanity... always of the imbecile kind? Or is insanity, at its worst, mollified by the respectful treatment which it meets, as vicious horses by kindness?

"... Here is a people without lunatic asylums. Well, their lunatics are few or harmless; what a comfortable coincidence! If insanity among *us* is caused by strong passions in one class and by intoxication in another, while the Turkish populations are nearly free from both... it implies a higher average morality.... Add to this there are no abandoned women here."

Five months after the first attack of fever Newman was taken ill of a far worse one, which gave a great shock to his nervous system. He was in real danger of losing his life this time, possibly because, Dr. Cronin being absent, there was no one to treat him. He suffered, too, greatly from continual sleeplessness. When he was recovering, Dr. Cronin, who by now had returned, ordered horse exercise for him, and Mr. Parnell very generously bought a horse for him.

In December, 1831, Mr. and Mrs. Parnell [Footnote: Mr. Parnell meant to have been married to Miss Cronin at Bordeaux, but this was found to be impossible, so he was obliged to wait till they reached Aleppo, where the ceremony took place in the early part of the year 1831.] went to Ladakia to help Mr. Hamilton, whose health had more or less broken down, secure a vessel to take him to France *en route* for England. He determined to see him safely on board. Mrs. Parnell also insisted on coming with her husband. But the travelling was rough, and she had had a bad fall from her ass, and besides had been ill and had no doctor at hand.

Mr. Hamilton went away in the ship, but Mrs. Parnell became more and more weak, until at last she died. Immediately on hearing of her death. Dr. Cronin set out, full of sorrow at the loss of his sister, to see if he could be of any help to Mr. Parnell. Newman writes:—

"The brother and mother here are so deeply afflicted, that I ask: What does the noble–hearted bridegroom suffer, but so lately a bridegroom?

"I am astounded at the reverse. Two months back she was hanging over my pillow weeping and kissing me as a dying man; now am I in youthful vigour, and she is in her grave.

"What a meek and quiet spirit was she, active to laboriousness, though refined in person. Affectionate she was, very dear to me also, but unspeakable is the loss to others. This is the third wife taken from those whom I desired as comrades: one died in Dublin, one in Bagdad, now one in Ladakia...."

"No *blame* against Mr. P. ought to be mixed with sympathy for this melancholy event. His wife's brother, on medical grounds, saw no objection to the journey.... Few English ladies are in body so well adapted as she was to bear the inconveniences, the long weariness, or the dangerous exposures of Turkish travel."

At last the time was come for the journey to Bagdad. Francis Newman and his friends went with their own horses, and with European saddles and stirrups.

"The native broad travelling saddle overlaps the animal's sides like a table, and tilts both ways. To get up at the side without help is a feat almost impossible. Many a time Mr. Parnell got off to search after some article of food or convenience for old Mrs. Cronin. To get up again, his most successful way was to make a run from behind and *divaricate* on to the horse's tail, like a boy playing at leap–frog; but the beast was always frightened, and bolted before he was well on. You will imagine the rest!... but we were all equally ludicrous, and indeed it is quite a serious inconvenience."

The next entry mentions the return of Mr. Parnell. He told them that Mr. Hamilton seemed absolutely unable to learn a foreign language, and this undermined his spirits and health, and made him a depressing companion.

On 25th April Newman and his friends started from Aleppo. They had not anticipated such serious difficulties as befell them during this journey. In the first place, they were not aware of the habits of the camel (at all events, his habits in the spring of the year). They found to their consternation that they work from two or three in the morning and travel till ten. Many people, not natives, had assured them that camels never travel by night, so they were the more unprepared for this unwelcome fact. The night travelling might not have mattered for younger people, but on old Mrs. Cronin the discomfort fell heavily. She had to be "forced out of her bed at one o'clock in the midst of the sharp cold of the night, and then have to ride when she ought to sleep. The effect of it on her (for she did not sleep by day) frightened us so much that at last we bought the drivers over to our hours.... The caravanserai at Aintab is so disagreeable a place for Mrs. Cronin that we enquired for a private house, and... we have hired one at the absurd price of three–halfpence sterling! It has a large grassy yard, very convenient for our horses, We have now only four, with the ass...."

However, they were not long at Aintab, for they were summoned before the Governor and accused of selling four Turkish Testaments. Then, being unable to deny having done so, the Governor said, "You must leave Aintab immediately." He provided camels, and they had perforce to go, as they had been so dictatorially bidden. But this was not all. A mob of fanatics beset them, followed them out into the country, and then pelted them with stones—first with small ones, but later with bigger ones, which could easily have stunned anyone who was hit by them. Presently a man galloped up and tried to seize Newman's horse's bridle, but he beat him off with an umbrella. Some of the crowd called out that the Governor had ordered them to be killed.

By the time Newman returned to his party Mr. Cronin was lying on the ground, and his mother declared that her son was dying. He had been set upon by men who had come to attack them, and beaten with fists, clubs, and stones. They tried their best to kill him. However, to Newman's intense surprise he was not hurt inwardly, only weak from exhaustion and pain. This was an almost unhoped–for comfort, and it was even found that he could continue his journey before evening. By this time the crowd had entirely dispersed, for an official had been sent by the Governor, and eventually he was able to quiet the people and send them off. Many of the travellers' possessions were lost, many stolen, but, at any rate, though discomforts and dangers undreamt of had been theirs, at least they were none of them seriously hurt; and that in itself was a thing for which they felt infinitely thankful. At last the Euphrates was reached.

"We saw it first in splendid contrast to a chalk desert, the most odious place through which I have travelled. We had soft chalk crumbling under foot, into which the beasts sank over their fetlocks or deeper.... When we surmounted the last chalk hills the green valley of the Euphrates burst upon us.

"It runs in a lowland excavation, bounded by opposite lines of high hills.... This valley was rich in the extreme, with trees scattered in it like England; but the sides of the hills were well wooded.... The river is very turbid, as if with white clay; it is unnaturally sweet, does not taste gritty, and is painfully cold. We presume this is from the melting of snow water.... The river is deep, rapid, smooth, and (I judge) as broad as the Thames at

Blackfriars...."

He thus describes the raft they were having made to take them down the river to Bagdad:—"Rough branches of trees of most irregular shape and quite small are strung together crosswise by ties of rope, and under them are fastened a sort of flooring of goat–skins blown up like bladders.... On these is fixed a deck of planks. These rafts carry enormous weights and draw very little water."

In the *Memoir of Lord Congleton* the end of this journey is thus told:— "They reached Bagdad on 27th June, and were met by Mr. Groves, who had for so many months been anxiously waiting for their arrival, after sufferings neither few nor light on both sides. It is hard to realize what such a meeting would be after two such years of toil and suffering as the past had been."

SECOND PART—BAGDAD

No sooner had the missionary party at length settled down at Bagdad than more trouble fell upon them. Mrs. Cronin, who had suffered almost more from the troubles, discomforts, and dangers of the journey than perhaps her friends guessed, grew worse and worse. She told Mr. Groves "that she was come hither to die," and it proved to be true; for only a few days after her arrival she died, to the deep distress of her son. So already, besides the unceasing discomforts, dangers, and disasters which had befallen the missionaries, there had been the cost of these three lives— Lord Congleton's wife, Mrs. Groves, and now old Mrs. Cronin, worn out by the terrible weariness of their journeyings under such rough conditions.

There is one thing which has struck me very forcibly as regards Frank Newman's *Personal Narrative*, and it is this: Throughout the whole book there is no mention of actual missionary work—the aim and object of this journey into Syria. There are, it is true, allusions to their own private prayer–meetings (of course they were hardly what one generally understands by the word "private," but still they could not be termed public) and to the distribution of New Testaments, but no actual *teaching* is mentioned. Nor does Newman write his own views on the subject. The diary–letters are chiefly filled with descriptions of the "perils of the way"—it is more or less secular. To me this has always seemed strange, for there was no doubt that he was, with the others, filled with a very real religious Christian zeal *then*, although later his views unhappily underwent great change and alteration, until a few years before his death, when his earlier faith was restored. But this fact remains: but for one's own previous knowledge of the aim of this journey, one would hardly recognize the *Narrative* as a missionary's diary at all.

In the *Memoir of Lord Congleton* there is far more missionary spirit; but still, even there, there is but very little detailed information as to mission work. During their stay at Bagdad Lord Congleton and Mr. Groves did indeed "develop plans for missionary work" which it was hoped would soon prove successful. The former bought a large house in the midst of the city for mission purposes. At first they thought of working among the "Armenian and Roman Catholic Christian population," and also "among the Jews," but they found the Mohammedans in Bagdad "peculiarly bigoted." And they owned to themselves later that "Bagdad had proved a failure in a missionary point of view." Mr. Groves, who wrote the *Memoir of Lord Congleton*, indeed owns that, "To many who look at life superficially, these years may seem lost; but He who often leads us 'about' (Deut. xxxii. 10) ... has purposes of which neither the one led, and still less the lookers–on, have any conception.... Thus to some these years of toil and sorrow *will* appear a mistake."

It is impossible to doubt the earnest faith and missionary zeal of these few who had come out to "do the Lord's work" in the East. But to many Churchmen it will be difficult to reconcile the words of Mr. Groves, that "the Coming of Christ, the powers of the Holy Ghost, were truths being brought before the *Church of God*" when it is remembered that they had practically severed themselves from the *visible* body of Christ's Church on earth, and were themselves (without Divine authority as delivered once to the Apostles) celebrating each Sunday in their house the Lord's Supper.

Constant mention is made in the *Memoir* of the open persecution which the mission party suffered in Bagdad, and of "the impossibility of access to the people." There were a few converts to Christianity made, but only a few; and the disappointments were many and grievous.

Then, too, their party was lessened by the departure of Frank Newman and Mr. Kitto for England. No reason is to be traced for this decision of Newman's, and it is not easy to understand what it could have been. It happened during the spring months of the year 1833, and shortly after his second proposal to Maria Rosina Giberne and her second refusal. He had written begging her come out to Bagdad, marry him, and work with them there. No doubt her refusal was a bitter disappointment to him, and possibly he wished to go back to England (he said in his diary he did not know how long he might stay there), and try if he could not persuade her personally. But if he thought this, he was again disappointed, for his meeting with her (as I see from some papers written by my aunt and kindly supplied me from the Oratory, Birmingham), was of no more avail than before. She mentions having met him shortly after his return, and it is evident that it was a meeting not devoid of awkwardness on her part and disappointment on his.

To go back to the letters from Bagdad, after this digression, Newman gives a very graphic account of the rafts used for travelling on the river from Moosul.

[Illustrations: PERSIAN LADY AND PERSIAN SMOKING DATE, 1827 FROM PERSIA IN "MODERN TRAVELLER" SERIES BY JOSIAH CONDER (pub. 1830)]

"The rafts used for descending the river consist of a rude deck fastened to a flooring of blown–up goatskins.... They are used for swimming bladders as in the ancient world. They serve for barrels to carry water.... The skins are also used in the bazaars ... for butter, treacle, honey, etc.... The raft is not rowed, except barely to keep it in the stream. It keeps twisting round and round, like a stone in the air;... but ... you have all the freshness and life of a vast streaming river and all the tranquillity of a mere pond.... One day, a man who wished to go down the river on our raft swam to us on a goatskin.... As a Thames wherry to a Thames steamer, so is a goatskin to a raft.... It has no prow nor stern.... If driven ashore it may burst many of the skins, some of which indeed from time to time need to be blown and tied afresh.... The oars are enormous, as in English barges. In our small raft two men at a time rowed.... I cannot tell you now of Mr. Groves's plans. I have a great deal to learn. The political state of this city, from within and without, is the very reverse of satisfactory." Then there follows a sentence which seems to imply that Mr. Groves was expecting too much from his "*monthly* visits" to the Arabs in the way of moral results. Also there follows a delightful account of the native doctor's methods of dealing with his patients. He "contracts to *cure* the patient ... for a definite sum, which is paid to him at once. If the patient thinks the price too high, the doctor lets him get worse; and when he applies anew, of course raises his demand. Nothing can be recovered if not paid down. Mr. Cronin" (the doctor travelling with them), "with all his practice at Aleppo, got fees only once or twice the whole time. He and Groves both despair of it here."

English patients when they use to their doctor the familiar phrase, "I put myself entirely in your hands," little think how completely and practically this was understood by these Bagdad doctors, who considered that a dollar in the hand is worth two promised *after* treatment of a case, and who, when they once had patients "in their hands," held them tight!

It is clear, I think, from the following entry that Newman did not approve thoroughly of Mr. Groves's methods of learning Arabic, any more than he seems to do of his "monthly visits" to the Arabs. He says that a friend of theirs, who had recently joined them, had studied Arabic and Persian twenty–eight years, and is an accomplished Orientalist, yet he "ridicules English notions of learning." Our religion, poetry, philosophy, science, are so opposed to everything here "that, he says, nothing but long time in the country can make an Englishman intelligible on religious subjects." To confirm this theory that a perfect knowledge of the language of the people to be taught is an absolute essential in a missionary—it is known, for an absolute fact, that missionaries have been eight years in India preaching until even they became convinced that sometimes they gave a totally wrong impression of what they were trying to teach to the natives, and therefore gave up all further efforts at teaching until they had learnt the language more *thoroughly*, and had it at their finger's—or, to speak more correctly, tongue's—end.

Eventually Mr. Groves came to the conclusion that for a long time to come "the wisest method" was to "avoid controversy with the Moslems." He formed schools not on the ground of "attending to the rising generation," but to aid him in the language ... give him opportunities of "trying his wings (as he calls it) against Christian errors, and exciting the attention of Moslems. Indeed, several (chiefly Persians) have come privately and begged New Testaments to send to their friends in Persia. At present I conceive he has nearly the whole Christian population here in his hands." And later, "Groves has not at all disappointed me, do not think that from anything I have written. He is what I expected from his book, and a great deal more. He has a practical organizing directing energy which fits him to be the centre of many persons, especially since it is combined with entire unselfishness and a total absence of personal ambition or *desire* to take the lead which he does take. He is very sanguine.... I am apt to be sadly faithless, and to see nothing but difficulties."

Perhaps his lack of conviction that this effort at missionary work *could* make its way in spite of so many great difficulties, as well as his own bad health (he states that he had not had a single day of real health since they have been at Bagdad), had something to do with his decision to return to England.

In August, 1832, Newman had a big class of boys every afternoon to whom he taught English and Geography; he mentions that "into the latter" he puts "a vast miscellany, physical, political, historical," from his knowledge and power of talk.

On 18th Sept., 1833, he left Bagdad. There is no entry in his diary between this and the last one in August, 1832, four months earlier. No word of his parting with his friends; no word of his reluctance to give up his missionary work.

But there is, I think, a good deal more in these words written on 18th September than meets the eye:—

"I am on my way to England for reasons partly personal" (I think this hints at a hope not altogether dead, which had been his close companion through his two years of absence), "partly connected with the interests of my Bagdad friends, *and my imagination is in England.*"

In his journey through Teheraun and thence to Tabreez, he passed through the celebrated rock of Besittoun. The sculptures there are said to represent the conquest of Darius Hystaspis.

"Our caravan did not go close enough to see the sculptures; we were probably half a mile off, but the muleteers were careful to point to them and talk of them. So too in going from Babylonia into Media by the ancient pass of Zagros, they were eager to draw my attention to the sculptures in lofty, apparently inaccessible rocks. 'Your uncle made those,' said a muleteer. At first I did not understand, but I found he meant by my uncle some infidel. No true believer, he said, could have done it.... The pass must be very ancient, and it is by far the noblest work I have seen in Asia."

The next letter is from Constantinople, 9th April, 1833.

"I am on my way to England, but do not know how long I may stay there." In his journey from Erzeroom to Scutari, he says he "became a mere animal"; he could only think of his horse's feet and his horse's footing. He never felt secure, for this reason: that the Tartar's horse, behind whom he rode, in the "ladder road" [Footnote: A "ladder road" is made by the horses all following each other in one track, and each trying to step in the steps made by the first horse.] beside the precipices, through the snow, "fell eleven times with him," and more than once fell over him. Frank Newman says his fear of falling prevented him from being able to admire the scenery, when, as often, it was grand and striking. "The Tartar starts at a fast walk, gets gradually into a shuffle, and studies the pace and power of all the beasts; at last he takes a sharp trot, but slackens before any of them lose breath. His great problem is, that the *weakest* horse of the set (who really sets the pace) shall come in well at last.... I never imagined I could have gained a power of sleeping for an hour, or two hours, and at last even for ten minutes ... in our last week, in which I had no regular night sleep. He" (the Tartar) "could not sleep, for he had two horses carrying gold ... but he dozed famously while on horseback. Dr. Kidd used to tell us that the wrist, the eyelid, and the nape of the neck went to sleep before the brain—a charitable excuse for one who drops a Prayer Book in church from drowsiness. I wish I could get Dr. Kidd to tell me whether the knee does not (at least by habit) remain awake after the brain is asleep, for I never saw the Tartar loose in the saddle even when he was all nidnodding." Then comes again the suggestion of the doubt which beset Newman that the way in which his mission party at Bagdad, and some Church Missionary workers at Constantinople laboured, was not a way which could long endure. That difficulties in the future inevitably must come as lions in the path. "Constantinople itself looks to me like mere card–houses—bright blue and bright red; and they are not much better. By being perched up so steep, they force themselves on the eye.... Perhaps I am out of humour: Constantinople is so dreadfully dear to one who comes from Asia (I pay ten piastres, or half–a–crown, for my mere bed—full London price). It is also very chilly and raw.... Yet I do enjoy the bed *with sheets*, it is an inexpressible luxury. How I have longed for it, but in vain, when suffering fever, to be able really to undress! But I must not write of such matters, nor of more serious ones that distract my judgment and distress me.

"I have seen the American Missionaries here. He" (Mr. Goodall) "gives himself entirely to promote the *self–reform* of the Armenian Church. This fundamentally agrees with what Mr. Hartley, of the Church Missionary Society, told me was the Society's proceeding against the Greek Church.... It also agrees with Groves's plan at Bagdad. I cannot censure it: I must approve it: yet I have a painful belief that it cannot long go on in the friendly way they all design.... This zeal of the Americans for Turkish Christianity is a new and striking phenomenon."

The last entry in the *Personal Narrative* occurs on 14th April, 1833, before Newman had left Constantinople. Very shortly after he departed, and not very long after, all his connection with this two years and a half missionary journey was a thing of the past.

It had been more or less a failure as far as regards outward consequences. Of that there seems no doubt. But there is also no doubt that it made its mark in spiritual matters in the minds of many. No doubt that it altered for some their spiritual landmarks and rubicons. No doubt that the subject of this memoir came home seeing religion from a different standpoint.

Archdeacon Wilberforce reminds us in one of his sermons, preached at Westminster Abbey, that the astronomers who built the pyramids of the Nile pierced a slanting shaft through the larger pyramid, which pointed direct to the pole–star. Then, if you "gazed heavenward through the shaft into the Eastern night, the pole–star alone would have met your gaze. It was in the ages of the past; it was when the Southern Cross was visible from the British Isles. Slowly, imperceptibly, the orientation of the planet has changed. Did you now look up into the midnight sky through the shaft in the Great Pyramid, you would not see the pole–star. New, brilliant space– worlds would shine down on you. But the heavens have not altered, and the shaft of the pyramid is not lying, or unorthodox. A new view of the heavens has quietly come, for the earth's axis has changed its place."

Very slowly too, sometimes, the axis of a personality changes its place. It may be that an entirely new point of view faces it. Some other view of life "swims into its ken." The mental eye can no longer see through the old means which served it in years gone by for lens. It is, as it were, looking at a new place in life's sky: for a time it is quite unable to reconcile its old ideas of religious astronomy with the new ones. What then? The sky is the same; but there are many ways of looking at it; and many spiritual atmospheres which cloud the outlook. Frank Newman could not reconcile at this time, nor in those which were coming, his old Calvinistic tendency of thought with new ideas which were forcing themselves in upon him. At the very end of life he saw the star of Christianity again, but this missionary journey which had just, for him, terminated, seemed to be more or less the rubicon which divided him from his old faith, and from the rationalism to which he drifted during the years while he was at Manchester, and University College, London.

CHAPTER IV. HIS MARRIAGE: HIS MOTHER'S DEATH: HIS CLASSICAL TUTORSHIP AT BRISTOL IN 1834

In Francis Newman's diary is this entry:—"On June 27th, my birthday, I first saw Maria Kennaway at Escot." [Footnote: Escot, Ottery St. Mary, S. Devon, now in the possession of the present Sir John Kennaway, M.P.]

Evidently the attraction between them was mutual, for the engagement followed quickly, and they were married the same year.

Maria Kennaway was the daughter of the first Sir John Kennaway, who was born at Exeter in 1758. In 1772 he sailed to India with his brother, the late Richard Kennaway. In 1780 he received his captain's commission, and in 1786 Marquis Cornwallis made him one of his aides–de–camp. I quote from *New Monthly Magazine* for 1836, which gave an account of some incidents in the first Sir John Kennaway's life at the time of his death. [Footnote: I am indebted for this account to the courtesy of the present Sir John Kennaway.]

[Illustration: MARIA KENNAWAY FRANCIS NEWMAN'S FIRST WIFE From a miniature PHOTO BY MESSRS. WEBSTER, CLAPHAM COMMON BY KIND PERMISSION OF SIR JOHN KENNAWAY]

"In 1788 Lord Cornwallis sent him as envoy to the Court of Hyderabad to demand from the Nizam the cession of ... Guntoor. In this mission he was eminently successful, not only obtaining that which he came to demand, but inducing the Nizam to enter into a treaty of offensive and defensive alliance against Tippoo Sultan. For this service His Majesty was pleased to create him a baronet (1791), and he received a mark of still further approbation from the Court of Directors (East India Company) in a vote which they passed to take out the patent of creation at the Company's expense." Later, Sir John arranged a definite peace between the Nizam's Commissioner and the Mahrattas with those of Tippoo Sultan. From this time forward Sir John remained as Resident at the Court of the Nizam. But as his health had suffered greatly from the Indian climate, he came back to England in 1794, and the East India Company voted him "the unusual grant of a pension of L500 per annum" on his retirement from official duties.

Soon after his return to England he met and married Charlotte Amyatt, and went to live at Escot, Ottery St. Mary. Here their family of twelve children was reared. Sir John, though his official life was over, yet busied himself in many local matters. He acted as deputy–lieutenant and as colonel–commandant of local militia and yeomanry. Then later, in advanced age, there fell upon him a great trouble: he lost his sight entirely. Curiously enough, his brother (who had served in the Civil Service of the East India Company) suffered the same deprivation.

Everyone who remembers her describes Maria Kennaway, Sir John's daughter, as possessing great beauty and attraction. She had hitherto spent her girlhood in the daily service of the poor around her home. She and her sisters started village schools in the neighbourhood, and taught the children constantly the religious duties in which they themselves had grown up.

Maria Kennaway—a Plymouth Sister as regards her religious profession—was a girl of deep and earnest faith. After her marriage to Francis Newman, it became a real grief to her to find that he was drifting further and further away towards agnosticism. Loving him devotedly as she did, her constant prayer was that he might return to his former faith: that the "cloud," as she called it, which was over him might be dispersed, and that he should believe as she did.

Like Moses, she never in this life saw her "Promised Land" (she never doubted that he would *die* in faith), for when she died in July, 1876 (devotedly nursed by her husband), she knew that *he* thought, as he bent over her at the end, that it was probably a *last* farewell for both.

I give here, as it seems an appropriate place, Newman's letter (to Dr. Nicholson) on his wife's death:—

"15 Arundel Crescent, "Weston–super–Mare, "*21st July*, 1876.

"My dear Nicholson,

"For more than forty years I have been in possession of a heart that loved me ardently: that happiness is no more. But I kept my treasure ten years longer than I had any reason to expect. Yesterday we committed my beloved to the grave....

"I saw her declining in strength through failure of appetite, but ever hoped for finer weather and change of air to restore her. But the fine weather came too late to restore her. From want of blood her heart became fatally weak, and she died just as her brother did, the late Sir John Kennaway, through failure of the heart and consequent mortification of the feet. I now believe that local death began on the night of the 5th. Her sufferings in the feet were great, and we could do nothing to allay them. Her breathlessness (also from weakness of the heart) we could aid by fanning. She knew she could not recover, and only prayed for 'release.' Her prayer was granted early on Sunday morning, 16th July.

"Of course I feel very desolate, and to live quite alone in declining years [Footnote: Some few years later he married his first wife's devoted friend and companion who had lived with them for eleven years, and who took the greatest care of Newman till he died in 1897.] seems unnatural and unhealthful; but I cannot form any decisions at present. I am conscious of excellent health and unbroken strength, and after forty years of happy love should be very ungrateful to repine.

"By God's help I mean to be cheerful and active....

"I am, your affectionate friend,

"F. W. Newman."

This is the epitaph Newman had placed over his wife's grave:—

"With no superiority of intellect, yet by the force of love, by sweet piety, by tender compassion, by coming down to the lowly, by unselfishness and simplicity of life, by a constant sense of God's Presence, by devout exercises, private and social, she achieved much of Christian saintliness and much of human happiness.

"She has left a large void in her husband's heart.

"Obiit, *16th July*, 1876."

Newman always spoke of his wife as "the most affectionate and tender- hearted of mortals." There was always a very great affection between them. His letters all show this. Their married life was a long intercourse of happiness, *un*-"chequered by disputes."

46

[Footnote: "Marriage is one long conversation, chequered by disputes."—R. L. Stevenson.] Still, there was not (as is shown, I think, in many ways) strong community of interests. For in all Newman's laborious philological studies—his learned lectures, articles, and researches, scriptural and literary, his speculations in the realms of deep thought—she was to all intents and purposes practically outside his mental door. She was never greatly inclined to join in the society of his learned friends; but this was more from a sense of modesty, because she was afraid of not being in sympathy with them; because she thought that she was not clever enough.

She had the greatest admiration for her husband. It is easy, of course, to understand that when Frank Newman came back from his missionary journey he was just the sort of young man who would take a girl's fancy. It was a thing not to be surprised at that she fell in love with him. She was keenly interested in home missionary work among the poor villagers of her own home. She knew that he had come through great dangers in his journey to the Holy Land as a missionary. He had not then definitely cast aside his old beliefs—that was to come later; *now* he was on the brink of it, and he was alone on this inward, personal brink. *She* would not yet be aware of it. Very probably he seemed a hero in her eyes, because of all the dangers he had braved to preach the Gospel, and because he was one of the most intellectual men of his day: had taken high honours at Oxford, and had given them up for the sake of what he believed to be right.

In the beautiful little Devonshire town of Ottery St. Mary, very possibly he was the greatest man who had come across her life's path. He very evidently cared for her; the inevitable next thing seemed to be to care for him. At that time his name was in everybody's mouth. Miss Frere wrote, in 1833, that "the brother of Mr. Newman (John Henry Newman) is a young man of great promise, who has left the fairest prospect of advancement in England to go as a missionary to Persia."

At any rate, Destiny had brought them together, and they were married.

As a woman said once to me, "There is no choosing in love"—once the *meeting* has happened, all free choice is at an end.

Mrs. Francis Newman was not very strong, and later in life developed greater delicacy. It will be remembered that Newman's mother and sisters were living at Oxford at this time, and he was anxious some time later to bring his bride to see them. Unfortunately she fell ill, and the treatment given for her illness proved quite a mistaken one; consequently her recovery was much slower than it need otherwise have been. The journey was, besides, a tiring one for her in her state of health. They had to go from Bristol to Oxford, for by this time Newman was settled at Bristol College as classical tutor. He had previously been tutor in Dublin for a short time.

In 1836 Francis Newman went through the ceremony of Baptism at a chapel in Bristol. I say advisedly, "went through the ceremony," for I believe both he and his brother had received the rite in early childhood, when their father was alive.

Mr. George Hare Leonard, University College, Bristol, has kindly sent me some information as regards Francis Newman's work at Bristol, as also has Mr. Norris Mathews, the City Librarian of the Municipal Public Libraries there.

From them I learn that the college at which Newman was classical tutor was, not "Queen's," as has once or twice been asserted, but Bristol College. It was founded in 1831, and only existed ten years. Mr. Hare Leonard tells me that it was held in a large house in Park Row, and that it had some very distinguished pupils, Sir Edward Fry, the late Sir George Gabriel Stokes, [Footnote: Sir George Gabriel Stokes, Lucasian Professor of Mathematics at Cambridge since 1849, and Fellow and President of Pembroke College, Cambridge, was born in 1819; senior wrangler, 1841. President of Royal Society 1885. Contributed many mathematical papers and lectures to the Royal Society and other societies at Cambridge University, Aberdeen, Edinburgh, etc.] and Walter Bagehot being amongst them.

At this time Newman was a member of the historic Baptist chapel at Broadmead. I think it must have been in this chapel, indeed, that he was re–baptized (as I mentioned a little earlier), and some of the congregation anticipated his becoming one of the sect of Plymouth Brethren.

Perhaps it is not generally known that Bristol College undertook to give religious instruction on Church of England lines to those boys whose parents wished it (I quote now from Mr. George Hare Leonard's letter to me): "This was not obligatory upon all, and there was a fierce attack on the college by certain of the clergy, and Bishop Gray was hostile. In 1841, under the influence of Monk (Bishop of Gloucester and Bristol), Bishop's College was founded close by, and the older and more liberal college was unable to stand the competition, and came to an end."

I quote here [Footnote: By the kindness of Miss Humphrey, Lensfield, Cambridge, who gave me this extract from a memoir of her father.] an account of the school life of the Vicar of St. Mary Redclyffe, Bristol:—

"In 1835 he went to Bristol College, a school that no longer exists, of which Dr. Jerrard, his brother William's friend and a mathematician of some note, was principal.... He remained for two years at Bristol College, and considered that when there he owed much to the teaching of Francis Newman, brother of the Cardinal, a man of charming character and great attainments (afterwards made manifest in many ways), who was then lecturer in elementary mathematics, and subsequently corresponded with him" (the Vicar of St. Mary Redclyffe) "on mathematical subjects when both had become famous."

This all seems to point, I think, to the fact that Bristol College had certainly a distinguished roll of names in its short ten years' record.

1836 was the year of Mrs. Newman's death—Francis Newman's mother. His wife was so alarmingly ill that he was not able to be present at his mother's funeral; and so the last time he saw her alive was on the occasion when he brought his bride to introduce to her at Oxford.

Miss Mozley says of his mother: "She was a woman content to live, as it were, in the retirement of her thoughts. She had an influence, though not a conspicuous one, on all about her. The trials of life had given a weight to her judgment, and her remarkable composure and serenity of temper and manner had its peculiar power. Under this gentle manner was a strong will which could not be moved when her sense of duty dictated self–sacrifice."

A month after her death Cardinal Newman had written: [Footnote: *Letters of John Henry Newman*, Anne Mozley.] "Of late years my mother has much misunderstood my religious views, and considered she differed from me; [Footnote: As of course she did.] and she thought I was surrounded by admirers, and had everything my own way; and in consequence I, who am conscious to myself I never thought anything more precious than her sympathy and praise, had none of it." He goes on to say: "I think God intends me to be lonely.... I think I am very cold and reserved to people, but I cannot ever realize to myself that any one loves me."

Those who have read Miss Mozley's *Life of John Henry Newman* will remember how passionately devoted to her two sons Mrs. Newman was. Once or twice she said that though "Frank was adamant" when she had wished to get closer in touch with his interests and sympathies when he was quite a young man, yet she was always *quite* in sympathy with her eldest son.

Probably as time went on and she saw the latter drifting ever further and further into religious views with which she had never been conversant, insensibly to herself, her manner changed when he spoke to her of how gradually the whole scope of his religion was widening and developing in a direction in which she felt it impossible for herself to follow him.

One wonders if she had had any knowledge of the growing agnosticism of her other son, but probably this was unlikely.

[Illustration: DR. MARTINEAU FROM THE PAINTING BY A. E. ELMSLIE]

CHAPTER V. FRIENDSHIP WITH DR. MARTINEAU

In the year 1840 Francis Newman was made Classical Professor in Manchester New College. That same year saw Dr. Martineau appointed Professor of Mental and Moral Philosophy at the same college. It will be remembered that for thirty–seven years Manchester New College had been at York, and had now but just returned to its name–place.

Here then began the friendship which lasted unbroken until death.

Both men were keen searchers—each in his own way—after religious truth. For both it was a subject that practically affected their whole lives. But while in Martineau the result was a deep theology which found its satisfaction in the fold of Unitarianism, in Newman dogma of any sort was practically an unknown quantity. He drifted further and further from revealed religion, until many of his letters and writings became to the Christian minds of some who read them exceedingly painful. It is true that before he died Mr.

Memoir and Letters of Francis W. Newman

Temperley Grey, the minister who attended him in his last illness, declared that there was a return to his original faith, but still nothing can alter the effect of the written word, and there is a passage in one of Newman's own letters which illustrates this fact very clearly. "It is a sad thing to have printed erroneous fact. I have three or four times contradicted and renounced a passage ... *but I cannot reach those whom I have misled.*" In those last nine words there is a world of unexpressed regret—regret which no after endeavour can eradicate. Both spoken and written words go to far mental ports, and very often–from being out of our ken—unreachable ones for us. No later contradiction can reach them and undo the once–made impression.

Martineau and Newman were not of one mind in the matter of religion. The letters which passed between them show that; but they show, too, that no dispute separated them. If for a time some painful passage in a letter of Newman's troubled his friend, the matter was dealt with with straightforward candour and unfailing forbearance and gentleness. There were no harsh words between them. Both of them were naturally, innately sweet and kindly in disposition. Even in matters of dispute which concerned that subject which occupied so large a part in both their minds, difference of opinion could not "separate very friends."

It will be remembered that the year before the regular correspondence between the two began, Martineau had written a paper criticizing Newman's *Phases of Faith*.

Before giving Newman's letters, perhaps a few words on Martineau himself would not be out of place here. He came of an old Huguenot family. Mr. Jackson, from whose biography of him I am quoting, says that Gaston Martineau, who, tradition tells us, was a surgeon of Dieppe, came to England after the Revocation of the Edict of Nantes in 1685, and that though first he went to London to live, yet that eventually he settled down at Norwich, and here all his children were born. The youngest of them became the father of James Martineau, the theologian. He was born in the same year as Francis Newman, and died just seven years before he did.

In the bringing up and early training of both men there was a large element of Puritanism. Many of the most severe Calvinistic doctrines held sway in Newman's home life, and even if the atmosphere was a little less thickly charged with religious thunderclouds in the early environment of Martineau, yet certainly, from all accounts, Sunday was pre–eminently a day that "hid its real meaning and brightness behind a frowning face." I cannot help quoting here a story which a little reveals the sort of religious atmosphere which brooded over the day and the point of view brought to bear on it by James Martineau's mother when he was a boy. The mother had gone to church one Sunday evening, and left word in her little home circle that they were to read the Bible.

When she came back she put the probing question to James: "What had he read?" His answer was: "Isaiah." She at once replied that he couldn't have read the whole; and he answered promptly, "Yes, mother, I have, skipping the nonsense."

From eight years old to fourteen James Martineau went, as a day scholar, to Norwich Grammar School. After school life he came to the conclusion that he wished to give his life to the ministry, and as, of course, the English universities were not open to anyone who refused to sign the Thirty–nine Articles, he was sent to Manchester College. Here it became evident to everybody that he was a student who would let nothing interfere with his work. His masters were struck by his accurate habits of mind and great perseverance in research.

In 1835 his ministry in Liverpool, as pastor in Paradise Street Chapel, began, and to his work here was joined his work at Manchester New College, which, as I mentioned before, began in 1840, the same year as Newman's own connection with the college. But when, in 1853, the college was transplanted to London, for four years Martineau continued to live as a minister in Liverpool, and yet he kept up his classes at the college (six hours by train from Liverpool).

In 1857 he was asked to come and live in town and devote his whole time to his college work, and this he agreed to do. There were not then many students, but among them were names which after years were destined to make famous, and among these were Alexander Gordon, Estlin Carpenter, and Philip Wicksteed.

In 1858 he was appointed minister to Little Portland Street Chapel. Formerly the congregation belonging to the chapel were rigid, unbending Unitarians. With the advent of Martineau began the newer, broader views of Unitarianism. Throughout the years which now were to be passed in London, Dr. Martineau's labours were unceasing as scholar, thinker, and theologian. It is said that, though he wrote and taught so much, yet he never let his reading be interfered with; he was always adding to his stores of knowledge. For fifty years he was recognized as one of the most profound thinkers of his day, as well as one of the finest writers.

The first letter from Francis Newman to Martineau, from which I quote, is dated December, 1850, from Brighton:—

Dr. Martineau from Newman.

"I seem to be out of joint with you in the two highest interests of man— Religion and Politics ... I am ... become a Republican by principle, for the continent Jefferson always held that constitutional monarchy was a simple impossibility in a large continental country where great armies were kept up; and I think the history of a millennium in Europe demonstrates it. All royalties were in their origin constitutional; but in the long run no dynasty ever resisted the temptation to overthrow the barriers which fenced it in. *Our* liberties seem to me rightly ascribed to the fact that we are insular, and need only a *navy* for protection. Sweden for the same reason is able to retain its liberties.... I think that in the order of Providence, royal power has served the purpose of uniting nations in larger masses than would else have held together.

"Where it has done this without destroying municipal organization it is clearly good in its result—as in Great Britain, Sweden, Germany; ... but having served this function, it seems to me that Royalty (unless it could again become elective) has done its work, and ought not to be regretted.... On doctrinaire grounds, either to unsettle it where it works well, or to desire to enforce it where it has violated its pledges and forfeited all claims to love and devotion, seems to me a mistake similar in kind.

     * * * * *

"Must not a time of weakness come when Austria is bankrupt—when an Emperor of Russia is a dotard or a child, when provinces of Russia become disaffected, or an army mutinies; or again, when France and Austria seriously fall out?... You see I am dosing you with some of my most pungent stuff, in proof that I trust your strength of stomach ...

"Your affectionate friend,

"FRANCIS W. NEWMAN."

Memoir and Letters of Francis W. Newman

In the letter which follows, Newman touches on two well–known personalities of his day—Frederica Bremer and Charles Kingsley. He mentions the fact of his having been engaged to meet Kossuth as the reason why the first attempt to meet Miss Bremer was unsuccessful. It will be remembered that Miss Bremer came to England in order to collect material for her *Life in the Old World*. (This year was also the date of Kossuth's first visit to our shores.) Miss Bremer was Swedish by descent, but Finnish by birth, for she was born in Finland in the year 1801.

As regards Kingsley, in 1850 he had published tracts on "Christian Socialism." *Alton Locke* had already come out and met with scorn on the part of the Press, though working men—who recognized Kingsley as their truest friend—welcomed it gladly. In 1851—a year of great trouble and distress all over England—he thought out plans to drain parts of Eversley (his parish), for there had been many cases of fever there, and Kingsley was pre–eminently a *practical* Christian. He was also far ahead of his time (as all great men invariably are), and he saw clearly how inseparably close in this present world is the connection between physical matters and spiritual. He recognized that if a man is *living* in unsanitary conditions, it affects in a very real though inexplicable way his spiritual life. He could trace the connection in a parishioner's life history between bad drainage and drunkenness: later on—though it might perhaps be very much later on—a "bee–in–the–bonnet" of his child: and he saw in this unhappy, unfortunate Little Result the outcome of someone's sinful failure in his duty to his neighbour in years gone by, when the first insanitary conditions were allowed to live and be mighty.

In some senses drainage, therefore, has a decided effect upon the spiritual life of men and women. Everyone probably will remember Dr. Nettleship's resolute assertion, that "even a stomach–ache could be a spiritual experience."

And so Kingsley pushed forward the drainage improvements in his parish, and considered it, what in very truth it was, a fitting subject for the energies of a parish priest, at work night and day for the betterment of the souls and bodies of his parishioners.

I cannot avoid quoting here Francis Newman's own strongly expressed views on drainage of the land:—

"Now, the drains being out of sight, it is morally certain that defects will exist, or be caused by wear and tear, unseen. In one place evil liquids and gases will percolate; in another evil accumulations will putrefy. Instead of blending small portions of needful manure quickly with small portions of earth that needs it, we secure in the drains a slow putrefaction and a permanent source of pestilence; we relieve a town by imposing a grave vexation and danger on the whole neighbourhood where its drains have exit; we make the mouth of every tide river a harbour and storehouse of pollution; and after thus wasting an agricultural treasure we send across the Atlantic ships for a foul commerce in a material destined to replace it....

"It was quite notorious forty years ago that the refuse of the animal was the food of the vegetable, and ought to be saved for use, not wasted in poisoning waters. How could well–informed men delude themselves into an approval of this course? Only one explanation occurs: *they despaired of returning to Nature*. They assumed that we must live by artifice, and they entitled artifice 'Science.'"

I return now to the letter from Newman to Martineau:—

Dr. Martineau from Francis Newman.

"Southampton, Wednesday, "*8th Oct.* 1851.

"My dear Martineau,

"Your interesting letter was sent to me by Monday afternoon, and first told me that Miss Bremer was in London, which I learned only by a pencil note on the outside, '142 Strand.' That evening I was going to see my two sisters—one returned from the Continent, and one come from Derby. And on Tuesday morning I was engaged to come hither to meet Kossuth! So I fear I have missed Miss Bremer. But, from to–day's news, I fear there is no chance of K. arriving till next Monday or Tuesday; and I shall probably go back to–morrow. I will *try* to see Miss Bremer immediately, but am much disappointed.

"I have had a little correspondence with Mr. Kingsley lately—rising out of a recent lecture of his, the practical results and practical principles of which gave me great pleasure. He says he has 'done his work' of protesting and denouncing capitalists, and now hopes to give himself to *construction* and practical creation; and much as I fear some of his generalizations, I hope great good from his purely excellent aims, and the amount of aid he can command. He agrees most heartily with my denunciation of large towns as the monster evil, and takes the matter up agriculturally thus: *No country can be underfed while it returns to the soil what it takes out of it*"—[The italics are my own. Is not this sentence of infinite value to us to–day?]—"for, in the long run, the soil will always give back as much as it receives. Every country impoverishes itself which pours into the rivers and sea the animal refuse which ought to be restored to the soil.

"No community can avoid this prodigality, unless its inhabitants live upon the soil. Therefore towns ought not to exceed the size at which the whole animal refuse can be economically saved and directly applied to agriculture.

"To me it seems that every reason—moral, political, agricultural, economical, sanitary—converge to this same conclusion; and I apply *Delenda est Carthago* to every city in Europe.

"On the subject of masters and servants, he says, 'Masters should be considered "*infamous*" who hired servants by the day or week, and not by the year; or who dismissed old servants without any other reason than to lower wages; but such a thing, to be possible and effective, must be *mutual*. The servant must have no power to leave a good master in order to *raise* his wages. But at present, while the servant is under no bonds to the master, and *does not like to bind himself*, it seems to me quite impossible to treat the masters as having any moral responsibility for the servants more than for foreigners. When we buy tea, we cannot ask whether the Chinese get a comfortable livelihood by selling it at that price.' That is an extreme and clear case to which we approach in every commercial transaction in proportion as the other party claims that the relation shall be one of mere marketing....

"Ever yours affectionately,

"Francis W. Newman."

The next letter, which is dated September, 1851, and which was written just after Newman's return from his Swiss tour, goes on with the same subject as the last, and also touches on the evils of *suddenly* introducing machinery; while it shows clearly that, in the long run, better wages are gained for the worker by its means—"Machinery is in every light the friend of the poor." He says very truly, "The first great want of the workmen is better morality and more thriftiness, *not* better masters or higher wages." Putting quite aside the question of whether "higher wages" are not needed by the workman, nothing can be truer at the present time than this fact, brought thus before us by Newman. It *is*, beyond all question, these faults which run through the bulk of the labouring classes (as we term them)—lack of the true spirit of morality and thriftiness.

It is difficult altogether to account for the reason why the lack of these characteristics is so much to the fore to–day, or to think of the remedy which shall reach and cure them. But that it is a presence in our midst is a self–evident fact. No one who has travelled much in France (to name only one other country), but is aware how vast is the gulf which divides the ways of living of our own labouring classes and of those which obtain across the water. There, thriftiness is the rule. They use a far simpler diet, and one which the land supplies them with, and are content. There is a far more healthy tone about them, even if it be a rough one, than there is among our own poor. I am constantly in France myself (it is the country of my own ancestors), and I have never failed to be struck by the absence there, in the country, of the vice which disfigures so often the home life of our villagers. You do not see there the sights that make the streets on Saturday evening in England a degrading scene. When the French villager is happy, he can be it without the aid of drunkenness. And as far as the cultivation of the land is concerned—well, we need only look at home in our "French Farming" schemes to–day and we shall find that when we want to come "back to the land," to find out how much care and industry will bring out of it, we have to send for a Frenchman to show us his country's secrets of manuring the land, so that the soil becomes precious and will yield, even from so small a space as a quarter of an acre, incalculable riches in the way of marketable goods.

As regards what Newman says about the work_women of England, it is impossible to agree with him. It is most assuredly not the case in thousands of instances that "there are *no* good workwomen out of work, or earning low wages," nor that "those who cannot get good wages are women who have *spent their prime in idleness* ... and sew badly."

One has but to refer to the statistics with which the Christian Social Union supplies us, as well as other societies, to have this idea quickly negatived. Mrs. Carlyle's experiences and Mrs. Newman's were evidently involuntarily misleading.

There was a certain impulsiveness in discussing many subjects to which Newman seems to have been peculiarly subject. He was sometimes so led away by it as to dogmatize inaccurately or over–forcibly.

Memoir and Letters of Francis W. Newman

Dr. Martineau from Francis Newman.

"My dear Martineau,

"... In a day or two I am meditating a visit to Froude, who is in Wales, and too much in solitude." [Froude was then preparing or writing his *History of England*. It will be remembered that Cardinal Newman's influence over him at college decided him later on taking Holy Orders, but he never went beyond the diaconate.] "Gladstone's letters just now are a powerful stimulus to public opinion.... Not the Socialists only, but numbers of workmen besides treat it as *an abstract wickedness* in a master to offer lower wages than are at any particular time existing. They have never any objection to a *rise* of wages; so I cannot say they treat the existing rate as a divinely appointed amount; but they do not see that if they are unwilling to bind themselves not to strike for a rise, they ought to concede in the master a moral right to lower.... What is to be done with those who will go on enunciating and propagating dangerous general maxims as abstract axiomatic truth?... *Your* method of making the masters determine how many *shall enter* a trade will succeed; but I do not see that it will succeed in ejecting. In the years of railroad excitement the London newspapers were enormously overworked, and a great increase no doubt took place in the numbers of printers (perhaps also in their wages); now the printers for some time have been in comparative depression.... I do not contend that *all* lowering of wages by masters is merciful and just, but that *some* may be; whereas the Socialists and Co. instantly declaim against *all* or *any* lowering, without entering into any details as to present or past history of the trade. When I said that machinery is in every light the friend of the poor, I do not think I overlooked the occasional mischief caused by its *sudden* introduction.... The effect of machinery is in the long run a steady rise of wages as well as a cheap supply of goods: the advantage to the poor is universal and permanent, the evil is partial and transitory. Moreover, the evil is immensely aggravated by their perverseness. Three generations of hand–loom weavers have been propagated in spite of the notorious misery it must cause. Machinery does *not* raise the rate of profits or interest; it *does* raise the rate of wages: compare Manchester and Buckingham in proof.... I do not think I am *at all* carried into reaction by unjust attacks on capitalists, but I am very strongly by the [right or wrong] belief that the first great want of the workmen is better morality and more thriftiness, *not* better masters or higher wages. I have not dared to print half of what are my convictions on this head.... The sufferings of the poor from bad air and bad water are quite a separate chapter. High wages do little to cure this. Indeed, in Manchester the workmen habitually prefer to save a shilling a week in house rent and spend it in beefsteaks, when the shilling would have got them a healthy instead of an unhealthy lodging. Bricklayers' wages are at present high in London; what is the consequence? I have at present a bit of a dwarf wall building in my garden. The men leave their work; I complain; the builder replies: 'Men will not come to work on a Monday without much trouble.' I fear this *means* that they drink on Sunday and are very 'seedy' on Monday morning. The very men who are excited by high wages to drinking and idleness will make a violent outcry when a fall of wages takes place, and *moreover* will get the ear and sympathies of Maurice and Co. for their outcry."

"Maurice and Co." of course refers to Frederick Denison Maurice, who was the principal mover in the Christian Socialism of the day, as he was in all social reforms. He had met with much abuse and opposition, but still there were very many who called him "Master." Amongst these last was Charles Kingsley, who had been one of his pupils, and who had been very greatly influenced by his opinion in religion and social matters. [Footnote: Kingsley (see memoir) said to Maurice, when opposition was fiercest against him: "Your cause is mine. We swim in the same boat, and stand or fall thenceforth together."] Neither man could bear the narrowness of "parties" in religion. They always demanded more toleration, broader views, and refused to be bound by narrow creeds. It was owing chiefly to Coleridge that Maurice took Holy Orders. He was born in that year of great men, 1805, and by 1851 his socialistic ideas were well known to the world.

"As to the milliners and tailors, my wife has the same experience as Mrs. Carlyle, that there are *no* good workwomen out of work, or earning low wages. Mrs. Wedgwood tells me that the Ladies' Committee could not get women to make the shirts.... Those who cannot get good wages are women who have *spent their prime in idleness*, and cannot work well enough to satisfy ladies. They sew badly, and get a poor pittance from the shops. As to tailors, I give more for a coat by four or five shillings than I did twenty–five years ago.... Until our national morality is much improved, and our moral organization repaired, there must be a large body of persons without any trade, art, or connection who will throw themselves into what seems to be the easiest art, and by their numbers will swamp it...."

"Ever your affectionate

"Francis W. Newman."

It should be mentioned here that in 1853 Manchester New College was moved to London, but that it was not until 1857, that Dr. Martineau went to live in town, in order to devote his time chiefly to the important work which devolved upon him in connection with it. This he continued to do until 1885. Newman had been appointed in 1846 to the chair of Latin in University College, a post he held until 1863.

The next letter of this period, addressed to Martineau, gives one an insight as to the effect of beauty of scenery upon Newman. He was far removed from the ordinary point of the rapid traveller of to–day, who only seems to want to cover great distances at rapid speed, and can therefore have no conception at all of what we might call the "atmospheric environment" of a place, which can only be felt by quiet moving, as Newman expresses it, "from point to point," to "see how aspects and proportions change."

Dr. Martineau from Francis Newman. "Grisedale Bridge, "Patterdale, near Penrith, "*31st July* 1854.

"My dear Martineau,

"I have been faithless in not writing to you before now....

"We are more delighted than ever with Patterdale. Probably enough you know the beauties of *your* neighbourhood so well, and esteem them so highly, that you turn as deaf an ear as I do to all praises of other parts. I have so strong a sense of the inexhaustibility of beauty, that it aids me to repress the restlessness which is kindled by other persons' praises of what is unknown to me....

"Unless I had *my own* carriage I get little pleasure from touring. What I want is to stop at the beautiful places, and go from point to point and see how aspects and proportions change; this in fact you seldom do well except on foot and at leisure. The walks here are inexhaustible, for persons who can carry with them their book or other occupation, and stay out four or five hours; but you want reasonably dry weather, else indeed the swampiness of the mountains greatly lessens the number of feasible or pleasant walks, besides impairing the beauty.

"I only get a newspaper once a week, and in such a crisis feel hungry for news as the week goes on." [The "crisis," of course, was the near approach at this time of the beginning of those hostilities which were to end in the Crimean war.] "Lest the Eastern question should flag in interest by lingering, lo! the Spanish insurrection breaks on us. I do not yet dare to hope European benefits from Spain: should such be the ultimate result, it will be a striking illustration how incalculable is the *course* of events, while the general end is not very obscure.

"Mr. Charles Loring Brace, of America (who, you may know, was imprisoned in Hungary), sent to me an introduction from Theodore Parker. It is highly probable he had one to you....

"The post summons.

"Ever yours, "F. W. N."

Harriet Martineau, sister of Dr. Martineau, was fifty–three years of age when Newman wrote to her brother about her illness. Practically for the whole of her life she had been more or less of an invalid. Even as a girl she suffered so much from deafness and wretched health, that she was hardly ever free from anxiety and depression. Nevertheless she did not let her ill–health prevent her from earning her livelihood by writing. Before she made her name by the publication of her stories on political economy, she experienced endless difficulties in her efforts to get publishers for her books. But no sooner had these stories appeared than her fame was assured, and money came in, so to speak, by handfuls, so that all financial troubles were altogether at an end.

From 1839 till 1844 she was so terribly out of health that no treatment produced any effect, until someone suggested that mesmerism should be tried, and this succeeded so well that she recovered a certain amount of strength and was able to go on with her writing. Nevertheless, that it did not wholly restore her health is evident from the fact that in 1855, when Newman was writing to her brother, he mentions her "formidable fainting fits" and daily pains in the head. "Her letter tells me," he says, "how very bad she is, that every day she feels shot in the head"; but he goes on to say that he does not despair of her better health because (as indeed her numerous books testify), her "body is so subject to her mind." It is, I think, necessary to remember that in 1844, when Miss Martineau tried mesmerism as a cure for her continued ill–health, mesmerism was practically taking its first steps in the English medical world. This science of healing, which began to be recognized in England about the middle of the eighteenth century, through the medium of the afterwards discredited Mesmer, has "in its day played many parts" and had more names than one. In the first instance it was called mesmerism, then animal magnetism, while to–day, when it has forced its way through incredulity, distrust, and opposition of all sorts, and come to the front in very truth, it faces us as a power which bids fair to be more and more with us as time goes on under the name of Hypnotism.

Perhaps few people remember the name of the man who really brought animal magnetism into prominence in the middle of the last century. Yet James Braid, the Scotch surgeon, who then lived at Manchester, and pursued with untiring thoroughness and perseverance his studies in the then little– known science, was really the shoulder that pushed hypnotism into our midst. It was Braid, indeed, who caused the name of "hypnotism" to eject that of "mesmerism" in England. He was never properly appreciated during his lifetime. But if he was not, he was only one of numerous examples which are always being brought up before our eyes (among those of our countrymen who have rendered their country signal services), who illustrate the famous English quotation, "Thus angels walked the earth unknown, and *when they flew were recognized* "

Braid, however, proved effectually that the mesmeric phenomena depend altogether on the physiological condition of the person operated on, and not on the power of the operator.

Dr. Martineau from Newman.

"7 P.V.E., "*17th Feb.*, 1855.

"My dear Martineau,

"You will believe that the state of your sister's health gives me much concern. She has kindly written twice to me. The second letter tells of formidable fainting fits, which I cannot explain away; yet, as I told her in my reply to her first, her symptoms *in general* are so similar to my own that I cannot but hope her physician views them too seriously, and *does her harm by it.* I, on the whole, believe that my own heart is unsound organically (distended), but my experience certainly is that the less I attend to it *in detail* the better, though I must in prudence avoid impure air and other evils. Her second letter tells me as a decisive proof how very bad she is, that every day she feels *shot* in the head.

"Now this is exactly the symptom I have for nine months been struggling to subdue, and as my wife knows, I am, week by week, balancing whether to put myself under a doctor for it.... The spasm which distresses me comes at the crisis when I ought to go to sleep, and so wakes me up. I could not get rid of it even in the summer, on days on which I had least mental effort, and was in all other respects conscious of great vigour....

"I went to a physician to complain of *sleeplessness* and got the reply that it was my *heart* that was diseased.... Your sister's body is so subject to her mind that I do not despair that, either through mesmerism restoring sleep or in some other way, she may rally far beyond her present expectation. I know a lady who was dying of brain fever, and could get no sleep until the physician called in a mesmerist; this gained sleep for her, and by that alone she recovered without medicine."

Dr. Martineau was one of the founders of the *National Review* in 1855, and frequently contributed articles to it. This next letter treats mainly of the proposed lines on which the magazine was to be run—its politics, points of view, etc.

Dr. Martineau from Newman.

"*14th June*, 1855.

"My dear Martineau,

"I have seen with interest that your scheme of the National Review is resumed, and I am told that you and Walter Bagehot are the political editors. Supposing that your politics are not essentially different from those of the *Westminster* the *Review* is of *practical* interest to me, in spite of my unfortunate collision last year, for which I hope you have forgiven me. I wrote in the last *Westminster* the last article on the "Administrative Example of the United States," and in the forthcoming number I have written the second article on "International Immorality." I wrote them freely, and indeed could not comfortably take money from Chapman in his present circumstances, but I would much rather write for the *National Review* if I am admissible.... I value *forms* of government in proportion as they develop moral results in individual man; and if I *now* am democratic for Europe, it is not from any abstract and exclusive zeal for democracy, all the weaknesses of which I keenly feel, but because the dynasties, having first corrupted or destroyed the aristocracies, and next become hateful, hated, and incurable themselves, have left no government possible which shall have stability and morality except the democratic. In England my desire is to ward off this result, to which, I think, our aristocracy are driving fast by uniting their cause with the perfidious immoralities of the Continent.

"Your political prospectus seems to me to be delusive by its vagueness. I mean, that it is no sort of security after misunderstandings between editors and writers. I think it is liable practically to lead to the result that one man's mind seems undesirably to assume the authority of a confederation;... but where Truth is sought, this is not easily borne. Have you considered whether you may not do as the *Revue des Deux Mondes*, which admits independent essays with the writer's name signed? I value the convenience of anonymous writing, and I do not wish to see it destroyed; but it is undoubtedly abused and overdone, and I think every movement in the opposite direction has its use."

I think that when reviewing many of Newman's ideas—ideas considered as strongly tending to socialism of a sort—it is wise to bear in mind these words in this letter: "If I *now* am democratic for Europe, it is not from any abstract or exclusive zeal for democracy, all the weaknesses of which I keenly feel." For they show very clearly that his was a mind which refused any party labelling. The reform was the thing with him, and the means by which this was brought about were only secondary and subordinate.

In September, 1856, Newman was at Ventnor; and though apparently still suffering from his heart and indigestion, found that he was able to bathe in the sea with much pleasure to himself. He gives voice to his surprise that, in those days, there should be so strong a feeling against "mixed bathing," as the term is: and he quotes articles and letters which he had seen in which disgust was expressed at "ladies bathing within reach of telescopes" and "at the indecency of promiscuous bathing"! This excessive over–prudishness, which has always, since early Victorian days, distinguished England, possesses as much vitality (even when, happily, dying) as that of the conger eel, whom no killing seems really to kill!

The earlier part of the letter deals with the disputes of the "three tutors against Dr. Hawkins," Provost of Oriel in 1830, and also with the proposal that his brother, John Henry Newman, should be made third secretary of the local Bible Society.

In the *Letters of Rev. J. B. Mozley, D.D.*, edited by his sister in 1884, there is a good deal of information given about the Oxford of that day, and this account of the dispute in 1830 occurs in one of Dr. Mozley's letters from Oriel College:—

"All sorts of rumours have gone abroad respecting the differences between the tutors, and it has received a most amusing variety of versions. It has been described as a strike for advance of wages or more pupils, which of course has fitted well into the probable falling off of the college consequent on the Heresy: at Tunbridge, a friend ... was told, the junior fellows had combined to turn out the Provost! For my part, I think it no more use trying to send abroad a correct account of it, for it is not easy to make it obvious to the meanest capacities, and everybody nowadays seems to feel himself justified in contending that to be truest which is the most consonant to his understanding.... I take it there is little doubt of H. Wilberforce being elected here, to Oriel, next year ... he is considered sure of his Double First...."

Of the Rev. Mr. Hill, mentioned by Newman as the "old secretary of the Bible Society," Dr. Mozley speaks in connection with the constant opposition and ill–humoured references to Pusey which at that time were rife at Oxford.

As regards "Bulteel" of Exeter College, Dr. Mozley thus speaks of him: "Bulteel's sincere belief is that there is a new system of things in the course of revelation now, as there was in our Saviour's time, and that God has given him the power of working miracles for the same reason as He gave it to the Apostles—in order to convince unbelievers.... There can be little doubt that Bulteel is partially deranged. I should not be much surprised if, before long, he attempts miracles of a more obvious kind."

As regards Hurrell Froude, Fellow and tutor of Oriel College, he, John Henry Newman, and Pusey were all three close friends in 1822. Hurrell Froude exercised a strong influence over J. H. Newman, and it was he who was one of the leaders in the Tractarian movement in 1833. He was a man of wonderful genius and originality, and it was a distinct loss to the world when, in 1836, he died. I cannot help quoting here the "private critique" written in 1838, and quoted by Miss Mozley in her volume, with reference to his *Remains*:—

"It is very interesting and clever, but I must say I felt as if I was committing an impertinence in reading his private journal–probably the most really private journal that ever was written.... I am very curious to know what kind of sensation his views will make, uttered so carelessly, instead of in Keble's, or Pusey or Newman's grand style."

With respect to Dr. Hawkins, the Provost (whose influence was in many ways a powerful one with J4 H. Newman), I quote two passages from letters of Dr. Mozley. One is dated 1836 and the other 1847 (during the Gladstone Election):—

"The Provost alluded in the most distant way to the sore subject (the condemnation of heretics) last Sunday. He observed that it was a disgusting habit in persons finding fault with other people's theology. Nothing so tended to make the mind narrow and bitter. They had much better be employing themselves in some active and useful way. This is laughable as coming from the Provost, who has been doing nothing else but objecting all his life." And:—

"The Provost has behaved very characteristically. He has been for once in his life fairly perplexed; and he has doubled and doubled again, and shifted and crept into holes; at last vanished up some dark crevice, and nothing was seen but his tail. One thought one was to see no more of him, when, on one of the polling mornings, he suddenly emerged, like a rat out of a haystack, and voted for Round. The Heads, in fact, have been thoroughly inefficient. The election has literally gone on *without* them. They have done nothing."

Dr. Martineau from Francis Newman.

"*18th Sept.*, 1856.

"My dear Martineau,

"Your welcome letter finds me still here. I certainly did not contemplate that I was speaking for the public ear on such a subject. I have a pain from it (chiefly from a sense, perhaps, that I should not like my brother to know or suspect that the information came from me), yet I cannot blame your proceeding, or question your right, so carefully and tenderly as you guard against objection.... The Rev. Mr. Hill, Vice–Principal of St. Edmund's Hall, was the old secretary of the (local) Bible Society. The Rev. Benjamin Parson Symons (now warden of Wadham College) is he who proposed and carried that my brother should be a third secretary.

"I think I told you that Symons was the *second* secretary; but I now doubt whether the second was not Rev.——Bulteel, of Exeter College, then an evangelical preacher of St. Ebb's Church in Oxford, much attended by Edmund Hall men. The after vote rescinding my brother's secretaryship was proposed by Benjamin Newton, a young Fellow of Exeter College, if this is of any importance.... The affair of the three tutors against Dr. Hawkins was told me exactly as I had it from my brother's lips; but the whole must have been strictly public. The other tutors were Robert Isaac Wilberforce (since Archdeacon and Roman Catholic), Richard Hurrell Froude, known by his *Remains*; and a much older man, Dornford, now a rector in Devonshire, who adhered to Hawkins. This took place in 1830, when my brother was only twenty–nine, Wilberforce his junior, and Hurrell Froude *my* junior in the University; probably my equal in age, i.e. then twenty–five; so it was *young* Oxford versus old. When the three tutors resigned (whose youth was a result of the Oriel Fellows going off so quick), Hawkins brought into the tutorship young Coplestone, as he was called—a nephew of the Bishop;... I almost think that for a time he resumed lecturing himself: but it will not do to say so.... I have here found out (after more than ten years' cessation) that I can swim as well as ever, and without discomfort to my heart. I am becoming quite zealous for my daily swim, even when (as to–day) the south–west gives us rather too much sea, to the chagrin of the bathing men. Perhaps you have seen various letters in *The Times*, etc., on the indecency of promiscuous bathing, etc. I cannot understand why they all direct their attack to the wrong point, and insist on driving people into solitudes and separations very inconvenient, instead of demanding that, as on the Continent, both sexes be clad in the water. Last year I saw an article that expressed disgust at ladies bathing within reach of *telescopes*! There is here such a colony of foreigners, that I hope they may teach this lesson. Besides the Pulszkys, who are a family of twelve persons, there are seven of Kossuth's household, a large family of Marras (Italian), three of Janza (Viennese), two or more Piatti's (Italian), who keep company together, and very many of whom bathe stately. Mrs. Pulszky is not well this year for swimming; but last year she swam daily, with her husband and an intimate male friend at her side. He will not let her swim in the sea without him, and is amazed at English husbands consenting to abandon their wives as they do. Mrs. Walter, her mother, is a devoted bather, and whenever the breakers are formidable has the aid of one or other male friend. It is a new fact to me, that the Viennese ladies, as a thing of course, are taught to swim in the Danube. There are regular teachers of swimming for both sexes, and a sort of diploma is granted to those who swim well enough to be at home in the water." [This is a phrase that was used to me; it now occurs to me that it may have been merely *metaphorical*, when the teacher says *Macte virtute*, etc., and concludes his lessons.]

"Of course, our climate does not allow the facilities of tropical waters (where alligators and sharks, however, are not facilities!); but the sea is fit for bathing with us as many months as the Danube, though I suppose never so warm as the Danube at its warmest.... If I could be with you at Derwentwater again, I think I should be less indisposed to try an oar. Indigestion or sleeplessness, not exertion, seems to be the chief enemy of my heart, which yet cannot bear exertion when so suffering. I am giving myself abundant ease, and never enjoyed myself with so much 'abandon.' We both like this place extremely.

"With kindest regards to all around you,

"I am, very affectionately yours,

"F. W. Newman."

In 1857, as I mentioned before, Dr. Martineau came up to London to live, having been asked by the authorities of Manchester New College to take more share in the work there than he had hitherto done. He was made Principal of the College in 1868, and held the post until 1885.

There is something in the letter which follows which must have made a very special appeal to Martineau—for this reason: that there is in it a passionate "abandon" quite foreign to Newman's usual style. He seems to have given rein to a sudden impulse of enthusiasm for his friend, and his letter, from start to finish, is full of it. He is evidently longing that Martineau should find in his London audience all the appreciation which his great talents deserved. And perhaps this is the thought which prompted those sentences which seem to urge him to curb the powerful steeds of his intellectual vigour, and not to give so lavishly or in such unstinted measure as in his sermons he had hitherto been accustomed to do. Newman says that in his preaching "there is *superfluous* intellectual effort." He adds that from " *intellectual* persons "he has heard the complaint that the "effort to follow is too great"; and he entreats him to prepare each sermon "with less *intellectual* effort, though, of course, not with less devotional purpose."

Dr. Martineau from Newman.

"7 P.V.E., "*30th May,* 1857.

"My dear Martineau,

"Perhaps you are already pulling up your tent–pegs: rather a heart–breaking work, especially to those who so love beauty and have surrounded themselves within doors with so much. You *need*, dear friend, a broad and fruitful field in London for your spiritual activity to recompense the great—the very great—sacrifices you must make in parting from all that you have loved in Liverpool. I have felt this so deeply that I never knew exactly how to *wish* that you might come to London; and, indeed, this place, so emphatically *dissipated*," [that is, *mente dissipata distracta*] "does not prize its great minds so much as smaller places would. ... Beloved friend, you know that great expectations are formed of you. It is hard, most hard, not to let this draw you into great intellectual effort, from which I fear much. For your literary lecturing, of course, I have no word of dissuasion. But let me assure you that in your preaching there is *superfluous* intellectual effort. It would be spiritually more effective if there were far less perfection of literary beauty and less condensation of refined thought and imaginative metaphor. I hear again and again from *intellectual* persons the complaint that the effort to follow your meaning is too great, and impairs both the pleasure and profit of listening to you. I myself am conscious that wonder and admiration of your talent is apt to absorb and stifle the properly spiritual influence, and when I *read* your sermons, I often pause so long on single sentences as to be fully aware that I could have got little good from *hearing* them. I know that no two men's nature is the same, and habit is a second nature. Do not imagine that I wish you not to be yourself. (There is no danger of that.) But I am sure that by cultivating more of what the French call 'abandon'—by preparing with less *intellectual* effort for each separate sermon—though, of course, not with less devotional purpose—and by letting your immediate impulse have a large play in comparison to your previous study, there will be less danger of overworking your mind and fuller effect on those who are to benefit. ... I dare say you received from me the new volume of *Religious Duties*. Its author seems to me *primitively* to have belonged to what you call the class of ethical minds, but to have passed beyond it, and now to be at once Passionate and Spiritual. And is not this the natural and rightful thing, that though we begin with a fragmentary, we tend towards an integral religion? This book has been to me most delightful and profitable, and I trust you will also find it so. Such a revelation of a pure, tender, ardent spirit is itself an inexpressible stimulus, and has given me quite a flood of joy and sympathy.

"The doctrine of immortality so unhesitatingly avowed (?) affects me as nothing from Theodore Parker on the same subject ever did. The love and joy in God flowing out of it is so spontaneous and kindling as to make me long to say,—I now no longer *hope* only, but *I am sure*. In any case I do rejoice that others can so believe, and I pray that if this be a mere cloud over *my* eyes, it may at length be taken away. Not that I have any deficiency of *happiness* from this, but I have a great deficiency of *power*, and I am painfully out of sympathy with others by it.

"I want to cultivate, if I knew how, rather more free communication with those who supremely love God as the Good One, and who will bear with me! I much need this, if I could get it. But however shut up I may seem, believe that a fire of love for you burns in my heart. With warm regards to Mrs. Martineau,

"Your affectionate friend,

"F. W. Newman."

I should like to quote here words illustrative of this side of Newman's personality, that side which reveals him "at once passionate and spiritual," longing to attain to religious truth, and not railing against the forms of dogma which have led other men into "the kingdom of heaven," as was his too frequent habit. These words were written by him when he seemed to himself to have reached some measure of spiritual intuition, and there is great beauty in them:—

"None can enter the kingdom of heaven without becoming a little child. But behind and after this, there is a mystery revealed to but few, namely, that if the soul is to go on into higher spiritual blessedness it must become a *woman*. Yes, however manly thou be among men, it must learn to love being dependent; must lean on God, not solely from distress or alarm, but because it does not like independence or loneliness.... God is not a stern judge, exacting every tittle of some law from us.... He does *not* act towards us (spiritually) by generalities... but His perfection consists in dealing with each case by itself as if there were no others."

And now, before concluding this chapter, I take two much later letters written by Newman to Martineau; one is dated 1888 and the other 1892. The first one is written quite clearly—which is wonderful when one remembers that he was then eighty–three—and the other, four years later, is cramped and not so easy to decipher. Still, in the first of these letters he himself says, "I have to write as slow as any little schoolboy... and cannot help some blunders." He had been to Birmingham on the 20th June to see Cardinal Newman, and mentions how travelling by rail tried his head. The latter part of the letter relates to a big dinner composed chiefly of Anglo–Indians and their *attaches*. There is one lighted sentence near the end which brings before one's mental eye his often–expressed "Mene, Mene, Tekel Upharsin," with regard to the Indian Empire, our past misgovernments, and our present failure to recognize old promises: "The glorification of our Indian policy only made me melancholy."

The "degree" which Martineau was to receive was no doubt his "Doctor of Divinity" degree which he took in 1884 (Edinburgh). Dr. Jowett, it will be remembered, was, throughout his whole life, closely identified with Balliol College. He was Fellow in 1838, tutor of his college from 1840 till 1870, when he was chosen as Master. Ruskin (to whom reference is made in the second letter) gave the larger part of his originally large fortune to the founding of St. George's Guild. This was intended to be a sort of agricultural community of "old–world virtues" for young and old, "and ancient and homely methods." One of his great aims was the promoting of home industries. As regards Newman's reference to politics at the end of letter No. 2 in 1888, Gladstone's Government was but just *breathing* after the sharp tussle they had been through with the Home Rule party, with Parnell at their head. In 1886 Gladstone had brought in the measure which was to give Ireland a "statutory parliament." This was practically the signal for a disastrous rent which tore his party in two, and was the precursor of their defeat at the next General Election.

Dr. Martineau from Newman.

"*6th July*, 1888.

"My dear Martineau,

"I did not know that the day of Oxford Convocation was June 20th. I was engaged to the Worcester College Gaudy for the 21st. Had I known that on the 20th you were to receive the degree, I should have been tempted to come and 'assist,' though I have always had an instinctive hatred of such mobs.

"I was at Birmingham on the 20th to see my brother. The noises on the rail greatly affected my brain and stomach. Noise was increased in the bedroom at Oxford, beside which heavy goods went to the rail, and I had two bad nights, partly from that cause, aided by the mental excitement up to midnight." [It is not difficult to understand this "excitement." The meeting between the brothers was never devoid of a certain mental reticence. It must almost have been impossible to forget the fact that about the subject on which each had always been most keenly exercised, they were worlds apart.]

"When I reached home I thought myself *quite well*, but soon found I could not write a word without one or more blunders in several letters, and a needful epistle became a heap of unsightly blots. This is only exaggeration of a weakness becoming normal with me. I have to write as slow as any little schoolboy. My housemaid was alarmed without my knowing it; but mere rest and sleep in some days removed my wife's alarms. But I still am forced to write very slowly, and cannot help some blunders.... On the morning of the 22nd I called on Jowett, who instantly said, 'Tonight is *our* Gaudy; you *must* come to it.' I had to beg off from my Worcester College host. (I was on my way to see friends in a neighbouring village.) I sat down to dinner with 102 guests; such a company as I never before *looked* at. I name chiefly high Anglo–Indians and their various *attaches* (members of Balliol College): *oi peri* Lords Northbrook, Ripon, and Lansdowne, three Viceroys of India, and Sir Gordon Duff, late Governor of Bombay." [It will not have been forgotten that the part played by Lord Lansdowne and Lord Ripon in 1833, with respect to the Bill for the discontinuance of the East India Company's trade, was not a very distinguished one.]

"Many smaller stars, Mr. Ilbert of name well known, and (long ago to *me* well known) General Richard Strachy, eager for bi–metallism. He began, but alas! could not finish his elucidation to me, how it would relieve Indian finance, without *anyone* losing *any_thing, or any lessening of payment, or dismissing officers, or the English Government paying anything, nor any unlucky last holder of coin or paper losing. The miracle (as to me it seemed) was to be wrought, not by a double standard—that was an ignorant mistake—but by a single standard metal, composed of gold and silver in fixed ratio. I was not happy enough (or unhappy enough) to learn how this was to result; but his eagerness and confidence were to me a surprising phenomenon.*

"A Worcester College man told me that your *Types of Morals* had already left a *strong* impression on younger men. I think there has not yet been time for the second great book and work.

"The glorification of our Indian Policy only made me melancholy. I hope you now get full and real rest. Though I *feel* as in perfect health, I have to say to myself, *Non sum qualis eram*, and take warnings. Pray, do you the same.

"Affectionately, to you and yours,

"F. W. Newman."

"In London vegetarianism seems going ahead. I have, still struggling through the press, *Reminiscences of Two Exiles and Two Wars*. The Quakers will be at once pleased and angry if that is possible."

Dr. Martineau from Newman.

"*19th Aug.*, 1892.

"My dear Martineau,

"I seem to have allowed you to get quite out of my sight. This is a result of my practical renunciation of London, the place which seems too exciting for me. I do not wonder that you so early take refuge in far Scotland. I so mortified my dear friend Anna Swanwick last year by my sudden retreat from the overstrain of her house, that I did not dare to repeat the trial this year; indeed, I should deeply alarm my wife by attempting it, and, alas! dear Anna herself proved unable to sustain herself—due, I suppose, to the self–imposed task of her new book. Though I am myself (foolishly perhaps) reprinting a tract on Etruscan, I see how many things are better left to younger minds. I am here (near Bewdley, Worcestershire) to make personal acquaintance with a remarkable man who has made marked advances to me for more (I think) than three years. He *was* a protege of Ruskin's and member of St. George's Guild. As such he was (apparently) reared under Emerson, Margaret Fuller, and Carlyle more than under Ruskin, and heard all the side of English Agnosticism. But with the growth of his own mind he became dissatisfied, and now for fourteen years he has given himself to a fruit farm of four and a half acres, with a cow and kitchen–garden and pigs! and abundant poultry, and looks the type of the future English peasant. His wife and one trusty woman manage dairy and cookery with eminent

73

success, and various sales, while he is cow–milker and gardener, student also of fruit and of the soil. *It is to me an interest as a foresight of the future.* He is a *student* of our hardest literature, and employs no labourer under him. Ignorant of foreign tongues, he reads German translations and Jowett's *Plato....* A school friend of Mr. Braithwaite lately sought my acquaintance.... He tells me that Mr. Gladstone lately gave to the world the utterance that among the possibilities of the immediate future he now sees, rather than any general Agnosticism, a simple recurrence to the simple Judaic Godhead. I *wish* well to Gladstone's new Cabinet, but fear that the trickiness by which he led Parnell's folk to aid Salisbury's overthrow will arouse a fatal resentment. If he espouse the Indian claims, that may save him. My best regards to all yours, and earnest wishes.

"Your affectionate friend,

"F. W. Newman."

Mr. Estlin Carpenter wrote lately to me to say that he does not know of any evidence to prove that Newman and Martineau were "acquainted, or at least intimate," before the former became tutor of Manchester College. He says their correspondence ended in 1892, and he imagines that Newman's "declining health during the last two or three years made further writing impossible," but that their warm regard for each other, up to the very end, was unalterable.

CHAPTER VI. FRANCIS NEWMAN AS A TEACHER

Francis Newman was certainly one of the greatest mathematical and classical scholars of his day. So that when the authorities of University College secured him for their staff, they knew that they could have obtained no better man for their purpose.

As a teacher he showed an infinite fertility of method in dealing with the young men who, there for the purpose of learning, yet did not always *want* to learn! He had, in especial, that rather vague and narrow definition of genius—"an infinite capacity for taking pains." He "took" them always with any scholar who had failed to grasp his meaning in some one of his instructions. He could put the whole matter in some absolutely new light—take it from an utterly different point of view; so that, while giving another chance to the slow–witted, he did not keep his whole class waiting. The quality of teaching is not strained. It is doubtful if it is capable of being learnt, if not in the first instance, in some measure, innate. Lying dormant in a man's being—even if, perhaps, its presence is unrecognized by its owner—it can certainly be developed by him when he is conscious of it. But if the power in embryo be absent, it is a difficult matter indeed to attain by effort any capacity of which one has not already the beginnings in oneself. Indeed, a famous writer of another age has written the word "impossible" against this attempt.

Frank Newman could, and would, take any trouble to help any dull student over some mathematical or classical stile, but he was not an adept at quickly getting into touch with that Presence which has moved, in whimsical measure, through the ways and by–ways of this life since the world began with coat of many colours, upon which the sun of merry imagination was always sparkling, and cap and bells which could for the moment ring sudden, spontaneous mirth across the shadows of the darkest day. If in medieval days it could cross the cell of some grave and reverend monastery, and guide the hand of some sculptor busy at his gargoyle for some majestic church, surely it could, with the greatest ease in the world, cross the threshold of some crowded class–room where a learned, absorbed professor was endeavouring to gain the attention of a number of young men rejoicing in their youth and on the look–out for the first suggestion of the Spirit of Humour. Frank Newman was not quick at appreciating the quips and cranks, the—to others—irresistibly mirth– provoking sallies of humour. He was not quick at seeing a joke. And when middle age was well past with him, he did not always see when he had himself been provocative of an upset of gravity on the part of the students. He did not always discover in time the pranks and designs for diverting the course of true knowledge in which the average young Englishman loves to indulge. He had not a very close focus for this sort of thing, and probably the reason was, that he was so absolutely absorbed in the subject which he was teaching or upon which he was lecturing. But in teaching a mixed class of boys or young men it is a *sine qua non* that one possesses a "mind's eye" with easily adjustable focus, as in a photographic camera; otherwise one cannot keep in mental touch with those members of the class who "come to" play "and remain to" distract the attention of fellow–students. Another reason why Newman did not appeal to these non–studious ones was attributable to the fact that he was, in many ways, very eccentric both in manner and dress. Now, everyone who knows the average English boy at all, knows that if there is one thing he cannot stand it is eccentricity. To be eccentric is to be taboo. As regards the "correct" thing to wear, and the "correct" thing to do and how to do it, he is generally quite as particular as the average young woman over fashion. And anyone who offends in these respects has his name written upon the ostracisic shell. If it happens to be a master—well, his peculiarities are quite enough to divert the boy's attention successfully from the weightier matters in which the master is vainly endeavouring to instruct him.

Sir Alfred Wills, Mr. Winterbotham, Sir Edward Fry, Mr. William de Morgan, and others, to whose kindness I am indebted for many reminiscences of Professor Newman as a teacher, tell me that he had many eccentricities which perpetually aroused their sense of humour. Sir Edward Fry tells me that his manner, when he himself was at college in 1848, was "somewhat nervous, perhaps even a little irritable, and he was not exactly popular as a professor. But his lectures were very interesting and stimulating." He adds that he was "a very brilliant scholar, with a tendency towards eccentricity."

This eccentricity showed itself in various forms, but one very noticeable one was that of dress. I am told by a friend that he often dressed in the onion fashion—three coats one over the other, and the last one—green! That he often wore trousers edged with a few inches of leather, and that his hats were not immaculate. Well, perhaps it has never been quite understood from what part of old and unfashionable attire the Spirit of Humour winks at one with such twinkling fun in the corner of its eye that laughter is irresistible. But none the less, few there are of us who have not—though it may be against our steadier and wiser judgment—at some time or other caught sight of that wink, and laughed spontaneously. To everyone who saw it, when the relics were collected and placed in his old house in Cheyne Row, Carlyle's old 'top' hat was irresistibly funny. Nothing loses caste more completely than a top hat when it is behind the time, and the shine is off the silk.

Sir Alfred Wills mentions, in the reminiscences which follow, which he has kindly sent me, that at one time Newman "took to walking from his house" (in town) "to the college and back in cap and gown." This, however, was not such a startling vagary of costume in a London street as was that of a certain professor of my acquaintance, very absent-minded and dreamy, who, intent on making some abstruse point clear to a young lady pupil, walked one evening round and round a London square with her, talking earnestly, and attired in his top hat and dressing-gown!

As regards Newman's teaching of Latin, Sir Alfred Wills says that "much the best thing that" he "got from" him "was the practice in writing" it. He tells us that his lectures showed signs of the most profound research, and that he took untiring trouble in explaining any difficulty which had arisen. If the difficulty had been that of some member of one of his classes, he would not keep the whole class waiting while he went over the difficult part of the lesson again, but he would approach the subject from an altogether different point of view, and throw, for the class *in toto*, a new light upon it.

Of course it was not only in Latin that he wished to make pupils think of it as a "spoken language," for Mr. Darbishire tells us that "one of his special endeavours was to accustom his students to deal with Greek *as a spoken language*" [Footnote: It will be remembered that Francis Newman introduced the "new" pronunciation of Latin.] (as, for instance) "in reading Greek plays." Mr. Darbishire further tells us that Newman was accustomed to have a series of meetings in his study for conversation in Latin.

As regards old methods of teaching Latin, I should like to quote from a paper on "Modern Latin" which Francis Newman wrote in 1862, because there is very much in what he says which shows where the failure of the old system comes in:—

"In general the old method was one of repetition: *it dealt immensely in committing Latin to memory*. Ridiculous as was the system of giving to boys a Latin syntax in the Latin language, it at any rate did accustom them to the reiteration of a small number of words expressed in very simple sentences, and conveying knowledge of *immediate utility*.... While I nevertheless believe that at most schools the boys still learn grammar by heart, I venture to remark that the newer method of teaching, so far as known to me, has immensely lessened the *quantity* of Latin which is thus learned....

"Further, it seems to me that we want what I may call a Latin novel or romance—that is, a pleasing *tale* of *fiction* which shall convey numerous Latin words which do not easily find a place in poetry, history, or philosophy. Nothing has struck me as being so much to the purpose as an imitation of the story of Robinson Crusoe, which brings in much that is technical to special occupations—as in nautical affairs—carpentering, fowling, pottery, basket–making, agriculture, etc.... If anyone had genius to produce in Terentian style Latin comedies worthy of engaging the minds and hearts of youth (for I can never read a play of Terence to a young class without the heartache), I should regard this as a valuable contribution."

I pass on now to some reminiscences, kindly contributed by Sir Alfred Wills, of the professor in relation to his University College students in 1846:—

"I have a very distinct recollection of the personality of Mr. F. W. Newman. He was appointed to the Professorship of Latin in University College in 1846, and I entered the college in October, 1846, and attended his first lecture and all those he delivered in the course of that session.

"He was of middle stature, very well made, with a face that always reminded me of the type of the North American Indian, with which I was familiar from Mrs. Catlin's book published in 1841. His complexion was dark, his hair very black and with no tendency to curl, and he wore it long, and his nose was aquiline. He differed from the Indian type, however, in that his face was rather narrow than broad.

"His voice was particularly clear and 'carrying,' and every syllable could be heard. I ought to have added to my description that his eyes were blue, bright, very expressive, and his smile, not very often seen, peculiarly sweet and engaging. He was decidedly eccentric. At one time, in dirty winter weather, he wore trousers of which the lower six or eight inches were of black leather; and at another time, upon what occasion I forget, he took to walking from his house to the college and back in cap and gown. There was a 'Cap and Gown' movement among the students, or some of them, in the session 1847–8, but it was not upon that occasion, for I remember seeing him in the streets in cap and gown, and during the session 1847–8, I was at home in bad health, having overworked myself. He would now and then, very seldom, ask some of the students to breakfast at his house. It was an odd mixture of hospitality and formality. He never seemed quite at his ease on such occasions, and I have a very distinct remembrance of one of these occasions.

"It was in singularly gloomy and bitter weather in the winter or very early spring of 1849. We were rather a large party. There was no fire either in the room in which we assembled or in the breakfast room; and I have not often been colder. There was only one guest who was not a student, and he was a certain Herr Vukovich (that was how the name was pronounced) who had been Hungarian Minister of Justice during the short period when Kossuth was supreme in Hungary.

"When he came in, Professor Newman said: 'Gentlemen, this is Herr Vukovich, lately Minister of Justice in Hungary,' and then turning to Herr V., he added, 'I shall not introduce these gentlemen to you by name, as it would be of no interest to you; and besides, you would forget their names at once'; and then he went off at score with, 'I have never been able to understand, Herr Vukovich, how it is that you have never introduced the Bactrian camel into Hungary,' and then proceeded to enlarge upon the admirable suitability of the Bactrian camel to the climate, soil, roads, conditions of Hungary. Herr V. *looked* very much as if he had never heard of the Bactrian camel.

"During the whole of the session 1846–7, Newman's lectures were the wonder of all who heard him. We read with him some of Cicero's letters to Atticus, and his stores of information of every description—antiquarian, philological, historical, and literary—were absolutely marvellous. I have never destroyed or lost my notes of them, and I feel sure that they would justify all that I have said. We all felt that we had secured for the college an intellectual giant. I had the great advantage of being, during my first session, in the senior class in both Latin and Greek, and we had for our Greek Professor Mr. Malden, who, I should think, was unsurpassed for sound and elegant scholarship, and in whose lectures I delighted from first to last during my two sessions (1846–7 and 1848–9), but certainly during the first session, Professor Newman's lectures were those which made upon me the deepest impression, which remains unimpaired to this day. It seemed as if no trouble was too great for him to take in preparing for them and as if nothing which could throw any light upon a set of letters, which are often obscure and difficult, ever escaped his eagle eye or his profound research. When I returned to college in 1848, I met with a profound disappointment. I have been asked for my recollections, and I must make them truthful. Professor Newman was at that time much engrossed with his theological and religious works.

"*The Soul* was published in 1849, and whether that may account for the change or not, the fact is that the lectures of that session presented a marked contrast to those of the earlier session, and I don't think I am exaggerating when I say that they were dry and jejune to the last extent. And I felt throughout that session that much the best thing I got from it was the practice in writing Latin, which was always an important part of his teaching, and in which he was a master himself. I am sure it is true that days often passed without there being anything in the lectures which I cared to preserve or even to note. I had that year, however, the privilege of reading the Nicomachean Ethics with him as a private pupil, and found him as good in Greek and as interested in illustration as I had previously found him in his Latin lectures.

"I forbear to touch upon his private character. That impressed itself insensibly upon us as worthy of the highest respect. But it was simply from the natural effluence of a noble character, for we came rarely into anything like personal intimacy with him. He was reserved and even shy, and I doubt if any of us knew much more of him privately than I did—which was not much."

I think these reminiscences of Sir Alfred Wills bring before us very vividly the sort of intercourse which existed between professor and pupil in those days. It reveals Newman as a man with whom the pupil would not feel altogether at his ease—towards whom he would not be moved to get into close sympathy, and this, perhaps, very largely because of a certain stiffness and formality of manner which unavoidably erects a barrier before any natural, spontaneous conversation.

Sir Edward Fry mentions Newman's manner as a "nervous" one, but says that his lectures were very stimulating, leading one to infer that even if the delivery was not arresting or impressive, yet all this was made up for by the force and brilliance of the matter itself.

It will be remembered that, at any rate, in his Oxford days, J. H. Newman had not an impressive manner either.

We come now to some other keenly interesting recollections—those of Mr. William de Morgan, who has kindly written them for this memoir. Mr. de Morgan tells me that his father and Francis Newman were old friends, but they were widely apart on religious questions, and that he remembers "when the Martineau controversy was at its height" he said to him: "Newman and I were very old colleagues, and I loved and respected him. But if I had been supposed to have any official knowledge of Newman's views about Christianity derived from my position as a Professor, I should have thrown up my situation long ago." And Mr. de Morgan adds: "This had reference to the absolute agnosis on religious views which was the banner U.C. nailed to the mast in old days." He says he remembers, in his boyhood, that there were many religious discussions between his parents and Francis Newman, but that he was far too young to understand what they were about then, and remembers them consequently but vaguely.

"When I came to see more of Newman as a Professor in class, I had arrived at the condition of a pert and very foolish boy of sixteen who had made up his mind to be an artist and failed altogether to take advantage of the splendid opportunities before him. I attended Newman's classes; saw him every day; might have acquired the knowledge of much of the Latin classics. Somehow I missed my chances, and I cannot now recall a single instance of my availing myself of the interviews he accorded so gladly to any attentive student to get at difficult passages, and so on. In my time I suspect his classes included a larger number than usual of bad and idle young scaramouches, who deserved to be turned out of the class, instead of the sort of over-forbearance their Professor showed. I feel sure now that a more truculent character than his would have enforced order better, with advantage to the weak and wavering pupils. He treated boys too much like human creatures—and some of us were as mischievous as monkeys. I recollect a particular instance illustrating this fact and his forbearance.

"The weather was bad, and bad colds abounded. One day Newman ventured to remonstrate gently with the victims of catarrh—indeed, the noise was awful. But he had the indiscretion to add: 'Gentlemen, if you cannot wipe your noses, I must really ask you to blow them outside the door.' Of course the results were awful! The young imps rushed out incessantly into the passage, and made noises like motor-cars. If the Professor committed an error of judgment in his first edict, he certainly made up for it by the way he kept his temper. In this he was really perfect. But the boys presumed on it, of course. I remember that one of them, instead of attending to his *Juvenal*, wrote a long poem about this nose incident, which passed from hand to hand.

"There was another incident about that time which I fancy others may remember better than I. It was snow time, and the schoolboys in the playground were pelting papers in the college precinct. Newman passed by, and a heavy volley all but destroyed his umbrella, which he used as a shield. A few days after he came into the Common Room with a new umbrella. 'See what a beautiful present I've had,' he said, 'from my young friends across the railings.' I have an impression that it was a guinea umbrella bought with penny subscriptions; but this may be another story that has got mixed with it."

Sir Edward Fry writes, in response to a request from me for his recollections of Newman:—

Memoir and Letters of Francis W. Newman

"I attended Professor Newman's senior class on Latin literature for two or three sessions in 1848, and I have a very vivid remembrance of him; at that time he had not assumed a beard, and his clean–cut features were not obscured by hair, as in later life. His lectures were very interesting and stimulating. If I may venture to express an opinion on the point, I should describe him as a very brilliant scholar, with a tendency towards eccentricity.

"We read whilst I was with him some three or four of the early works of Livy, and some of the histories of Tacitus; and his expansion of the Constitution of Rome, both at the early and later date, was of very unusual excellence. Such was my memory, and this has been confirmed by a reference to my notebooks which I have made in consequence of your note. I think his estimate of character did not always agree with that of Tacitus. Other subjects which I recollect as having been expounded were the relation of Latin to the Celtic group of languages, and that everlasting question, the relation of the Etruscans and the Pelasgi.

"Once a week Newman used to give out a piece of English prose to be rendered into Latin; these he corrected, reading also to us his own version. Since your note I have looked at such notes of his lectures as I can find, and at his corrections of my Latin prose."

Mr. Talfourd Ely, writing on Francis Newman as a teacher, says "he was most careful and conscientious in his work. He was refined and even fastidious in literary taste. To the ordinary undergraduate, such as myself, he seemed too little like other men. We did not understand his genius, and were too apt to judge him by peculiarities of garb and speech. Like many other scholars, he could hardly keep in touch with young athletes, and probably did not care to do so. But personally I was greatly indebted to him, and I can never forget his generous help and kindly thoughtfulness."

Mr. Winterbotham, also pupil of Francis Newman, says:—

"I was more keen on mathematics than classics, and was not what he would have considered a promising pupil. My brother Edward, who was a year my senior, was not much better.... My recollections are confined to the peculiarities of his dress and manner: the rug with a hole in the middle for his head, which formed his outer garment in winter. The complete suit of dark grey alpaca, *tail* coat, waistcoat, and trousers, which he donned in warm weather.

"His remonstrance to the class on the indignity inflicted on him by the boys at the adjoining school, who snowballed him and broke his umbrella, was followed by his request that they would 'use their influence with the boys' by way of protecting him in future, and his recognition of their efforts next day, when he exhibited a new umbrella presented to him by the boys.... For dear old De Morgan [Footnote: Father of the Mr. de Morgan who contributes his reminiscences, and old friend of Newman.] I had a great regard, and I was better able to appreciate his marvellous powers as a mathematician."

Here is a short reminiscence by Professor Pye Smith:—

"Newman was a small, dark, slightly-built man, with black moustache and beard, and a doubtful affected manner. He made us read long passages without comment, and rarely went beyond the translation. I do not think I ever spoke to him (or others of his class). The memory of his teaching would, I think, be most valuable in correcting the Latin verses we made for his comment and correction. The only professors at that time whom I got great benefit from were Aston Key, De Morgan, and Masson."

The next reminiscence belongs to a much later date in the Professor's life. In 1863 he was no longer teaching at University College. Mrs. Kingsley Tarpey says she remembers him first in the summer of 1874 or 1875. Her descriptions of him, his opinions, and his life as she knew it are full of keen interest.

[Illustration: FRANCIS NEWMAN IN MIDDLE AGE FROM PHOTO BY JOHN DAVIES, WESTON-SUPER-MARE]

In the quotation from a letter which follows, Professor Newman's own views on teaching at the college are given:—

"You say there is a complaint that '*as the students cannot be got to prepare their work* the lessons *have come to be* mere prelections from the professors.' I am not aware of any change in the pupils since I have been here, except that my classes are smaller, in part owing to the removal of Coward College and the rivalry of the new institution in which it is now comprised; in part (I happen to know) from dread of my personal ... influence; in part, I suspect, from the working of London University, which I think bad; and others must add, whether worst of all is, my own want of judgment in selecting subjects, and the mode of the treatment. Undeniable it is that my classes are smaller, that my half-dozen best scholars are decidedly below the half–dozen best I had in the first year or two. But if I am myself to blame, it is, I think, *from the very reverse process* of that implied in the words above quoted, viz. I often question whether it would not be at once wiser and more right to raise my teaching to the small minority of my best pupils, and ignore the many who come in on my classes unprepared. I have of late suspected that I allow the University so to drag me down into school teaching that the abler and advanced students are driven away from me. Moreover, I am getting quite sick of going again and again over elementary books in mere school fashion.

"To vary this, I have this term given one day a week in my senior class to lecture *on* books, viz. 1st, on Horace's *Odes*, which nine out of ten have already read, and which I myself read with the junior class last session (having engaged to do this before I guessed that the University would select the same year for B.A.), and many of the junior class being this year in my senior class. 2nd, on the *Epistles* of Cicero, which are enormously too long and too difficult for pupils to read, and in which, nevertheless, candidates for honours at B.A. are liable to be examined. I conjecture that somebody has seen this announcement of mine in our prospectus, and imputes it to a *relaxation of discipline* in my pupils (indeed there is little enough, and always was, in the majority of mine; they only want to scrape through their degree, and the University kindly keeps its real demands at a minimum). On the contrary, it is an effort of mine to make the lectures less unworthy of my more advanced pupils. I may add that I have *always* lectured more or less in this way on Cicero's *Letters*.... At the same time I avow my entire dissatisfaction with things as I have them. In June I have to print and publish the books in which I will lecture from October to June next, *while I have not the slightest idea who will be in the classes*. In August, out comes the statement of University books for the following year, which often increases my confusion. It is easier to complain of this than to remedy it."

It is not difficult to understand Newman's point of view as regards the almost impossibility of keeping in hand in one class a team of students— some eagerly desirous of going forward into the real study of literature, and others only anxious to "scrape through" for the purpose of obtaining their degree.

Mrs. Kingsley Tarpey's reminiscences begin thus:—

I think it was in the summer of 1874 or 1875 that Professor Newman first came to visit us. My mother had been much interested in some articles of his on vegetarianism, and had corresponded with him on the subject, and when the Annual Conference of the Vegetarian Society was held in Manchester later on, he stayed with us. This visit was the beginning of a very warm friendship with our family, which lasted close on twenty years. During that time my mother corresponded regularly with Professor Newman, but unfortunately only some eighteen or twenty of his letters have been preserved. There is scarcely one of these, however, that does not contain something of permanent interest and value.

I remember very well, in the days when we used to have visits from him, that Professor Newman was looked upon by very many as a mere faddist. His extreme views on several subjects no doubt took him out of range of the sympathies of the "man in the street." But it is strange to find, on looking through these letters, how advanced opinion is coming into line with his so–called outrageous ideas of a generation ago. It would have given him keen pleasure, if he could have lived till now, to see the strides that have been made of late years in the Women's Suffrage movement, and the admission of women to public bodies. In social and moral reform, and in the Temperance movement also, the progress has been very marked, and we may soon have an Act prohibiting the smoking of tobacco by young boys—a matter on which Professor Newman had very strong views. Last, but not least, the Vegetarian movement, in which he took so keen an interest, has gained new vigour from the advocates of the simple life.

I remember that on the occasion of his first visit we children regarded him with mingled awe and curiosity. His quaint appearance and his formal, deliberate manner of speech made him seem to us like a being from another world. We were at once fascinated and repelled, and I think he became at first the object of our constant, though furtive, observation. But his unvarying gentle kindness and extreme simplicity very soon won our confidence, and later on an accident made us his fast friends and admirers.

It happened that the second or third time that he came to Manchester for the annual meeting of the Vegetarian Society, my father and mother were away, and it fell to the younger members of the household to entertain our distinguished visitor. It was an occasion looked forward to with trepidation and misgiving, but we need not have felt alarmed. No one could have been more genial in his attitude to the youthful housekeepers. He would chat easily and pleasantly with even the youngest of us, and he always managed to find some interesting topic. Sometimes he would give us an account of the doings at the Conference during the day. I remember some curious facts about some of the members. One man ate nothing but apples, and considered them a complete and ideal food for man. Another varied his diet between roots and nuts. He carried assorted strange nuts with him in his pocket, and after his speech he presented some to the President. Our Professor brought them home with him and wished us to try them, but I am afraid that, with the conservative instinct of young animals, we distrusted the unknown, and we did not venture. The Professor considered that our molar teeth clearly indicated grain, roots, and nuts as our food, and the incisors as clearly suggested fruit, but at that time he was in some doubt about the canine teeth. At his request some of us gravely cracked nuts with him, and after the experiment we agreed that human beings more naturally crack nuts with the back teeth, where leverage is most powerful. A suspicion remained that our pointed fangs *might* have been used to tear flesh!

During this same visit it was suggested that the Society should change its name to one that would describe it more accurately, "Vegetarian," strictly, implying that the members would eat only vegetables. There was much difficulty in finding a portmanteau word that would convey vegetables, eggs, and milk. Professor Newman much disliked the idea of calling it the VEM Society (the name that was afterwards adopted, I think); his proposal was "Anti–creophagite," or "Anti–creophagist." But he could get no support for this name; members objected that no one would know what it meant or how to spell it. Professor Newman had been pained to learn that only two or three people in the hall knew the Greek word.

He was very much interested in language, and it was characteristic of him never to pass a word that he did not know. He had a great dislike and contempt for *slang*, and he deplored the growing use of it, and the impoverishment of the language that resulted. But dialect words, or old words that lingered in some parts of the country, while they had dropped out of common speech, interested him greatly. One day a younger sister of mine brought him a footstool as he sat reading, and in offering it to him called it a "buffet." It is not a word in common use, but I think we had adopted it from the nursery rhyme about "Miss Muffett, who sat on a buffet." The Professor was on the alert at once.

"That word is quite new to me," he said. "Did you say 'bussock'? I wonder is that a Lancashire word, or does it come from Ireland? 'Bussock'! Will you spell it for me, please?"

My sister was far too young and too shy to correct him, and after faintly murmuring "buffet" again, she ran away in extreme confusion. I am afraid "bussock" went down in the Professor's notebook as an interesting variant of "hassock."

In this connection some delightful stories were told by Dr. Nicholson, of Penrith, an old friend of Professor Newman's and of my father's. The Professor was staying at Penrith, and the two friends had been walking up a steep path. When they stopped to rest, the doctor was regretting that his climbing days were virtually over.

"The truth is," he said humorously, "we are neither of us as steady on our pins as we once were."

"Pins, Nicholson, pins! What are *pins*?" asked Professor Newman gravely.

On another occasion they were out walking together and the first Lord Brougham passed them in an open carriage. Dr. Nicholson remarked upon Lord Brougham wearing "goggles," and Professor Newman said, in his gentle deliberate way, "Now, Nicholson, may I ask what you exactly mean by 'goggles'?"

The Professor wore hats that in those days were considered amazing: large white or light grey hats made of soft felt. On one of his visits to Penrith he had walked up from the station to the house, and he was followed by a crowd of little boys shouting "Who's your hatter?" which was a catch-phrase of the time. The Professor described to Dr. Nicholson what an extraordinary interest the boys had shown. "They repeatedly asked me," he said, "to tell them who was my hatter, and really, Nicholson, at the time I could not remember the man's name."

Miss Nicholson, of Penrith, adds another story which should have place here.

"My own chief recollection of him," she writes, "is of a day when he and the second Mrs. Newman came into Penrith with me, where I had some shopping to do. On the way into the town Professor Newman said, 'You do not seem to be very clear as to the history of John Brown and the battle of Bull's Run.' I said I was not very clear about it, so he began from the beginning, so to speak, and the story of John Brown lasted till we reached home again. I went into shops to make my purchases, and on each occasion as I came out Professor Newman took up his tale just where he had left off. He showed no annoyance at the frequent interruptions or at my inevitable lapses of attention. His wonderfully clear, distinct enunciation, and his marvellous memory for facts, never faltered."

There was an extraordinary absence of humour about Professor Newman that made him at times unconsciously very humorous. I wish I could remember the quaint wording of an advertisement of his for a cook in a vegetarian paper. There was a long and precise account of the services required for "the smallest possible family," and application was to be made by letter to "Emer. Prof. F. W. Newman," etc. We thought some of the cooks might be puzzled to know what Emer. Prof. meant. I remember also an artless post card he wrote after one visit explaining that he had forgotten his *teeth*, and asking to have them sent after him.

He had a very odd theory about baldness in men. It sounds a little like a joke, but I believe it was meant in all seriousness. He had observed that men with a very strong growth of beard were more liable to go bald early than those who had the hair on the face thin and scanty. He described this as a kind of *landslip*, I remember, and his idea was that human beings could only have a small crop of hair, and that a good crop on the chin meant a failure higher up. And that, he thought, accounted for the fact that women rarely go bald.

At the time of the visit I have described, our whole family had become enthusiastic vegetarians—indeed, I may say the whole household of fourteen, for the servants had followed suit. This was a great pleasure to Professor Newman, for it was through his writings that my mother had first become interested in the subject. He had great hopes at one time that she would also share in some other crusades of his against alcohol, tobacco, vaccination, etc. etc. He sent her a great number of leaflets and pamphlets on all these subjects, but though my father was a non−smoker and almost a total abstainer, he was so from habit and inclination and not from any pledge, and I do not remember that the Professor made any convert except myself. I came across a bundle of tracts of his which no one seemed to be reading, and I devoured them all. For some years, from about the age of fifteen, I was an enthusiastic follower of Professor Newman, even in his most extreme ideas. I am afraid he never became aware of this, however, for of course it was only with the older members of the family that he would discuss such questions.

The most enjoyable visit we ever had from him was also the last of any length that he paid us. I think it must have been in the summer of 1879 or 1880, when we were living in the country a few miles from Manchester. It was then I first learnt what a delight a country walk might be. He joined some of the younger members of the party who were taking the dogs out for a run, and I do not think two hours were ever spent by us in a more interesting and fascinating way. He had the rare and charming gift, in talking to young people, of making them feel that he regarded them as equals. And though he was imparting knowledge all the time, he had the air of being really more interested in what they had to contribute. That walk was a revelation to me, a kind of treasure trove of natural science. Hitherto my love of nature had been almost entirely aesthetic and poetical, and this walk with the Professor gave me a new pleasure and a new interest in country life.

I should run into great length if I were to set down all the little traits and incidents that go to make up the memory of that gentle and charming personality. His eccentricities were entirely lovable, as we knew them, and even when he meant to be severe his unconsciously humorous way of putting things took away the sting, as when, one day at lunch, he pointed at a jug of claret and asked, "What is that ugly black liquid? I say ugly and black because I believe it to be some kind of wine."

He had kind and courteous ways with women, and he surprised one by his thoughtfulness in domestic matters. There was no subject too small or too remote for his consideration. I remember his showing us a new scientific way to build a fire, lighting it from the top; and it is upon a lesson of his on rural sanitation that I have based my own management of those matters in our country home. I have a pleasant memory of his holding a skein of wool for me to wind one wet afternoon, and of his telling me the while of his observations of a family of *bugs*. He was travelling in the East, and at some place where he stayed was much distressed by vermin. At last he discovered that a procession of bugs came out nightly from a certain crack in the plaster, and by removing the paper he could get a very good view of the colony with the aid of a glass. He did not disturb them, it is needless to say, but watched them during his stay, and learnt many curious things about their habits and customs. He formed a very high opinion of their intelligence, I remember.

One day he came in and found my mother and some of us sitting sewing; he asked if he might read to us, and said that his mother and sister used to like him to read to them when they had work to do. I do not remember in the least what he read to us, though I am sure it was appropriate and instructive; but I remember well that he stood while he read, and that his delivery was as clear and as careful as if he had been reading to a large audience.

After his second marriage we saw him but little, but my mother heard from him now and then, and he often sent her articles he had written. In the last years of his life he wrote but seldom. I give extracts from letters over a period of about eighteen years.

FRANCIS NEWMAN IN PRIVATE LIFE BY MRS. BAINSMITH, SCULPTOR

My father and mother were very great personal friends of Newman's, consequently I saw a great deal of him during my early girlhood.

My father was the late George Bucknall, of Rockdene, Weston–super–Mare, and for many years was a great invalid. He suffered from locomotor ataxy. Professor Newman lived just across the road from our house: we could often see him walking about his garden, or sitting at his library window, and very often he came across to our house to discuss his books or letters with my father.

As a young girl I remember the great fascination of his courtly, genial manners. I shall never forget my first interview with him. It happened on my return home from school for the holidays. Being much distressed at having to change from the old pronunciation of Latin to the "new," it occurred to my father that I should ask Professor Newman to help me. So I went in to see him. He was sitting by the fire in large fur–lined boots made of felt, and wearing two coats (for he always found it difficult to keep sufficiently warm). When I stated my difficulty, he went to his shelves with his wonderful smile (the room was lined from floor to ceiling with books) and took out his translation of the *Iliad*, and read it to me. Then he said quite casually, "Now I will read the same passage to you in Latin." And he proceeded to read it aloud in a musical voice of exquisite charm. I cannot express the pleasure which this gave me, nor how it set me at my ease with him from that moment. He gave me a very warm invitation to come again, and he would gladly help me in any holiday work I wanted to do.

I was always specially struck with his way of talking about religion. He was very reverent in what he said, and it was evident that he was at heart deeply religious. I mention this because in later years it has been often a shock to me to find him condemned by others for doubting revealed religion.

Memoir and Letters of Francis W. Newman

The Professor's special views on foods were very strong, and he had a great dislike for the custom of rearing cattle for food. Once he gave a dinner party to show how many choice courses could be served with vegetarian recipes only. As my mother was ill at the time, I was invited to go with my father. I remember the delightful way in which he received us. He presented the "youngest lady" (myself) to the "oldest gentleman"— the late Professor Jarrett, who was an old college friend of his, and who was staying with Newman. I remember the awe with which I gazed at him. Mr. and Mrs. Dymond, Mr. and Mrs. Temperley Grey, and Mr. and Mrs. F. G. Comfort were among the other guests.

Once, when he was talking to my mother, he said: "You are wearing a nice coat" (a black fur one). "I suppose it is very dear? How much a yard do you think it would cost?" As he spoke he looked down at his own coat (the outside one of three), and said: "I have had this coat twenty years and cannot match the cloth." This was not to be wondered at, for it was a long hairy one—quite green with age. Another day I came into the room and heard the Professor say to my mother quite seriously: "I never can understand how it is that my hat always interests the idle little boys in the street. They say as I pass them, 'Where did you get that hat?' Everyone wears a hat of one shape or another, and I really fail to see why *mine* should be so very interesting."

He was wearing a soft felt hat with a very broad brim, set far back on his head; and with his peculiar American–looking beard and thin grey locks that came down over the high Gladstone collar which he always wore, and a black and white shepherd's–plaid scarf wound round his neck and twisted over in front with its ends tucked into his waistcoat, he looked sufficiently odd.

I remember once running as fast as I could to catch the post, and as I started I saw the Professor in front of me, evidently bent on attaining the same object. Great was his glee when at last I did overtake him (though I had some difficulty, for he ran well even at the age of seventy), and he said, "I thought I would give you a good race, but you have caught me up after all!"

One day he called just as I was going for a ride. He gave me quite a lecture on the dangers of the side–saddle, and said very earnestly that women ought to ride "astride" (at that time this was a thing *incompris* in England). He declared that women in other countries were accustomed to riding thus, and that it was the only safe method of riding.

At the time of his brother's being made Cardinal, some ardent admirers of the Professor's in Australia sent him a very beautiful silver inkstand. His delight and pleasure in receiving such a present was great. But that people should think of him in that way was a great surprise, for his humility as regarded his powers was a very noticeable fact about him always. The design of the inkstand was one of great beauty and good workmanship. It represented ostriches standing under a palm tree, and beside them was an exquisitely made silver feather for a pen.

[Illustration: FRANCIS NEWMAN EMERITUS PROFESSOR OF LONDON UNIVERSITY Enlargement of photograph of the bronze bust done from life by Mrs. Georgina Bainsmith, sculptor, of St. Ives, Cornwall, which is now in University College, London.]

One afternoon my father, mother, and I were all sitting reading, when the door opened and the Professor walked in. He held his hat in his hand, and a large rug was fastened round his shoulders like a shawl (over his three coats), and in his hands he held a small brown−paper parcel. As he came in he said, "I don't know why your maid did not announce me—I see she is a stranger"; and then turning to my mother, who had been ill, he said, "My cook has made a new vegetarian dish for my lunch to−day, and I requested her to make some for you, as I am quite sure it will suit you." The dish turned out to be delicious—one of those which his wonderful vegetarian cook was so constantly inventing. [Footnote: The parlourmaid, on being reprimanded for not showing Newman into the drawing−room, said she thought she was only to show "gentlemen" into the drawing−room!]

Newman had a theory that plants feel pain, and that we should treat all vegetable life as if it were sentient, and care for it accordingly.

The Professor was always ready to respond to any appeals for the advancement of the Woman's Suffrage movement. At that time it was very unpopular, but whenever we had meetings in favour of it at our house he was always the moving spirit.

At Weston−super−Mare Newman lived a life of great seclusion, and I believe I was the only young girl who visited him constantly—indeed, ours was the only house to which he came almost daily. Once when he was very ill, I think I was the only visitor admitted; and as Hannah, his old servant, ushered me in with a smile of pleasure, I heard a curious sound. On looking back to the hall door I saw a huge netting hanging from where the letter–box should be, trailing along the floor like a huge sausage, crammed full of letters of enquiry for the Professor. Hannah told me "the master had not been able to attend to them."

I had long possessed a great wish to devote my time to the study of modelling, and my father's great wish was that I should devote myself to Art. In 1885 I gained the distinction of a silver medal at Taunton Exhibition for modelling some flowers in clay on vases, with low relief panels. This pleased the Professor very much; and when, one day, I told him how keenly I wanted to model a bust of his head and shoulders, he smiled, and said, with an odd boyish, shy sort of pleasure, "Was he good– looking enough to be immortalized?" and added he would be delighted to sit to *me* for his portrait, though he had always refused to sit to others to be photographed.

So he used to come and talk to my mother, and thus I was able to work at my modelling with ease. Great was my delight when I found I possessed power over the clay, and was succeeding in making a portrait which everyone considered a good one. The Professor insisted on my being very particular over the collar and the scarf. (His collars always had to be made for him, as he could not buy in shops the kind he wore.) In later years of hard student life that followed, for me, with the added distinction of other medals, nothing ever came up to the excitement caused by my portrait of the Professor. The bust [Footnote: This bust is now standing in the general library of London University, with this inscription:—

"FRANCIS WILLIAM NEWMAN
(brother of the Cardinal),

Emeritus Professor of University College, London.
Natus June 27, 1805. Obiit October 4th, 1897.
As an expression of the great esteem and affection in which he was held
by all who knew him, this bust (modelled from life by the
Sculptor) is presented to this University by

GEORGINA BAINSMITH, Sculptor, "St. Ives, Cornwall." Aug. 1907.] has always been one of my greatest treasures; and after the lapse of years that have gone by since it was first modelled, I still revere and reverence his memory and his truly beautiful life. Whatever he wrote, *this* is what his actual life and deeds expressed strongly: "*he lived to do good.*" This is what impressed me most as a young girl, and my life has been richer and nobler for the honour and privilege of knowing Francis Newman.

Georgina Bainsmith, *nee* Bucknall. St. Ives, Cornwall.

[Illustration: ANOTHER VIEW OF THE BUST IN UNIVERSITY COLLEGE (OF FRANCIS NEWMAN), ON ITS PLINTH BY MRS. GEORGINA BAINSMITH, SCULPTOR, OF ST. IVES, CORNWALL The Reproduction is by Mr. J. C. Douglas, of Strives, Cornwall, and was photographed from the clay before it was cast.]

CHAPTER VII. LETTERS TO ONE OF HIS GREATEST FRIENDS, DR. NICHOLSON

Dr. Nicholson, a native of Barbadoes, was only fourteen years old when his father, Rev. Mark Nicholson, came to England. [Footnote: I am indebted for these facts of Dr. Nicholson's life to some printed data kindly sent me by his daughter.] He was sent to a private school at Bristol, and went on to Oxford, where he took his B.A. degree. Later on he went to study Oriental languages at Gottingen; and there he became the pupil of the famous Dr. Ewald, Professor of Oriental Languages. At the end of his work there Dr. Nicholson obtained the Ph.D. degree. The Professor and he became close friends, and a correspondence began between them, on Dr. Nicholson's departure, which lasted unbroken till the Professor's death. He was perfectly conversant with Latin and Greek, and also Arabic, while Hebrew was almost as familiar a language; and as for his knowledge of Sanscrit, Ethiopian, Gothic, Chaldean, Syriac, French, German, Spanish, Italian, Danish, it was as perfect as could be. He had, in the truest sense, the *gift* of tongues. Sixteen languages, indeed, he had mastered besides his own. He had, in very truth, a perfect genius for them. And it was no slipshod attainment with him to learn any one of the sixteen; for by the time he had mastered a language he practically knew it inside *and* out. He loved this study perhaps more than any other, because it gave him a truer insight into Holy Scripture. Many articles on the Hebrew Scriptures were contributed by him to *Kitto's Biblical Encyclopaedia*, and there are many allusions to these in Newman's letters which follow. He translated Dr. Ewald's *Hebrew Grammar*, and thus it became well known to Englishmen.

[Illustration: DR. JOHN NICHOLSON FROM A PHOTO TAKEN AT GOTTINGEN BETWEEN 1855 AND 1860 BY KIND PERMISSION OF MISS NICHOLSON, PENRITH]

Dr. Nicholson lived for forty years at Penrith. He did not care to go much in society; he was too true a student for that. For the two studies (and social life *is* certainly one) are so diametrically opposed regarded as pursuits, that it is almost impossible to make the day long enough to devote oneself to both. "Love to study" might very truly have been recognized as his life motto, even as it was that of one of the greatest students at Harrow a few years ago, Rev. Thomas Hancock, for both men cared nothing for fame. Dr. Nicholson was a man of strong religious tendencies, and though he was in no way narrow in his views of other religious societies, yet he was decidedly most in touch with the Anglican Church. As a politician he was a Liberal. Fifty years ago he married the second daughter of Captain Waring, R.N., and had six children.

He died (in November, 1886), as Rev. E. W. Chapman, Vicar of Penrith, said, "in perfect peace, with our Lord's Name and our Lord's last words on his lips. His presence in the town, his loving sympathy with poor people, his kindly greeting to all who knew him, we shall miss very much...." He added that "his whole life was spent in the study of Holy Scriptures...."

Francis Newman was his lifelong friend, and the letters which follow will plainly show that it was a friendship of kindred spirits: the friendship of two who had a great many interests in common, and were therefore in close touch with each other.

To Dr. Nicholson from Francis Newman.

"*17th Feb.*, 1843.

"My dear Nicholson,

* * * * *

"I hope you will not bother your little boy with any foreign language too soon. *Soak* him well and long in his native English, or he will never come to any good, I fear. If he sees a father in love with German, he will of himself quite early take to it. The great difficulty (I should expect) will be to secure that it may not be too early. Of course you see about the Anti–Corn Law doings? I think I shall before long be as fanatical as anyone about it: I rage the more inwardly because I have no vent. I am eager to sign a solemn league and covenant about total and immediate repeal, which I suppose and hope they will get up...."

The next letter in order refers to "Berber," a language bearing some relation to the Arabic, over which Newman was at work with his dictionary. It also touches on his own ill–health and enforced idleness. It is dated from Manchester, October, 1843:—

"I have been suffering indisposition which was aggravated in reality by overrating its importance. My medical adviser said it was organic affection of the heart; in spite of my great incredulity ... I took other advice afterwards in Derby, where I went to see one of my sisters, and am now assured that it was nothing but 'the great sympathetic' that disordered the heart. I was nearly three weeks in the country and in idleness, and gained much benefit from it. I spent much indoors time in learning to use water–colours, and got a nice pony to ride, and was a great deal in the air, and very early to go to bed; and took no medicines but tonics and a colocynth pill on occasion. Myself and wife both return much better. I believe I knocked myself up by excitement of mind over the Berber and working at my dictionary, At Prichard's advice I have lately written to Bunsen to ask his aid in getting the dictionary published. I think it may be of use, as adding one more known language in North Africa to those already accessible, which are, I believe, Arabic, Coptic, Gheez, and Amharic."

In June of the same year he says, in respect of Kitto's *Encyclopaedia*: "Your *Ahasuerus* shows you to me as an invaluable contributor to him: I could not have written that (if I had had the learning) without an attack on Ezra and Esther about the word!... Mr. Jowett has sent me (at Bunsen's and Prichard's request) the chief part of the transcript of the Berber MS. in the possession of the Bible S——. I suppose I must do my best now to get deeper into the language."

In May, 1845, Newman has been greatly interested in translating into Greek, English verses "to test the *possibility* of retaining any Greek accent such as the books mark in singing." He has tried translating "Flow on, thou shining river" in Greek, so that it might be sung to Moore's own tune. One does not come across in his letters much reference to music, nor does it seem as if he had any great taste for it—at any rate, not in the same way as had Cardinal Newman, who had a real passion for it in earlier years.

The later part of the letter has to do with the much–vexed question of the "Maynooth Controversy."

Newman writes from "4, *Cavendish Place*, 12th *May* 1845":—

"My dear Nicholson,

* * * * *

"I venture to enclose two tunes for the Sapphic metre, Greek and Latin, to which my sister, at my request, has added an accompaniment. Will you be so kind as to get Mrs. Nicholson to play the piano while you sing it, and tell me what is to be said to it? While dabbling in some of these tunes, I have translated divers scraps of English poetry into Greek, experimentally, especially to test the *possibility* of retaining any Greek accent, such as the books mark, in singing. It seems to me a clear impossibility, whether emphasis or sharpness of note predominated in the accent. I have translated 'Flow on, thou shining river' to Moore's own tune, so as to retain Greek accent *as well as* quantity in exact agreement to the music ... the commonest metres puzzle me most....

"I wonder what you think of the Maynooth Controversy? To me it has been so puzzling a one that I have been heartily glad that nothing obliged me to express an opinion.

"Some things seem clear to me: (1) That a measure for cutting down the Church of Ireland, as by Lord Morpeth's Bill, would have been, and would now be, far better in every respect than this of Sir R. Peel; (2) that the present is a mode of perpetuating the *sinecure* Church of Ireland by paying the Romish, and real Church, out of English and Scotch funds. Hence it is popular with many Irish Protestants, of which Sir R. Peel *boasts!*" [Francis Newman seems to forget, in his frequent allusions to "Protestants", that there was a National Church in Ireland, as in England, long before the word which sprang into being at the Reformation had found its feet.]

"If they (the Government) were pleading that a Romanist people ought to be allowed to support their own Romish clergy, they could justly claim that we, as a Protestant people, would not interfere on the ground of our dislike to Romish doctrine. But when they demand to support Romanism out of common funds, they implicate *us* in the question, whether (on the whole) *that* religion contains more truth or error; and I think they *force* those who see it in black colours to urge the No Popery cry. So far, I am disposed to justify the Anti–Maynooth war. Sir R. Inglis may be a bigot in his view of Romanism ... but I think he is *not* 'out of order' in intruding the religious demerit of Romanism into a parliamentary discussion. If this measure had been thrown out, I fear Ireland would have been awfully embittered. Yet I hope the fierce opposition will stop any future scheme of keeping the sinecure church untouched and endowing the priests with imperial money.... Thus I halt between two opinions."

In November, 1843, Newman touches briefly upon the Oxford movement thus:—

"You do not seem to know that the *Record* has been making a fuss this last month about the Bishop of Oxford's public declaration that he never requested my brother to suppress Tract 90. All he did was to suggest that 'the publication of the Tracts be discontinued,' which meant that there was to be no No. 91. The Bishop indignantly disclaims the idea that my brother had been disobedient.

* * * * *

"I am, for a week past, resting from Berber, having written to M d'Avezac in Paris to ask whether a report I heard is true, that he is preparing a dictionary of it. I have ordered an Amharic grammar, too, and want to compare them, but I abhor the Ethiopic type!.... I cannot get Kitto to tell me whether the sale of the *Cyclopaedia* is satisfactory."

As regards Irish affairs:—

"I have lately spoken at a meeting of the Friends of Ireland, and have sent to the *Guardian* newspaper here, [Footnote: Manchester Guardian.] in reply to their demand that I would specify some plan, a paper on *Fixity of Tenure* for the cottiers of Ireland. I feel no doubt that this must ere long become the great Irish question, of even more interest than the ecclesiastical one...."

And in March he gives more news of his "Berber":—

"I am again at work at the Berber MS., which I have not touched since the 1st October. The Royal Asiatic Society have accepted my offer to edit it. At present their pages are occupied with the history of Darius Hystaspis from the rocks at (I think) Besittoon, near

Hemadon—the most curious document which recent research has brought to light, and, I am told, confirming in detail the accounts of Herodotus."

The two following letters to Dr. Nicholson deal chiefly with matters connected with John Sterling (who had recently died) and with Newman's arrangements for adopting one of his children.

Perhaps most people are familiar with Carlyle's biography of Sterling, but it may be as well to say here that he was a brilliant writer, a Liberal in politics, and interested himself keenly in General Torrijos and his group of Spanish exiles. When at college, at the age of nineteen, he came under the influence of Julius Hare, his tutor. When he was twenty–six he again fell in with Hare at Bonn, and here came to pass one of the mistakes of his life. Chiefly through Hare's influence he took deacon's orders, and he worked under Hare at Hurstmonceaux for the best part of a year. Very soon afterwards he began to feel the breach growing wider between his own convictions and those taught by the Church. He never, consequently, took priest's orders. Through grievous ill–health his winters were passed at Bordeaux, in Italy, or at Madeira. He died at Ventnor 18th Sept., 1843.

"While riding to–day I was meditating on the continual strain which the pulling of my horse made on the left arm, while the right was idle; and it struck me that this might conduce to the size of the muscles on that side. Also my wife always leans on the left, as being stronger in her right arm.... The hardest work I am put to is holding an umbrella against a fierce wind; and in this my right hand certainly beats my left.... I have had no bad nights since I left Manchester, except two which I attribute to an excitement on meeting my sister, whom I had not seen for eight years.... I mean to return home next Saturday. Since I left you an important change of prospect in my domestic economy has occurred. I have accepted the responsible office of guardian to the eldest son (thirteen years old) of my dear dying friend Sterling, whom I went to see at Ventnor, Isle of Wight. The lad will come to Manchester next week, and in future live in our house, and I trust I shall love him as a son. He seems a very affectionate boy. His mother died about eighteen months ago. I found my poor friend on the whole stronger than I had expected, yet steadily declining: long since convinced that his case was hopeless (and indeed expecting his end sooner than those around him), yet thoroughly calm and resigned to the gracious will of Him Who had so ordained it. Not to mourn over talents so high and a will so upright thus prematurely to be lost to us were impossible, even did I not know how truly brotherly in affection is his heart to us. He will leave six orphan children. Yet this calamity is relieved by the tenderness of his brother to them, and by the existence of adequate supplies for all reasonable wants.... Tell your little boy that I have to–day been out with a nephew of mine (Johnny Kennaway) nearly of *his* age, and he rides a little white pony. It was almost too spirited for him, and I was once afraid it would run away with him; but I could not do anything to help him but pull up my own horse short and call to him to do the same....

"Believe me, my dear Nicholson,

"Your affectionate friend,

"Francis W. Newman."

This letter was written from Escot, Ottery St. Mary, Devon, [Footnote: His wife's old home.] in September, 1844.

In 1841 Ward of Balliol brought out a very strong pamphlet, and accused the Reformation of many changes in the English Church; as Rev. J. B. Mozley says in his *Letters*, it was "a kind of strong interpretation of No. XC, just as Pusey's ... is a mollifying one, proving that No. XC says nothing but what our divines have said before." As regards "the statute", the Hebdomadal Board had early in this year "proposed a new statute" for the conferring of B.D. degrees.

"*30th Dec.*, 1844.

"... I suppose you are busy with *Ewald's* [Footnote: Dr. Nicholson was the pupil of Ewald, and the first translator of his *Hebrew Grammar*.] *Grammar*.... I shall be more at rest whenever circumstances put me into that direct conflict with current opinion, which I dare not go out of my way to provoke, and yet feel it to be my natural element. My antagonism to 'things as they are'—politically, scientifically, and theologically— grows with my growth; and I believe that every year that delays change more and more endangers destruction to our social framework."

I cannot forbear quoting here from a letter recently received by me from a distant cousin of mine, Mr. George Grey Butler. He says: "I remember once at table Mr. Newman saying (when asked his attitude on various public questions), 'Oh! I am anti–slavery, anti–alcohol, anti–tobacco, anti– *everything!*' with a twinkle in his eye which caused an outburst of mirth amongst his listeners."

Rev. J. B. Mozley goes on to say, "Pusey will not take the test," (or statute) "that he has declared publicly ... Hussey the Professor, Eden, Baden Powell, and several Liberals, Price of Rugby, are all strong against it.... Gladstone is very strong, and thinks every exertion ought to be made against it."

On 7th Oct., 1844, Newman is expecting the arrival of the son of his old friend, John Sterling. "Edward Sterling will probably come to us to–day; his trunk is here already. I do not think you know that his father's earthly career is over.... Sterling's will is like himself. He has so strong a feeling of the wrong and absurdity of laying responsibility on people, and yet fettering their discretion, that he has left the fullest powers possible both to his brother as executor to manage his property and the other children, and to me over Edward. He has directed L300 a year to be paid me for Edward.... He was indeed a noble soul, and few know what a loss it is; but those few rate it high. As Captain Sterling (his brother) said, he had been accumulating wisdom all his life, and could he have lived twenty years more to pour it out he would indeed have left behind him a precious legacy.... Thomas Carlyle wrote a beautiful letter over him. His little son knows not at all what a father he has lost; and as for me, I want to tell him, but feel how hard it is."

In 1845 the taxes upon corn had caused great distress in England. But far worse was the trouble in Ireland; for practically, through the potato famine, owing to the thousands of acres which were blighted, there were literally thousands dying of starvation. Cheap food was far more difficult to get at there than in England, and at length at the close of the year Sir Robert Peel said he would repeal the Corn Laws altogether. In 1846 the Bill with this end in view passed through the House of Commons and House of Lords and became law. But the consequence of this measure was in effect the signal for Peel's going out of office, and his place was taken by Lord John Russell.

To return to Newman's letter.

"You perhaps know that the Liberals at Oxford are likely to side with Ward against the Heads. I do not see what else they can do; and I devoutly hope that the tangle will be irremovable except by abolishing subscriptions. Price of Rugby is all in a bristle about it. I much admire his spirit. Baden Powell protests *in toto* against the statute."

101

"*6th Nov.*, 1845.

"My dear Nicholson,

* * * * *

"Your news about the potatoes unfortunately is no matter of private information, but rings through our ears, and I am increasingly doubtful whether we are to hope for open ports. I believe the League is right in saying that Sir Robert's *next move* will be for an absolutely free trade; but *when* that next move is to be must depend in part on his colleagues; and the country must perhaps suffer much before they come over, or he gains boldness to defy their opposition....

"If you have been reading the *New Prospective*, I dare say you will guess that the article on 'Church Reform' is mine. I was not sorry to get it printed, even in such a quarter—(though I know no other periodical that is free enough to dare to print it. The *Westminster Review* is not enough in religious circles),—because I want to send it to Churches of various grades, and get their opinion. I fear I have expressed myself too sanguinely of Dissenting Co-operation. They seem to say they will support *nothing* that does not go to length of alienating the whole Church property to secular uses."

On 16th April, 1846, politics are touched on again.

"*16th April*, 1846.

"My dear Nicholson,

"I have sent one or two 'Leagues' of late to my brother-in-law in Devonshire, thinking that they had in them matter of instruction to him.... Does not Peel appear of late to have made himself as little as of old? Yet I rejoice in his obstructing a mere Whig ministry of the orthodox kind; and although his course has heaped misery on Ireland, nothing less severe, I imagine, would brace England up to the stringent remedies which alone can save that country;—nor are we *yet* screwed to the point!...

"I have finished the Berber MS. as far as the Arabic had been translated, viz. twenty-eight folio pages: four more remain, of which I cannot understand either the

Berber or the Arabic. I suppose neither could Mr. Hodgson understand them; for while he professes to have translated the whole of the Arabic, he has quietly omitted these. I naturally turn myself to your aid. I have quite ascertained that the Arabic and Berber *do correspond*....

"I am trying to move my house, i.e. to get into a new shell, further from the smoke. [Footnote: Newman had not yet left Manchester New College.] Edward Sterling's little brother, aged five and a half, is now with us; and especially for his sake I desire to have pure air.... I am sorry to say she" (Newman's wife) "is becoming more and more afflicted with rheumatism. I am about to send her to Malvern, where one of her sisters now is, to try a hydropathist physician there—a regularly educated man. As she must take little Johnny S. and her own maid, and another to help in bathings, and look after the child, it is quite a nomad eruption and waggon–load of Scythians.

"My sister's child, a boy of Johnny S.'s age, fell into the fire six or seven weeks ago, and was almost burnt to death. The poor little fellow endured agonies, but is at last nearly recovered.... It seems a wonderful recovery."

The next letter notifies his election as Latin Professor in University College.

"*London. 6th July*, 1846.

"My dear Nicholson,

"A few words just to say that on Saturday I was elected Latin Professor in L. U. C., and to thank you once more for your valuable aid. Hoping Mrs. N. continues well, and with kind regards to her, and the children,

"I am, ever yours affectionately,

"Francis W. Newman."

CHAPTER VIII. LETTERS TO DR. NICHOLSON FROM PROFESSOR NEWMAN DURING THE FOLLOWING YEARS: 1850 TO 1859

The first of special interest in this series of letters is dated March, 1850, and concerns Newman's Latin studies and also Indian and China affairs.

"Sir Charles Trevelyan is doing his best to introduce the English alphabet into Indian languages. He believes it, with me, to be of political, educational, and religious importance; but he seems to be opposed by all the English scholars. Edwin Norris says that even Sanscrit imported its alphabet from a foreign tongue. The number of primitive alphabets is so few, the diversity of languages so great, that nearly all tongues must have adopted foreign alphabets. I cannot therefore understand the almost a priori objections raised by the learned.... Do you attend to Indian affairs? The disbanding of our Native Indian armies, the prospect of a sure surplus in the Indian treasury, with the necessity of a conciliatory policy to all the Indian princes as soon as we are disarmed, seem to me as light pouring in through a dark cloud. But I am not easy (far from it) until we get out of this Chinese scrape. I have for years maintained that the more we fight against China the more we shall teach them the art of war; and unless we tear the empire in pieces by aiding insurrections, they must beat us at last, and become masters in the Indian seas. We cannot contend against three hundred and eighty millions of ingenious, industrious, homogeneous men under a single monarch with compact country, splendid rivers and harbours, unsurpassed soil and climate—if once we drive them to learn the art of war from America, as Peter the Great learnt it from Europe. But I seem to be *insanus inter sobrios*, for nobody accepts this thought from me.

"Hearty regards to you all.

"Ever yours,

"F. W. Newman."

It will be remembered that in 1851, though not until December, Louis Napoleon, nephew of Napoleon Bonaparte, had been successful in his aim of becoming President of the French Republic. But he had practically led his army through a sea of blood to reach this autocratic position. Later, in 1852, he made the French people designate him "Emperor of the French" under the title of Napoleon III.

Lord Russell had, with his ministers, brought their time of office to an end; and Lord Derby came in as Prime Minister at the head of a Conservative Party. He only remained in office a short time, however, and his successor was Lord Aberdeen, and Mr. Gladstone was Chancellor of the Exchequer.

In the letter which follows, Newman vindicates the honour of Kossuth, whose friend and helper he was when Kossuth came to England for funds to set going the new Hungarian revolution against Austria. With the views of Charles Dickens, of course, Newman had not the slightest sympathy.

"7 P.V.E., "*19th Dec.*, 1851.

"My dear Nicholson,

*　*　*　*　*

"I never see Dickens' *Household Narrative*, and therefore cannot answer; but I do not believe there is any 'alternative side' against Kossuth's character. (Dickens is, in my judgment, a foolish man; he writes on centralization and despotism like an Austrian: however, so does Carlyle often.) But all that can be said against Kossuth is, that up to the age of twenty–two or twenty–three he was a thoughtless young man, who liked hunting and gambling. Since that age he is irreproachable, the proof of which is, that the Austrian *Times* has not a word to say against him. Their libel about the Orphan Fund was at once refuted by Count Ladislaus Vay, but they would not insert Count Vay's letter, or even acknowledge it. I think, indeed, the Continental Republicans may be proud of their leaders.

*　*　*　*　*

"Lord Palmerston seems to me to be entangled in *routine* and old creeds, so that he does not do all the justice he might to his better wishes; but I also think he loves *place* better than to carry out those wishes....

"Ever yours heartily,

"F. W. Newman."

The letter in January, 1853, which is next in order, is largely concerned with Mazzini. As is well known, Mazzini was an Italian patriot and Republican, born in the same year as was Newman. When he was only sixteen, seeing the refugees who fled from the unfortunate rising in Piedmont, he determined then and there to rescue his country when he should be old enough to do so. He made "the first great sacrifice of his life" in giving up the study of literature (which he loved) for direct political action. He joined the Carbonari in 1829, though he was not in sympathy with their aims or organization.

In 1830 he was imprisoned by the Sardinian police. There, in his prison cell, he thought out his plan of action for his country, and on being released he went and organized the "Young Italy Association." The object of it was to teach the mass of the people first to know their rights, and then to obtain them. The end of all his efforts for his people as regarded himself was this:—

In 1832 he was expelled from the country, but he managed to remain hidden at Marseilles; and from that time for twenty years he led "a life of voluntary imprisonment within the four walls of a little room." In 1844 Mazzini accused the English Government of having opened his letters and told their contents to the authorities of Italy. This set the whole of England against him, but Carlyle defended him in great measure, and testified to the worthiness of his noble struggle for his country's freedom. Later, in 1848, when the Lombard revolt broke out, he took the part of the revolutionaries with vigour.

In 1852 he planned the revolt at Mantua, and in 1853 at Milan. Others were set going later. He had started in London (with Kossuth) the European Association, and issued in September, 1855, its "republican manifesto." He strongly condemned the agreement made in 1859 between Napoleon III and Piedmont, because he foresaw its inevitable consequences. Mazzini, Garibaldi, and Cavour were a trio who largely influenced their country's destiny. Garibaldi has been called the knight–errant; Mazzini, the prophet of Italian unity; and Cavour was the hub which formed the centre of the wheel of Italy's fortunes.

[Illustration: FACSIMILE OF LETTER FROM FRANCIS NEWMAN, DECEMBER, 1855]

"7 P.V.E. "Friday night, *28th Jan.*, 1853.

"My dear Nicholson,

* * * * *

"As regards Mazzini, I am both glad and sorry. I cannot pretend to know the *truth*, and fear to say what may unjustly disparage him; but he has fallen a little in my secret judgment. I am *told* (and I cannot test the assertion) that Mazzini wrote to Italy to *implore* his countrymen to be patient, and not to make any attempts at resistance, even though the best among them were slaughtered; and added: But if you will and must make your attempt *now*, then by all means I shall come—not to conquer with you; for of that I have no hope—but to die with you. Now I cannot learn whether this was simultaneously with his writing to tell us that he was in high hopes of success, and only wanted L3000 to turn probability into something like certainty. If it was simultaneous, he is not the less patriot; but he thinks 'the point of honour' requires he should tell a lie to his English friends in order to get the wherewith to die a martyr's death; and it makes it very hard to trust his simple truth in future. But if (as one friend of his thinks) Mazzini's own opinion has changed, it lowers one's notion of his discernment. In fact, it is scarcely credible to *me*. There are those, I find, who have lately helped him to money, expressly thinking it was a going to martyrdom, but believing he was bent on it, and that possibly he may now do more good to Italy by his death than ever he can do by his life. I cannot take this view. I believe the tyrants would have the good sense to destroy him so secretly that no moral effect should follow from his death; and if he utterly disapproved of an outbreak, I do not understand the 'honour' which should make him go to useless destruction when his life may be so valuable. It is not the same thing to an exile as to a soldier in a rank, for the exile necessarily comes too late. However, I do not know whether at this instant Mazzini may be disguised in Italy: he is so retired and so stealthy. I expect he will (be) betrayed sooner or later, if he plays so bold a game. Nevertheless I am glad that (for whatever reason) the Italians are still quiet. Louis Napoleon will certainly sooner or later get embroiled; and unless there were new facts unknown to me ... I earnestly hope they will wait. The Germans are a slow people; but they will move in time. Every German I see believes this.... 'We without them cannot be made perfect,' seems to me the clue to European oppressions. While stupid barbarism exists in masses, it will be the tool of tyranny against the more educated and refined and wealthy....

"Ever yours, "F. W. Newman."

107

In November, 1855, he discusses public affairs, with relation to Louis Napoleon, with Dr. Nicholson:—

"....I should indeed like to have the talk on public affairs which you suggested; but things have moved on since then! Friends of mine dread that the difficulties of French finance will precipitate Louis N. into a base peace. I argue,—it will then be into one so base that the French will not endure it. For the Russians *know* the French difficulties; and if proposals of peace come first from France, or if they see French action become slacker, they will yield *nothing*, and make sure of a peace which saves all their territory and reserves all their free action.... Only yesterday came the news of Omar Pasha's 5th November victory. Even if it be exaggerated, still the repulse at Kars and this new defeat make it impossible for Russia to make peace *now* without a humiliation such as L. N. cannot attempt to remove. It *may* so be that L. N. will be blown up by his finance and by popular discontent; it may also be that his difficulties will lead him to make popular concessions to the spirit of freedom, as is usual when great sacrifices are demanded of a nation; or it may be that he will get through with a struggle, putting French finance on a healthier footing than has ever been yet. But I think, if he stands, he *must* carry on the war; and the more he feels his dangers, the more vehemently will he resolve to stick at nothing necessary for success, and will bid high to get Sweden to join us, which means to despoil Russia of Finland and Poland.

"And if he is overthrown all Italy will rise, and after it Hungary, and after it Germany and Poland....

"It grieves me much that Kossuth has united his name with Ledru Rollin's; and altogether I think Kossuth is so *soured* by the misconduct of the Western Cabinets as to lose his soundness of judgment and fairness of reasoning.... Through 1854 his tone became more demagogic, less dignified, more defiant to authorities. He is now contemptuous to the British *nation* also, though I think it has throughout displayed precisely the sound instinct which he so often ascribes to nations, and from which he says a statesman must catch his inspiration. Our *nation* did not know what he knew—that Austria had given just ground of war to Turkey—that Turkey was ready in October, 1853, to ally with Hungary against Austria; nor could it know what were the military facilities for overthrowing Austria, nor whether the stubborn resistance of Louis Napoleon was what forced Aberdeen into his policy. But the nation since the Russian invasion of Hungary has practically felt how dangerous to all foreign liberty is the Russian power, and the absolute necessity of repressing and curtailing it; and this determination of the people has made the war a reality, has given power to that side of the Cabinet which alone was willing to go forward, has displayed itself equally in our lowest distress and our chief triumph, which Kossuth ought to honour....

"I doubt whether his union with Ledru Rollin is approved by any eminent Hungarian in England.

"While I regret all this, I yet expect Kossuth to be great again whenever action in Hungary recommences; but he cannot bear *in_action well; and, alas! I make no doubt his private resources cannot bear delays. I almost begin to fear that he covets to be driven publicly to America by our Government, as less ignominious than being starved into the same step. I cannot understand ... how he fails to see that if we weaken Russia we strengthen the chances of liberty, though Aberdeen would not allow his particular policy in 1853–4. We are doing so very much more than he asked of the Americans in 1852 that the tone he assumes is wonderful. And then to scoff as he does, as though we had done nothing in destroying the Russian Black Sea Fleet and overthrowing the whole prestige of their military superiority. To have been beaten by the Turks is still more humiliating.... I wonder whether you have any alarm about America. I should have some alarm if Nicaragua and the Mosquito land were the topic of quarrel; for I think the Americans would really fight us as a single nation to hinder us establishing ourselves on American soil south of them. They sufficiently dislike our northern position....*

"Very cordially yours,

"F. W. Newman."

* * * * *

We now pass to Newman's letters in the year 1856; and the first of this series speaks of the "Harry" who is mentioned elsewhere in this volume, as having been Professor Alleyne Nicholson, of Aberdeen. He was coming to stay with Professor Newman during term time:—

"7 P.V.E. R.P., "*28th Oct.*, 1856.

"The grammar used in University College School is *Key's Grammar*.... Hitherto, no particular Greek Grammar has been used in the school, but Greek has been taught through *Robson's Constructive Greek Exercises*, which, I presume, Harry ought at once to work at.... A Greek Grammar by Mr. Greenwood is expected to be ready by Christmas, and is to be brought into the school. It will be new *to all*; and Harry will be on a par with the rest about it.

* * * * *

"*Robson's Constructive Latin Exercises* ... are used in the school.... Give him" (Harry) "my very kind regards, and say that his little bedroom here looks to me desolate until he comes; but I cannot flatter him that I have anything to fill up the emptiness of heart he will feel when he loses not only papa and mamma, but also his faithful coadjutor in study— *Annie!* Seriously, you will have to consider about his evening *amusements*, for it will not do to be studying morning and night. What think you of giving a well defined time to *drawing* every evening? He has so much taste for drawing insects that he cannot fail in outline. We have a little room which we call 'the boy's room,' where he can put any of his Natural History collections which you think it well he should try, but we have *no butterflies to catch,—few even in summer.*"

* * * * *

At the end of July, Newman went to stay with Dr. Nicholson and his family at Penrith, and there are one or two notes concerning his journey tither. The next letter is dated 24th Aug., 1856. He wrote therefore when the Crimean War was still going forward. That war which, amongst mistaken policies, blundering Government tactics, and aimless ambitions, holds a foremost place. It was not till the end of the year 1855 that it came to an end. After the attack on Sebastopol, the French—whose army had suffered quite as much from the terrible winter and from disease, etc., as our own—succeeded in taking the Malakoff Tower. This made it impossible for the Russians to defend Sebastopol any longer, and in March, 1856, peace was proclaimed. Then followed Russian promises, which were made as easily as they were broken.

"7 Park Village, East. "*24th August*, 1856.

"My dear Nicholson,

* * * * *

"Events have proved that Russia, too, painfully knew her own weakness. Probably he" (Louis Napoleon) "already in December knew that she knew it, and the war was far too unpopular with the French to be continued except on a different policy, with new necessities and new prizes to be won. Our policy from March, 1853, to March, 1855, was so hollow and so silly, that no wisdom could afterwards bring things right, or make the results of the war worthy of the cost; but the *comparative* result in March, 1856, is so vast a gain over what nine out of ten of our statesmen (so called) were projecting to accept in March, 1855, that I cannot open my lips against the peace in itself. I could not in any case wish the war continued, except on new principles for worthier objects. However, Russia has really had a terrible lesson, and a great humiliation. That she could not take Silistria or Kars against Turkish troops, except by the accident of famine, will never be forgotten by German armies or statesmen.... The native Russian peasants and low persons do not *yet* know that the Czar was beaten; they suppose him to have conquered with immense cost; but the nobility knew the truth, and it will leak through to the lowest people, I expect, in the course of a few years. I think Europe has a respite of a quarter of a century from the incubus of Russia; and *if* in that interval the Hapsburgs are overthrown, all will yet come right. I fear we are still forced again (in spite of Mazzini and Kossuth) to regard the French as having the initiative of revolutions. I have resolved to give up all extra and needless effort of the brain, until I can really get rid of certain morbid symptoms, quite chronic, which distress me, so that my projected Latin analysis lies in embryo.

"... I have had satisfactory approval of my *Iliad* from my brother, Dr. Newman, a fastidious critic and practical poet, as also from other private quarters which I count much on; but reviews as yet do not notice me.... I have no high expectation of the very existence of the book becoming known, except slowly to many who might perhaps be glad of it if they knew it....

"Ever your faithful friend,

"F. W. Newman."

In October of the same year he thus speaks of the School of University College:—

"... The School of U.C. is remarkably full of pupils this season. My junior class has unusually *old* pupils; I do not yet know their quality. One (a Mr. Sassoon, a Jew?) [Footnote: Probably this was the father of the present Sir Edward Sassoon, second Baronet.] I mistook for a German, but he told me he is an Arab of Hindoo birth, and talks a little Arab and Hindostanee, but knows more of English than of any other language. His English is good, though the pronunciation is a little foreign."

In another letter, written this same month, he speaks of Mazzini as knowing that the "liberties of Italy cannot be safe without revolution either in France or Austria." That he feels it must come sooner or later, so that it would be better for Italy to act and suffer rather than to become "stupefied." Newman declares that the Governments know, and is the reason why they "hate Mazzini, since ... success in Italy will cause explosions elsewhere."

Newman goes on to say: "For myself I look at it thus. The deliverance of Italy *cannot* come by Governments (unless these are first revolutionized); it can only come by insurrection. No one from without can ever know or judge what is the time for hopeful insurrection: it must be done from within, and generally without plan. My sole question is, Is the cause legitimate? I find that it is. I leave Italians to judge of the time. Meanwhile every year I would give of my superfluity to the aid of patriotic effort.... To fail ten times may be necessary for success in the eleventh. If they were losing heart and becoming denationalized, the case would be bad; but it is the contrary. The fusion with Austria is impossible. The more they bleed the more they are united, and the more resolved.... My wife is cheered to learn that Harry will go to Mr. Bruce's on Sunday. A black spot had rested on her heart, I find, from fearing that he would go *nowhere* to church. I am sending you a corrected copy of my translation of the first chorus in *Antigone*, since you honour it by putting it into your *Sophocles*...."

"Ever your affectionate friend,

"F. W. Newman. "To Dr. J. Nicholson, etc."

Another mention of the translation I also insert here. He had been able to give far more time to it than if he had been in London, for he had in September been spending some time at Ventnor. "A youth introduced to me by Mrs. Pulszky is zealous in the Greek tragedians, and I have been helping him to a little *Sophocles* which put me up to translating the 1st Chorus after I had been reading it with him...."

Here is the translation to which allusion is made:—

"SOPHOCLES, ANTIGONE"

1ST CHORAL SONG

1st Strophe

"O ray of the Sun, the fairest
That over the rills of Dirke
To Thebe the seven–gated
Wast ever of yore unveil'd
The eyelid of heaven gilding;
At length thy splendour on us was shed,
Urging to hasty reverse of rein
The Argive warrior white of shield
And laden in panoply all complete,
Who sped in van of the routed.
Stirr'd from afar against our land
By Polyneikes' doubtful strife,
He like an eagle soaring came,
Screen'd by a wing of snow unstain'd,
With many a stout accoutrement
  And horse–hair crested helmets.

1st Antistrophe

"At mouth of the portals seven
Above our abodes he hover'd
With lances that yawn'd for carnage;
But vanish'd, afore his chaps
With slaughter of Thebes were glutted;
Afore the flicker of pitchy flame
Might to the crown of turrets climb.

113

So fierce the rattle of war around
Was pour'd on his rear by the serpent–foe
Hard match'd in deadly encounter.
For Jove the over–vaunting tongue
Supremely hates. Their full fed stream
Of gold, of clatter, and of pride
He saw, and smote with brandish'd flame
Him, who at summit of his goal
Would raise the peal of Conquest.

2nd Strophe.

"Foil'd in his frantic rush,
  Though still with blasts of hate against us raving,
  Down dropt he, torch and all,
And heavy struck the Earth, who upward spurn'd him.
  Such auspice of the war
To us was fair; and elsewhere new successes
  Befel, whereon the right
  Great Ares routing wheel'd the chariot–battle.

For, posted at the seven gates,
Equals to equals, seven chiefs
To trophy–bearing Jupiter
Payments of solid brass bequeath'd.
Save that the gloomy–hearted twain,
Sprung from one mother and one sire,
Planted with adverse dint the spear
And earn'd a fate in common.

2nd Antistrophe

"But now, since Victory
Mighty of name at length is come, delighted
  In car–borne Thebe's joy;
Henceforth forget we battle's past annoyance.

114

But through the livelong night
Let us in sacred band approach the temples,
  And Bacchus to the dance—
The god who shakes the soil of Thebes—be leader.

"But hither Creon, lo! proceeds,
Son of Menoekeus, newly rais'd
The sceptre of this land to sway.
Now at new tokens of the gods,
 Methinks, some sage device he plies.
Therefore to special parliament
Hath he by general summons fetch'd
This meeting of the elders."

The next letter largely concerns Persia. And it is necessary to remember that, in the early part of the nineteenth century, she began, at the suggestion of France, a most unfortunate war (as regards herself) with Russia.

In 1826 there was another war, and this cost Persia all the rest of her possessions in Armenia. The taxation of the people, which the rulers enforced to enable them to pay the expenses of the war, caused the former to rise in insurrection in 1829. The death of the Crown Prince in 1833 seemed the crowning blow to the fortunes of Persia, for he had been the only man who had seriously tried to raise his country from the depths to which she had fallen.

In 1848 the son of the Shah, who had, through the assistance of Britain and Russia, obtained the throne, came into office, and he resolved to put forward claims to Afghanistan and Beluchistan. When the ruler of Herat agreed that the Shah had claims, the English Government made the Shah sign an agreement in 1853 that he would give up pressing his claims as regarded Herat. But in 1856 the Persians retook this city, because they declared that the Ameer of Kabul was planning an advance on Herat. Thereupon a British army, commanded by General Outram and Havelock, was sent to Persia, and defeat after defeat for the Persians followed their arrival, and in July, 1857, they were compelled to give up Herat. Since then Persia has not ventured to lay her hand on the "key to India."

"7 P.V.E., London, "*19th Dec.*, 1856.

"Dr. Barth, the African traveller, has been re–seducing (me) into the Lingua Amazighana, which I had forsworn. I am not sure that something will not come of it—to me at least. I have already built a castle in the air, that sometime hereafter I shall become 'Professor of Libyan' to U.C.

* * * * *

"How dreadful is it that we should be able to get into a war with Persia, proclaimed *at Bombay* on November 1st, and nobody here knows why it is or what it seeks after; and the country's honour is committed while Parliament is not even sitting. And for this we throw up Italy and ... Switzerland? Have you seen Cobden's recent letters on Maritime War? I rejoice much in them, and think adversity has improved his tone. With hearty regards to Mrs. N. and all,

"I am, ever yours,

"F. W. N."

The letters at which we have now arrived are those written during 1857. The first is dated March, and I quote some passages from it to show the Professor's own views as regards evening home preparation for boys who are working at school during the day, because it seems to me that his opinion in this matter should carry weight:—

"I much dislike a boy having *both* his work at school and *then* evening work at home, when he is getting sleepy and ought to have relaxation. It is the nuisance of day schools, and quite hurtful to study, if there is nobody at home to answer questions. Besides, Harry" (this is Harry Nicholson, mentioned two or three times in these letters as attending University College School) "is so studious of himself that it is very much to be desired that he should have time for *voluntary* work. I regard this as having been very beneficial to *me* at school, where I never had work enough set me to fill up half my time."

The letter which follows is dated April, and in it we find that "Harry" had just returned home, and that his report had testified to his diligence and progress. At the end of the letter comes this little touch as to some of the schoolboy belongings which had been left behind in Professor Newman's house. "Harry has left divers snail–shells fastened on pasteboard. Perhaps he did not know how to carry them safely."

On 6th May mention of the owner of the snail–shells recurs again:—

"Mrs. Newman was rather disappointed at the unceremoniousness of my parting with Harry. It seems like a dream his vanishing. I suppose she is like Hecuba, grieved that she could not make the funeral of Hector. (I did not even kiss Harry *by proxy* for her!) Most gladly does she give him up to Mrs. Nicholson; and yet, I fancy, she wanted a funeral ceremony on losing him."

Throughout these letters belonging to the year 1857, there is no special mention of the Indian Mutiny. Yet it is impossible to doubt that it occupied a great place in Newman's thoughts. No one who has written on India and our relations with her as he has done, could have failed to have written his own strong views on the lamentable mismanagement which led to the Mutiny. But most probably the letters concerning it were either not kept by Dr. Nicholson, or else Newman asked for them back, as in so many cases he was accustomed to do with regard to his own letters towards the close of his life. He had a theory that letters should not be kept, and many people have told me that he asked for his letters back in order to destroy them. Happily, however, this is *not* the theory which everyone holds. Indeed, to many of us, the Past lies so near the written word, that *almost* it re–awakens between the folds of a letter; indeed, in many instances, the Past and Present only meet across it. In this sense it is the only thing that holds up the picture of the past before our tired eyes. *Litera scripta manet* is a living truth. The next letter from Newman to Nicholson was written on 20th June, 1857. On 8th June of this year died Douglas Jerrold, dramatist, satirist, and author. Mr. Walter Jerrold tells us that, in 1852, he had accepted the editorship of *Lloyd's Weekly Newspaper*. It was said of this that he "found it in the street and annexed it to literature."

His fortune as a writer began when he was only sixteen. His capacity for work and his perseverance in working were enormous. In 1825 he wrote great numbers of plays and farces; but beside all these, he contributed, as is well known, to *Punch* (at its first commencement in 1841), as well as to hosts of magazines and political tracts, etc. Newman alludes to Jerrold being in receipt of L2000 a year from *Lloyd's Weekly News*.

I pass over the discussion as regards the Newmans' proposed visit to the Lakes, and also his expressed delight in a book, many copies of which he had just given away—*Intuitive Morals and Religious Duty.*

"In truth, dear friend, I get happier and happier, and only am pent up and mourn to feel how I live for self alone. I sometimes think with a sort of envy how your knowledge of medicine and tender heart for young children puts you into near and kind contact with the poor. However, we have each his own talent, if only one can find the mode of wisely disposing it.

* * * * *

"I am sorry to see that Douglas Jerrold has not left sixpence to his family, though he was in receipt of L2000 a year (they say!) from *Lloyd's Weekly News.*"

In November another letter alludes to his Latin translations. He says he has been gradually inclining to the belief that Terence, Virgil, and Horace had "damaged" the Latin language in very much the same way as Pope did the English, as regards arbitrary style and method of writing cadences.

It is universally conceded that Horace was not a great thinker. As one of our modern English critics has said: "His philosophy is that of the market–place rather than of the schools; he does not move among high ideals or subtle emotions.... He carried on and perfected the native Roman growth, satire, so as to make Roman life from day to day, in city and country, live anew under his pen.... Before Horace, Latin lyric poetry is represented almost wholly by the brilliant but technically immature poems of Catullus; after him it ceases to exist."

As regards Pope, the critics of the end of the eighteenth century considered his style eminently artificial and forced. But to–day, according to Father Gasquet, we cannot but recognize his services to English poetry as invaluable. "He was virtually the inventor and artificer who added a new instrument of music to its majestic orchestra, a new weapon of expression to its noble armoury.... But one must admit that to the taste of the present age there occurs a certain coldness and artificiality in his portrayals alike of the face of nature and of the passions of man. He appeals rather to the brain than to the heart. Ideas and not emotions are his province.... To the metric presentment of ideas he imparts a charm of musical utterance unachieved before his time."

"*30th Nov.*, 1857.

"My dear Nicholson,

* * * * *

"I have of late been urged by a particular circumstance to make various trials of translation into Latin (lyrical, etc.) verse—an exercise I always used to dislike, and have never much practised. I now find my dislike was largely caused by the unsuitable and over–stiff metres which used to be imposed on me when I was under orders.... In English and Greek versification I have long been aware of the essential importance of this; but I have looked on Latin as too inflexible a tongue to be worth the labour, since nearly all the translations I have seen, pall on me as mere flat imitations of the ancients instead of having a smack of the original. I have been inclining to the belief that Terence, Virgil, and Horace have done damage to the Latin language, or at least to our taste; just as Pope was the ruin of English poetry so long as he was allowed to dictate the style and cadences. In Plautus, Lucretius, and Catullus the language has a flexibility and the metres a freedom which (as I think) academicians and schoolmasters have not duly appreciated, and which ought to impart to us (when we *do* do anything so absurd as to write foreign verses) a freedom at which we have not generally aimed. As to metre, I think it really a *folly* to insist on Horace's restrictions, which are entirely his own, being neither found in the Greek, which he copied, nor in Catullus; and which made the problem of *translation* so much harder (and he did not translate), that one has to sacrifice too much. I think we ought to construct our metres by selection from the Greek, just as Catullus or Horace did, not imitate them slavishly. I send you one specimen of my translation, to ask whether so many as seven lines together the same is *too monotonous*. If there were only four or five it would be as one of Catullus's. I dare say you have the original....

"With truest regards to you all, "Your cordial friend,

"F. W. Newman."

Pulszky, the friend of Kossuth and also of Francis Newman, was a Hungarian author, politician, and patriot. In 1848 he was serving under Esterhazy in some Government post;

119

but when he was suspected of revolutionizing in his native country, he took refuge in England. Pulszky went with Kossuth later to America. In 1852 he was condemned to death by the Austrian Government, but his fourteen years spent in Italy seem to have influenced the Ministers to pardon him in 1867. While in England (I do not know if he suffered from it elsewhere) he became a martyr to *tic douleureux*, that most trying form of facial neuralgia which attacks in such paroxysms of severe pain—attacks which seem brought on by the most trivial reasons, such as a knock at the door or by a sudden shake to the chair on which the patient is sitting, and which, as a rule, give no warning of their approach.

"My dear Nicholson,

"You remember that you kindly furnished me with your prescription for *tic douleureux* to give to my friend Pulszky. He told me a few days back that he sent it (I think a year ago) to the poor girl at Ventnor who was a horrible sufferer from it, and heard no more of it until this autumn when he was at Ventnor again. He was delighted to find she had been immediately cured by it, had had no returns, was made competent for work, and is in a servant's place. On my naming this, I have two urgent applications for the prescriptions. If you will a second time take the trouble to copy out the prescription I will keep it myself, and give copies to my friends without further coming upon you.... I have ventured to assert that the Nicholson who is so talked of as promoting the ballot in Australia is *not* your brother Mark.

"Do you know, when I saw in the *Illustrated London News* the face of the late lamented Brigadier Nicholson of the Punjaub, I thought it *very* like you. Is he possibly a distant relative?

"Ever yours heartily,

"F. W. Newman, "7 P.V.E." "*20th December*, 1857.

This remark of Newman's that he saw a strong likeness in "the face of the late lamented Brigadier Nicholson of the Punjaub" to his friend Dr. Nicholson is one of those arresting suggestions which seem to strike sudden light out of the flints of ancestry which whiten the road of life along which we have come.

That there *is* a distinct likeness in the two faces no one who had seen the portraits in Captain Lionel Trotter's *Life of John Nicholson,* and then looked at that of Dr. John Nicholson in this book, could have had a doubt. But, as it seems to me, there is even more ground for the likelihood of Newman's suggestion, if one tries to trace the lineage and land of the families of Nicholson in years gone by. I quote the following from Captain Trotter's *Life of John Nicholson:*—

"In the days of our Tudor sovereigns the family of which John Nicholson was to be the bright particular star had made their home in the border county of Cumberland." He goes on to say that the first to come over to Ireland was Rev. William Nicholson (in 1589), and he married the Lady Elizabeth Percy. Captain Trotter says there is a tradition that his two brothers went over to Ireland with William Nicholson. One settled in Derry, the other in Dublin. During McGuire's rebellion in 1641, his son's wife and her baby boy "were the only two in Cran–na–gael" [now known as Cranagill] "who escaped the common massacre by hiding behind some brushwood. In their wanderings thence they fell in with a party of loyalist soldiers, who escorted them safely to Dromore, whence they made their way across sea to the widow's former home at Whitehaven...." What became of this Mrs. Nicholson does not appear. "Her son William, during his sojourn in Cumberland, had become a Quaker." This was very probably due to his having been influenced by his intercourse with George Fox. Later on the former went back to Cranagill. There were three sons born to this William Nicholson, and Captain Trotter tells us that it was from the eldest (also a "William") that the famous John Nicholson was descended.

Now, it seems to me that it is not at all unlikely that there may have been some connection (as Francis Newman suggested) between the branch of the Nicholson family to which John Nicholson, of Mutiny fame, was related, who made their home in the "border county of Cumberland," and that to which Dr. John Nicholson, the lifelong friend of Francis Newman, belonged. The latter also belonged to a north country family who, I believe, settled on the borders of England and Scotland. Dr. Nicholson himself lived for a great number of years at Penrith, in Cumberland. So that, all things considered, perhaps Newman's conjecture, after he had realized how strong a resemblance there was in his friend's face to that of the hero of Delhi, was correct.

The next letters belong to the year 1858. In August, 1858, Newman was again devoting much time to Latin versification:—

"My chief time this summer has been employed in a new *furor* —Latin versification. I find that by choosing and adapting metres from the Greek fountain and not sticking to Horace, or even to Catullus, the language admits of translation from English closer than I at all conceived. I think I have done 1500 lines in all. I only translate short pieces and pleasing ones. I have been led to it by a practical object. I used to hate Latin versification, and indeed the extreme poverty and ambiguity of the language is laid bare shockingly by the process. Perhaps not really worse than in prose translation, but every metre (or almost every) deprives you at once of a sensible fraction of the already scanty vocabulary. One learns also how essentially clumsy and prosaic the language is in its vocabulary, though so compact in its structure.

"The Atlantic Telegraph, no doubt, already excites wild and impatient hopes in our Australians, of which you will hear an echo. It is indeed a critical event, as determining an immense extension of the telegraphic system....

"Ever yours heartily,

"F. W. Newman."

It will be remembered that the Crimean War broke up the Coalition Ministry which Lord Aberdeen had formed. This was due to the fact that the motion for enquiry into the state of our soldiers before Sebastopol was carried by a great majority against the Government. Lord Aberdeen resigned when this happened, and Lord Palmerston came into office, with Mr. Gladstone as Chancellor of the Exchequer. Then, when Palmerston acceded to the demand that a committee of enquiry should be appointed, Gladstone, who had opposed it before, thought he ought not to remain in the Cabinet which had now agreed to have the enquiry made. So he gave up office, but still helped the Government generally until after Orsini's attempt in 1858, upon Napoleon III's life. Perhaps it is necessary to recall here that Gladstone had taken up the cause of the prisoners—especially political prisoners— in the prisons of Naples in 1851. He spoke strongly on the terrible cruelties which were perpetrated there. In *this* effort to help forward an enquiry Gladstone threw himself most heartily.

* * * * *

"I send you to–day a Latin Grammar which I have found on my shelves. By the *binder's* ticket 'Penrith' I infer it to be Harry's. I hope I may congratulate him.... I never met Gladstone. He was a hero of mine for about a year. I hoped great things of him. After the letters on Naples and his Chancellorship of the Exchequer, I thought he had worked clear of the errors of his youth and was 'the coming man.' But in the Russian war his intense party spirit and endless mistakes have lowered his ... intellectual discernments.

* * * * *

"I am, ever yours heartily,

"F. W. Newman."

In December of this year Newman writes word that he has been working hard at Arabic for some time, because he has undertaken to teach a friend modern Arabic. He is again staying at Hastings, where he had been so constantly.

"20 White Rock Place, Hastings, "*30th Dec.*, 1858.

"My dear Nicholson,

* * * * *

"I am strangely thrown anew into sympathy with *your* studies. I have been working really hard at Arabic for some time—and why, do you think? Because I had the temerity to undertake (for philological reasons) to teach a friend modern Arabic. I could not have been so rash or so foolish as to undertake to teach ancient Arabic; yet I am almost driven on learning the ancient by the number of questions which have kept arising.... I have been looking up all my old MSS., and am surprised at the extent of my former attainments, very much indeed of which I had forgotten. But words come back to me with a pleasant rapidity, and I am delighted to find how much I have exaggerated to myself the gap between old and new Arabic."

With this letter those belonging to the year 1858 come to an end.

Memoir and Letters of Francis W. Newman

With 1859 begin Newman's criticisms on the policy and unscrupulous methods of Louis Napoleon.

The latter had made himself absolute ruler of France in 1851. Later on he annexed Savoy and Nice. In his campaign in Lombardy against Austria he was assisted by Great Britain. In May, when this letter following was written, Napoleon's Manifesto had just been published in the London papers of 4th May:—

"10 Circus Road, S. John's Wood, "*5th May*, 1859.

* * * * *

"I dare say you read Louis Napoleon's Manifesto in yesterday's papers. I wonder what you think of it. I find myself at variance with most of my friends, and with nearly all the newspapers *that I see* ; but the *Morning Chronicle* and the *Daily News*, of which I have only seen *one* article for a long time back, appeared to be maintaining what I hold. That we ought to be strictly neutral (not armed and threatening neutrals) seems to be an axiom; but at the same time I look at the crisis with much hope and little or no fear. To declaim against L. N.'s treachery is only a way of playing into the wrong hands, i.e. supporting Austria. He has pledged himself to expel her from Italy and not to seek dominion in Italy for France. If he fails he shatters his own power in Paris: so much the better, I suppose. If he succeeds, Italy is a certain gainer, and Europe through Italy. I say a certain gainer, because the existing oppression (testified by Gladstone and Clarendon) rests upon the aid of Austria, and is far worse than war, and worse than a transitory dictatorship of France; and the mischief of Austria has been that her power has been confirmed by European diplomacy; but if France proves treacherous, it will be against the protest of Europe, and her rule *cannot* be permanent. Besides, L. N. must almost of necessity give some aggrandizement to Sardinia. Lombardy, Tuscany, and Parma seem inevitably to rush into Victor Emmanuel's arms, if not also Venice, if the Confederates are victorious. Hence a stout power is interposed between France and Southern Italy. And is it not stupid to think that because L. N. is a bad, unscrupulous man, therefore he covets nothing but *territory*? He covets *stability* and the glory of liberating Italy; and acting with heroic moderation is the obvious way of winning to his side republicans in France and the diplomatists of Europe. *If* he acts thus, I think his dynasty will be permanent; if not, not, or hardly. The Papists already hate him, and he already distrusts them...."

It is impossible to read many letters of Newman's and not recognize the unfailing unselfishness with which he constantly gives up his own plans of seeing his friends, in order that his wife may go to those places for which she has a special affection. Not infrequently he gives up a journey much farther afield for the purpose of pursuing antiquarian researches because he knows how great would be her ennui were she to accompany him, and he is ever full of a tender concern that she shall suffer no unnecessary discomfort or trouble.

"*13th July*, 1859.

"My dear Nicholson,

"I had really hoped we might spend a few days at Penrith and have a chance of seeing you, for my wife talked seriously of Keswick and the neighbourhood. But when she began to remember in detail the climate of the Lakes, her courage broke down, and she said there was nothing did us good but the seaside, and especially the coast of Wales. So now we are starting for Carmarthen, Cardigan, Aberayron, Aberystwith, etc., a weary distance from Penrith.

"I told you I had undertaken the daring task of teaching modern Arabic (somehow) to a young lady. My lessons began in October (the second week), and ended with the second week of March, being broken by Christmas. About a fortnight ago she sent me a written exercise, in which I corrected a few grammatical faults, and then copied it out to transmit it to you, with my translation into English. I should like you to see a specimen of my *Roman* (?) character, and also to hear what you think of the capacity and power of the modern language as compared with the ancient.... I hope you are hitherto well satisfied with Italian affairs. The pamphlet of Napoleon III on Italy shows that in 1857 he definitely proposed to Austria a scheme for the total secularization of the Papacy. I now feel sure he will not stop at that. It also advocates a federation of all Italy—a wonderful proposal from a French ruler. No democrat would have proposed that."

In September he writes from Aberystwith, and relates how he is busy translating *Robinson Crusoe* from the Arabic.

"I am constantly reminded of you by the study which I have been rather closely pursuing here for nearly eight weeks, viz. the reading of *Robinson Crusoe* in Arabic. It is to me often difficult from several causes: (1) It is not pointed, nor even the *Teshdied* added; (2) I could not bring Golin's with me, and the dictionaries which I have are very imperfect; (3) the writer has most arbitrarily changed the details of Robinson's story, and makes it often incoherent and stupidly impossible; so that neither does the original help me much, nor can I rest on internal congruity to help me out."

It should perhaps be remembered here that the Arabs had a great contempt for the Grecian and Roman languages. Their own language was only printed in ancient classical form, of which the Koran is the most famous example, and the characters and symbols proceeded from right to left. In its most ancient form it is named "Kufic." There are only symbols for sixteen out of its twenty–eight consonants. Certain of our own words own patronymity from the Arabic languages—words such as algebra, alcohol, zenith, nadir, etc. These show clearly that the language did influence early intellectual European culture in no small degree.

To go on with the letter:—

"I am greatly encouraged by my success in understanding it" [the story of *Robinson Crusoe* in Arabic], "for it is a far more ambitious style and on far more various topics than I have ever before encountered; and when I get my Golin's I expect to get to the bottom of many words that puzzle me, though others are probably modern developments, especially quadrilaterals and words belonging to special arts. But there is a religious formula which recurs many times, every word of which is easy, and yet the whole of it is to me unintelligible. I suspect it is elliptical and allusive, and it occurs to me that it may be familiar to you; if so, I know you will have pleasure in explaining it to me. Whenever Robinson falls into distress and betakes himself to prayer, I meet these words:—

[Arabic]

and then follows the matter of sorrow. I also three times meet [Arabic] at the end of a sentence, where the meaning seems to be *et alia ejusdem generis*. I suppose it is an abridgment by initial letters. Can you help me to a solution? We have stuck here" [at Aberystwith] "longer than we intended; in fact, we should have left nearly a week ago, only that Mrs. N. caught a sharp cold, and the weather became suddenly so severe that I have feared to let her travel.... Probably, like all the world and his wife, you are yourself just now absent from home.... Do you not with me see that the Italians already are showing how vast a benefit L. N. has brought them? It is only the beginning of a vast revolution.

"I am, ever your true friend,

"F. W. Newman."

CHAPTER IX. LETTERS TO DR. NICHOLSON

In 1860 Sardinia, because it happened to possess the clever, far−seeing Count Cavour, had "dreamed against a distant goal"—the goal when his king should be made King of Italy, instead of only Sardinia. He only had to wait one year before his wish was attained. Victor Emmanuel, son of Charles Albert, King of Sardinia, was in 1861 proclaimed King of Italy, and nine years later he was head of the whole united nation. This is briefly touched on in Newman's first letter to Dr. Nicholson in January, 1860. He also spoke in strong praise of a book of Mrs. Beecher Stowe which he and his wife (then staying at Hastings to see the new year in, as they did the year before as well) were reading together. Mrs. Beecher Stowe was, of course, best known by her *Uncle Tom's Cabin*, perhaps the most popular American novel ever written. *The Minister's Wooing* was published in 1859.

[Illustrations: 20 WHITE ROCK PLACE, HASTINGS 1A CARLISLE PARADE, HASTINGS WHERE FRANCIS NEWMAN OFTEN STAYED, IN 1860 AND EARLIER From Photos taken in 1909 by Valentine Edgar Sieveking]

"1A Carlisle Parade, Hastings, *4th Jan.*, 1860.

"My dear Nicholson,

"A Happy New Year to you all! We are here, in the same lodgings as a year ago, having begun and ended the year in them. We have begun this year with hopes for the future brightly contrasted to anything for ten years back. For this, among men, I thank, first of all, Cavour and Victor Emmanuel, and secondly, Louis Napoleon. The hatred which the last incurs with the Austrian party and the Ultramontanists is, I think, a fair measure of his services and tendencies.

* * * * *

"I cannot get any solution from any of my books of certain difficulties in the Arabic phraseology of *Robinson Crusoe*, [Footnote: Hiawatha and Robinson Crusoe were very much used for Latin translations at the college by Newman.] and I want to ask your help; but I do not like to do so until I learn that it would not encroach too much on your leisure.

* * * * *

"We have been here reading aloud Mrs. Beecher Stowe's new tale, *The Minister's Wooing* with very great pleasure. I regard her as a real 'prophetess,' and am delighted at the enormous circulation of her works. I have been stimulated to try my hand at translating into Latin five of the most eloquent passages in the book, as a trial of the possibility of putting such things into that language. I am pleased with the result, although it is clear to me that without a development of the Latin vocabulary far beyond Cicero, Livy, Tacitus, and Seneca no one could ever be *fluent* and free to speak on modern subjects. One has to paraphrase and go round instead of speaking outright. I am thinking I ought to know something more about Arnobius and Lactantius, and see what sort of *development* they effected; and the resolution rises in my mind that I will look to this, being hitherto quite ignorant of them.... I suppose the 'Volunteer Rifles' are talked of at Penrith as elsewhere. I regard it as a breach of faith to transform these Volunteers into Light Infantry, which seems to be the darling idea of military men."

Later on, in February, there is another letter relating to Newman's Latin *Robinson Crusoe* and his own difficulties as to how to find out when are the times of spring and autumn in an equinoctial climate.

"I have been (as many others) a sufferer by the weather from slight bronchitis, exasperated by the coughs and noseblowings of the students, and by an ill–arrangement of the class–rooms. I had nothing serious, but enough to force me to spend my evenings in bed, from seven o'clock almost, and keep me three entire days away from college. I have been ... busy ... with a Latin *Robinson Crusoe*, rewritten quite freely (not a translation), that I have not been able to get back just now to Arabic; and have buried your letter in papers so deep that I lost much time the other day in a vain search for it.... In writing on Robinson's island I found my botany sadly at a loss, and have hunted the *Penny Cyclopaedia* diligently and uselessly to learn the simplest things, such as: To an equinoctial climate, when is the spring and when the autumn? Do the leaves fall twice, or not at all? When is the chief cold? Is it when the sun is lowest, or when the clouds are thickest? Or does it depend on hail and electric phenomena, or on local relation to great mountains?"

It will be remembered that in 1859 the outbreak of the war of the Italian liberation took place. Garibaldi—the Knight of the Red Shirt—though he had settled down as a farmer on the island of Caprera, was summoned by Cavour to fight for Victor Emmanuel. He and his *Chasseurs des Alpes* went into Central Italy as chief in command, and helped to complete the annexation of the Sardinian territories. It was in August, 1860, that he made his military promenade through Naples. During the next few years he was longing to march on Rome, but he also wished to foment the rebellion in Hungary, and not to let it come to nothing.

"10 Circus Road, St. John's Wood, "London, N.W. "*10th Nov.*, 1860.

"My dear Nicholson,

"I believe I have never so much as written from Wales or Clifton to you, to denote that I was not killed on the rail. In old days I suppose that every distant journey demanded this kind of 'receipt' from a traveller; but we now travel too much to make it natural. I am reading the Book of Proverbs in Arabic, in order to work myself up in the vocabulary of morals, and am pleased to find that I know nearly all the words, although the exact *form* of some is new to me.

* * * * *

"We may now congratulate one another on the 'definitive' fact of a constitutional King of United Italy. Louis Napoleon, in consenting to it, appears to me to have surpassed the limits not only of ordinary kings, but of ordinary statesmen. I find that even able and temperate French writers, such as Eugene Forcat, are shocked at it.... Louis Napoleon's ... enemies outside have been Germany, Spain, Russia, Austria, Naples, and the Papacy, and inside, all the Catholic clergy and the politicians.... Do you see Garibaldi's renewed solemn promise that his flag shall be joined to the Hungarian in effecting their liberation from Austria? What I hear and *know* of Lord Palmerston's intrigues against Hungary and *threats to Sardinia* if she dares to assist Hungary ... fills me with indignation and no small alarm. No doubt all that intrigue can do is now employed to induce Austria to *sell* Venetia, not in order to benefit Italy (though to this they have no objection), but in gratuitous enmity to Hungary, which (Lord Palmerston says) the English Government *will not permit* to be separated from Austria. This I *know* he avowed to the Sardinian Ambassador, and sent the English fleet into the Adriatic as a demonstration. Happily the war is now likely to be deferred till Parliament meets, and our ministry may be severely checked in time. I trust we are only at the beginning of magnificent results in Europe and in North America....

"Your true friend,

"Francis W. Newman."

1861 was a great year for the fortunes of America. Then it was that the Civil War between the North and South (United States) first began. The question seemed to be, how far the United States might really interfere with the doings of any particular State of the Union. The North determined that they would not allow the Union to be broken up, and so they fought. But really the true point at issue was a far bigger question than that, for it turned out that the real dispute had to do with whether slavery was to be allowed to continue, or whether it should be put an end to for good and all.

The North said it must cease, and after a war lasting five–years, this was the final decision upon which peace was made. England very nearly was brought into this war against her colonies, but happily not quite. It was probably due to Abraham Lincoln (who was most wise in his Presidentship) that this war was averted.

"*14th June*, 1861.

"The interest of American affairs almost swallows up with me those of Italy, Poland, Hungary; though I am on the whole in decided good heart as to them all, i.e. as to everything but India. Everywhere else the tide seems to me to have turned for the better; but in India that is by no means clear to me. I hope our Government has discovered its error as regards America.... The glorious patriotism and unanimity of the North none could absolutely foresee; but that the attempt to break up the Union would goad the pro–slavery faction of the North into intense hostility of feeling to the South, appeared to me so clear and certain that I predicted it in print. That their backers and merchants should so lavish their private fortunes for the war was more than I dared to hope. I think the Union gets a new heart from this time."

"10 Circus Road, London, N.W.

"My dear Nicholson,

"I hope that the capture of New Orleans, now fully attested, pretty well tranquillizes your mind, and justifies us in believing that we see the beginning of the end.

* * * * *

"Events have not even yet taken the scale from the eyes of deluded people here. I still hear on all sides the doleful lament that 'the successes of the North are much to be regretted, since they *can only prolong the war.*' Mr. Gladstone [Footnote: Then Chancellor of the Exchequer.] has just printed his recent Manchester speech, in which he sympathizes with the South, because he does not trust the soundness of the North in the cause of freedom!... I am calmly told that it is not for the *interest of England* that America should be so strong, and it is better for herself, and for us, that she break up! England may have all India, but the United States may not have one Mississippi, or keep the mouth of her own river. I have never felt so unutterably ashamed for my own country, for it affects public men and the press of London *on all sides*, with exceptions which may be easily counted. Are you not delighted with the progress of India for the better? It appears in the public news in many ways; but besides, I have papers from Oudh and Calcutta which interest me extremely, and give me the most cheerful hopes of the future. The change introduced by the extinction of the Company's rule is prodigiously beyond what I ever dared to expect in so short a time. I am beginning to print (for very limited circulation!) a Latin *Robinson Crusoe*—chiefly to please a lady–teacher, my favourite pupil. It is not a translation, but an imitation. My wife is just returned from Brighton, where I spent Easter—but did *not* go to the rifle review. I feel unable to take interest in it, until Secret Diplomacy is abolished. At this moment there is no security that Lord Russell is not intriguing against Hungary, while possessing liberal views for Italy."

It is necessary here, I think, to add that the Hon. East India Company had, so long ago as 1833, been deprived of its commercial privileges; but still its directors practically ruled India under the Board of Control, which Pitt originated. Later, in 1858, Lord Palmerston brought in a bill which was its death–blow. The Company was to be abolished, and the Home Government reigned in its stead in India.

In July, 1863, Newman severed his long connection with University College, and evidently looked forward with great pleasure to uninterrupted time for writing and studying.

"I am finally severed from University College, but do not as yet know how much difference that means, since this is my natural vacation. I suppose that next October I shall begin to realize the greatness of the change for good or evil. (The enclosed photogram makes my face dirty, and one eye too dark; yet seen through a magnifier it is really good.) I seem to have an Augean stable to cleanse in reducing my papers to simplicity, and burning accumulations of thirty years. I am not likely to write less, but perhaps more, in anonymous ways, which impedes one's concentrating oneself on one subject, if that be desirable: as to which I cannot make up my mind. The danger of overworking the brain I see to be extreme if one has one subject and that all paper work and private work.

"I have now got my house, to keep on with right to leave at a quarter of a year's notice."

As the following letters make much mention of the struggle through which the United States was passing, it is perhaps as well to give, briefly, a few details of the happenings which were then taking place.

In 1856, when the Republican army was first started to put an end to the extension of slavery, Lincoln, who was the most prominent man against the pro–slavery party, took the lead as the most active servant of the cause. But there was another, working perhaps more quietly, but quite as resolutely against slavery, whose name should never be forgotten. William Lloyd Garrison—a man of the same age as Newman—started in 1831 a paper called *The Liberator*, with no capital or subscriptions. This paper he carried on for thirty–five years until slavery was abolished in the United States, although he received constantly letters threatening his assassination. He came to England in 1833, and on his return he started the American Anti–Slavery Society. Before that was accomplished, however, in every way possible he had spread over the whole of the States pamphlets etc., urging on his people the pressing need of the abolition of the slave trade. Then in 1863 (July) General Grant's success in capturing Vicksburg gave back to the

Union the full control of the Mississippi river. By 1864 Grant was in full command of the Union Army. But *the* aim of the Abolitionists had been triumphantly attained before then, for on 1st Jan., 1863, President Lincoln declared that all slaves in the States then in a state of rebellion should be free. Only two years later this man, who had done so much to rid his country of a degrading trade, was assassinated.

The following letter is dated 4th Aug., 1863:—

"... I hope that you now, with me, believe that the era of Southern 'successes' (i.e. hard and HOPEFUL *resistance*) is finally past. I believe nothing now remains but the resistance of despair, which cannot long animate the masses. Hatred of the free negro may awhile move them. But, the Mississippi once open, the N.W. has no longer a party favourable to the South; and the exhaustion of the South is so marked and undeniable that the real end may be much earlier than the people think.... General Neal Dow (now a prisoner at Richmond) in his last letter to England observed that the moral end served by the prolongation of the war had notoriously been the immediate legal emancipation of the negroes in the Gulf States; but the further prolongation of it is to determine the future internal government and possession of landed property in these States as the guarantee for the future. But it is a hard wrench on the politicians of the North to consent to this. Lincoln and Blair evidently would still much rather export the negroes *if they could*. Lincoln will not do anything against the will of the blacks; but it is evidently his weak point to deprecate them as equal citizens."

In September, 1863, Newman and his wife were spending their holiday at Windermere. From there he writes:—

"I fear that the projects of Louis Napoleon in Mexico, and the consequent sympathies of the United States with Russia against Poland and France, make an imbroglio fatal to Poland. Now that, if the Russian Empire were organized into States possessed of substantive interior nationality (as the French plan is), this would seem to be a very lamentable result. The two Western Cabinets have so acted as to ensure that Russia and the United States shall each desire the aggrandizement of the other; and if Russia take a lesson of imperial liberality from America, her empire may terrify our grandchildren with excellent reason. But I believe that the interest of the nations, of the true people everywhere, will prevail over Cabinet ambitions as soon as slavery is effectually uprooted in America."

Never do the words "a" and "the" light up so vividly the significant gulf which lies between the absence and the presence of Fame than when the first qualifies in the first instance the name of some man at a time when he is not specially distinguished; and then, much later on, the second prefaces it as the mouthpiece of Fame. In 1863 Newman's mention of "*a* Mr. Grace, the *recent* celebrated victorious cricketer," proved that his world—wide fame had but then been in its initial stage.

Newman's counsel to Dr. Nicholson in *re* cigars as injurious to appetite and inflaming to the eyes, reminds one that though, as I have shown by his speech to Mr. Butler's family, he was "anti—everything," including smoke, yet he mentions constantly in his *Personal Narrative* that in Syria during his missionary journey there in 1830–3, the fact was that he himself smoked in the fashion of the country, and by no means disliked it in his own young manhood. He begins on the Temperance and Teetotal question thus:—

"Llandudno, "*17th Sept.*, 1863.

* * * * *

"I am reminded of it, by seeing to—day a statement made concerning cricketers, that no first—rate cricketer takes beer, ale, or spirits, which (it is said by the enthusiastic narrator) inevitably 'jaundice the eye,' nor tobacco in any form, (!) which induces a kind of stupefaction or negligence. The recent celebrated victorious cricketer, a Mr. Grace, it is said, will not take even *tea*; but prefers water. (I hope the water is better than that of Windermere!) Two months ago I was reading from a sporting newspaper about a rowing match on the Thames, and there learnt that if a rower is known to take beer or ale, it lowers the bets in his favour. In fact, no habitual drinker, though he drink *only* for health and strength (as he thinks), is regarded to have a chance of the highest prize.

"I cannot help thinking that both wine and alcohol and tobacco lower the vital powers, and that men are strong *in spite* of them, not by reason of them.

"Will you forgive me for suspecting that cigars lessen your appetite (which is less keen surely than it ought to be), as well as inflame your eye?"

Newman goes, in his next letter, to a much more intricate subject: i.e. cuneiform inscriptions.

He had been studying them for two months. Emanuel Deutsch, one of the great authorities on cuneiform inscriptions, gives us the following information as regards them:—

The writing itself resembles a wedge, and it has been proved that it was used by the ancient peoples of Babylonia, Assyria, Armenia, and Persia, as well as by other nations. It was inscribed on stone, iron, bronze, glass, or clay. The stylus which impressed the inscriptions on them was pointed, and had three unequal facets, of which the smallest made the fine wedge of the cuneiform signs. The first cuneiform writing of which we know dates from about 3800 B.C.

It was used first in Mesopotamia, and then in Persia, and the districts north of Nineveh. When it became extinct, for nearly sixteen hundred years, its very existence was absolutely forgotten. It was not until the year 1618 that Garcia de Sylva Figueroa, ambassador of Philip III of Spain, on seeing them, felt convinced that these inscriptions, in a writing to which no one in the wide world possessed a key, must mean something. Therefore he had a line of them copied. In 1693 they were supposed to be "the ancient writings of the Gaures." Hyde, in 1700, trifled with them, and gave them credit for being nothing more than the architect's fancies. Witte saw in them nothing but the disfigurations of many generations of worms. Others had their own speculations as to their meaning. But Karsten Niebuhr took a big step higher and nearer to their real meaning. He made out that there were three cuneiform alphabets, because of the threefold inscriptions at Persepolis.

In 1802 Grotefend, of Hanover, put before the Academy of Gottingen the first cuneiform alphabet. Then, among other great investigators, followed Rawlinson.

The first of these alphabets is Persian; the second the Median; the third the Babylonian.

Deutsch tells us that, originally, the cuneiform signs were pictures of objects drawn in outline on a vegetable substance, known by the native name of *likhusi*. He thinks it probable that the supply of this was not equal to the demand, for early in the Babylonish history clay was used instead of *likhusi*.

(This letter is undated.)

"My dear Nicholson,

"I cannot remember the longitude or latitude of my hearing from you or writing to you, and do not know whether I have to apologize for neglecting you, so absorbed (it seems) have I been. I cannot even tell whether I told you of my two months' devotion to Cuneiformism, and my study of the Medo– Persian and Scythian inscriptions as *promeletemata* of an article in the November *Fraser's Magazine*.

"I found the Assyrian useless to dabble in: it is so vast, so fragmentary, so embarrassed by dogmatic hypotheses and assertions, and deterring complications, that one must give oneself *wholly* to it for any chance of getting to its foundations. But I feel on perfectly solid ground in Medo– Persian or Scythian. Difficulties in them are like difficulties in Greek or Sanscrit: that is all. In the Assyrian, I do not yet know whether to believe at least half of the characters, and many fundamental alleged principles; and I get no satisfaction in what I read....

"The eight millions in the U.S. who are to be educated, stimulate me. I am dying to get into relations with some who will be practically engaged in it.... I was very gloomy about American affairs four or six weeks ago. The President seemed running fast to ruin. But his plans have happily broken down so early and so decidedly, that he is probably himself ashamed of them, and the people have rallied to oppose them. I now trust that all will come right."

"Benner, Dolgelley, "*20th Aug.*, 1864.

"My dear Nicholson,

"I dare say you duly received a copy of my Iguvine Inscriptions [Footnote: There is a town in Central Italy, Gubbio, which was anciently known as Iguvium or Eugubium, which possessed many medieval palaces (the Brancaleoni), and well–known Eugubine Tables.] which I directed to be sent to you. For the first time in my life I have published with the secret hope of what some call 'fame,' i.e. with the desire of gaining 'credit,' because such 'credit' is of first importance to aid me in pushing on my schemes in regard to modern Arabic literature in European type.... To put forward an Easy Instructor in modern Arabic and an Anglo–Arabic Dictionary, in European type, *with advantage*, I should greatly wish another journey to Turkey, but as I have no children to leave with my wife, and she would be killed with ennui if I took her, and would more than double the expense, I have not seen how to do it. Besides, I want money to publish my books.... General Grant's position between Petersburg and Richmond is become terribly anxious (my last news was his loss of six thousand men in attacking the fortresses behind the one which he blew up), and unless ultimately successful, the longer he tarries, the more complete will be his disaster.... I have always been despondent as to the Northern scheme for forcing its way through Eastern Virginia; and am not the better reconciled to it by Grant's campaign. There is no sound success for the North now, unless they put the 'coloured' race politically on equal terms with the 'whites,' and not to do so when 'colour' is legally undefinable, and when the only loyal citizens in loyal provinces are 'coloured,' is an alarming infatuation. I suppose they must suffer more and more, until they resolve that the slave owners of Kentucky, and the colour bigots of Illinois and Pennsylvania, shall be forced to yield to patriotic necessities. Perhaps until they put down Slavery and serfdom within their own limits, they are not to be allowed success against the rebels. Mr. Lincoln's gratuitous establishment of serfdom in Louisiana, and recognition of the pardoned rebels, as the only citizens worthy to hold power, has filled me with despair of him. It is now clear from his own avowals, that he will do no more justice to the coloured race than he is *forced* to do."

In a letter dated 24th November, 1864, he says:—

* * * * *

"I much rejoice that the Americans have made the Presidential election a trial of principles, not of persons. Such a victory as 213 to 21 seems to imply that the old 'democratic' party is henceforth killed, while the Abolitionists, who have voted for Lincoln and Johnson, are left quite free not to attack the Government as severely as they pleased for any shortcomings. I hope you have seen, or will see, the speech of Andrew Johnson at Nashville, proclaiming liberty 'full, broad, and unconditional' to every person in Tennessee. It is in so hearty and outspoken a tone as to double its value. '*Loyal* men alone, *whether white or black*, shall rule the destiny of Tennessee.' 'All men who are *for equal rights* are his friends.' Now that he is Vice–President–elect I cannot but hope a great change for the better in Mr. Lincoln's policy towards the free and freed negroes, for Johnson and Lincoln have been in intimate relations from the beginning.... Have you read details about the U.S. Sanitary Commission? It is a magnificent development of high historical importance to the future of wars, carrying out Florence Nightingale's ideas and wishes on to the vastest scale, and adding to it the tending of sick and wounded enemies."

Newman's next communication to his friend alludes to the Permissive Bill, and assures him that there is no fear that it can ever "hinder *legal* methods of getting liquor (for medicine, for chemistry, for art)." He adds: "The sole question is, whether by an agent of the public authority, who makes no gain by an increased sale (which we think the sound mode), or by a trafficker who gains by pushing the sale."

As regards America: "I now understand that the darkest moment for the North—the repulse of Burnside at Fredericsburgh—was the *only* thing that at last decided Mr. Lincoln to issue his proclamation of freedom.... He has been born and bred under a slave–owner's interpretation of the Constitution and of the negro–temperament, and ... seems to persist in his publicly avowed preference of *gradual* abolition. Could he have had his way, I predicted, and would still predict, twenty years of misery, confusion, with probably new war unfavourable to the North. Garrison has done his worst to aid the President, but Sumner and Wendell Phillips have (as I now take courage to believe) checkmated him. He will NEVER get his Louisiana and Arkansas reconstruction approved by Congress, and *colour–legislation* will be declared to be a violation of 'Republicanism.'... Yet Mr. Lincoln is a better President every half–year, and I fully count will at last give way to truth and necessity with a good grace.

"I have been actively working up my *Handbook* of Arabic. I also design a *skeleton* dictionary of Arabic–English. I have got a valuable book from Algiers (if it had but vowel points!). But I cannot publish until I have money to spare. Meanwhile I work hard to mature and perfect."

Late in September, 1864, he is again writing on American turmoils:—

"*Next June*, 1865, the debt of the U.S. will be about 400 million sterling, only half of what England had at the end of the great French War, when her population was not two–thirds nor her means one–fifth of the U.S., who (if once freedom and order is established over the whole Union) will be a focus of immigration three times as attractive as ever, with wealth multiplying twice as rapidly as ever.... I have no anxiety about anything *but the policy which is to prevail in victory....* It is frightful to me to hear President Lincoln avow that (against the morality of his heart) his official duty is to do nothing for the coloured race except under compulsion and to save the whole Republic from foundering. He knows they are subjects of the Union, and *owe allegiance* to it, to the point of laying down their lives for it; yet he does not know that those who owe allegiance have an indefeasible right to protection. He is conquering rebellious States, and does not know that the conqueror is thenceforward RESPONSIBLE for the institutions which he permits in those States, and believes it to be his official duty to respect the old institutions however inhuman, however against Republican Constitutionalism, and even when a violation of a treaty with France.... It is too clear that Lincoln will be a great drag upon everything decisive in policy, and especially where decision is most necessary, i.e. in vesting in the coloured race *power to defend their own rights*. When the war ends, it will be very difficult to hinder the Northern enthusiasm from collapsing and foolish statesmen from doing necessary work by halves."

In May, 1865, Newman writes these strong words: "President Lincoln was dead against the confiscation of estates, and bent upon restoring a powerful landed aristocracy, with a wretched dependent peasantry free in name only.... A far sterner nature than his was wanted, which understands that Justice to the oppressed must go before Mercy to the guilty; and I believe they have got the right man in Andrew Johnson."

In February of the year 1866, a great trouble and anxiety fell upon Newman while he and his wife were staying at Hastings. For nine or ten days she seemed to be dying. "We got her through the acute crisis.... I resigned her a full month ago, and have since not dared to hope that she can do anything but linger. Nevertheless her life is less distressing and more worth having than it was. She moves from her bed into an arm–chair; sits at table for dinner.... She talks cheerfully, and can enjoy seeing her sisters. When I look at her I fancy she is pretty well;... yet I feel that she might be carried off very suddenly. Indeed, this was her mother's case, who had the very same combination of disease, and retained much muscular strength to the last. We had two physicians at Hastings, and here she is under Dr. Garth Wilkinson. I have no complaint against any of the physicians: they seem to me all to have done all they could; but nothing that anyone has done has been of any use. It was by nursing, not by medicine, that she was saved through critical days and nights. The physician said she could not live forty–eight hours, and so we believed: and at her request I sent him away.... I have written so many letters that I forget to whom I have written: and it was indeed a tumultuous existence at Hastings. I have now a good night nurse and cannot say that I want anything; but a great shadow overspreads me."

The Doctor had evidently miscalculated Mrs. Newman's strength and recuperative power, however, for in June of the same year:—

"I am happy to say that she" (Mrs. Newman) "now looks very like herself, though feebler and liable (I fear) to relapse. But she is not only in comparative health, but gives a hope of acquiring more soundness in the next three months. I give up this house" (10 Circus Road, N.W.) "in a very few days, and have taken a house in Clifton—1 Dover Place—but it will not be ready for us until 1st August."

Nearly three months later, he writes:—

"I am at last in my new home, which is very pretty, very pleasant, with delightful prospect, and *perhaps* may suit me well; but I have sad trouble with a drunken house owner, who kept me twenty–three days out later than his contract,... and has given me roof and pipes either out of repair or insufficient, rat holes very troublesome,... cisterns and taps all in unsatisfactory state. Last night, for the third time in ten days, I have been inundated through two floors." But he adds more hopefully than the case seems to warrant," If I can get these matters right my house is very promising. ... After a few weeks here my wife's strength has increased notably, by no other doctor than a donkey chaise, and she now seems just what she was last summer....

"I have had a letter from Pulszky (to whom I had not written on this subject) telling me he is convinced that Bismarck put on a mask of fanatical reactionarism in order to win the confidence of the *King of Prussia!* ... It seemed to me certain, that when new States had to be incorporated with Prussia, despotic reaction would be *impossible*, much more if a German Parliament were summoned. And now the King himself proposes Universal Suffrage for all men above twenty–five and of unblemished character! This seems to make any English Reform Bill impossible, which is not far more democratic than any practical statesman here has yet imagined. Nevertheless, I am increasingly gloomy as to the near future of the English Empire. The Radicals seem perfectly blind as to its centres of danger, and the amount of foreign sympathy which insurrection in India or Ireland will now have. Andrew Johnson seems destined to involve the U.S. in new civil war. I grieve deeply for it."

The next letter shows Newman settled in at "1 Dover Place, Clifton." His Anglo–Arabic dictionary is finished, though revisions are to be added later. At the end of the letter he gives the names of those who, he hopes, may some day form a Ministry under Gladstone.

"*12th March*, 1867.

"My dear Nicholson,

"Our correspondence is so slack that I cannot tell what or on what I last wrote, nor where to lay hands on your last.... We have had severe weather all this month, and the snow continues all day since last night; but I am happy to say my dear wife is not the worse.... I remember vividly the spring of 1836, the first year of our marriage: the season from December to May was the severest that I take note of since the great historical winter of 1813 (1812?). This begins to remind me of 1836.... I had hoped that continued work at Arabic would explain to me certain fixed difficulties in the documents which I have studied; but a number of them, even where the printed text is quite clear, remain unsolved. I venture to trouble you with the only words which embarrass me in a rather long and complete narrative of the burial of Abd el Mejied and the ceremonial of installing his brother as his successor. If you can translate the line or half–line I shall be benefited.

"I finished my Anglo–Arabic dictionary three or four weeks ago, but I hope to enrich and revise it. Perhaps the course of public events surprises you as much as me. As the Whigs cannot afford to be outrun by the Tories, it appeared to me at first that I had been wrong in expecting a tough and lingering struggle. Yet it seems to me, in revising details, morally impossible for either Tories or a *Russell* Ministry to do enough to stop and satisfy the outdoors Reform movement. If *Russell* would retire, or were forced to retire, and Gladstone had courage and resolution to make a Radical Ministry, including Bright and Mill, Stansfeld, Forster, Milnes, Gibson, etc. (to which the Duke of Argyle would adhere), and were to dissolve Parliament if necessary—even so it would be hard to pass through the Lords a measure adequate to stop the clamour for more, and active agitation. I begin to relapse into my belief that there *must* be long conflict. Nothing seems to me worth a national Convulsion which does not give us new principles and new persons in the Executive Government. I incline to believe that we shall live to see Radicalism (of a grade far beyond what is popularly so named) in high office and carrying out its principles with energy."

It will be remembered that Lord John Russell had long tried to reform Parliament. In 1866 he had brought a bill for the purpose before the House of Commons. It was rejected, and with it the Ministry went out. Then, when Lord Derby became Prime Minister, with Disraeli as leader of the House, he found he could do nothing but introduce in 1867 a Reform Bill of a far more marked and definite character than the one which had "gone under" during the last year. This bill, however, passed in August, 1867, showing how the country in the meantime had become more and more ready for such a measure. Its conditions were that borough franchise was given to all rate– payers, and lodgers who used rooms of the annual value of ten pounds. But perhaps a great deal of the driving power came from the large numbers of the working–classes which were now added to the constituencies. In 1868 Disraeli, who had now become Prime Minister, retired when he found that the Liberal majority reached to over a hundred through the new elections. Then came the man of the hour, whom Newman had longed to see in that place—Gladstone, who took the office vacated by Disraeli. At once it was seen how far stronger was this new Ministry than the last, or, indeed, one might perhaps say than many "lasts." One of its first measures was the always–to–be–regretted one of the disendowment of the Irish Church. Disestablishment, which of course preceded disendowment, was in many respects a gain. The Land Bill followed in 1870, and the next year abolition of religious tests for admission to degrees and offices in the Universities.

"*15th April*, 1867.

"My dear Nicholson,

"I would not have you take any particular trouble about it, but if in your Turkish Dictionary you find (this) to mean *tax*, at your entire leisure (no hurry at all) I should be glad to learn how to pronounce the word.

"I received on Saturday from Washington a newspaper which contains very interesting news from North Carolina and Alabama. N. C. comes out 'square' for the Republican party, and Alabama avows Republican sentiments. Both accept negro suffrage and absolute equality of the races. *Coloured orators are prominent and acceptable.*

"I also have a very interesting letter from a coloured gentleman from New Orleans, saying that the last acts of Congress have quite quelled the reign of terror, and brought out the White Unionists, who did not dare to speak before; and they are much more numerous than he had believed. Although Congress has been pusillanimous in the extreme, and always deficient, both as to time and substance, and although the danger of reaction is not past, still everything is turning for the better since the last act of the thirty–ninth Congress and first of the fortieth, and I think we may now hope that the Unionists of the South, white and black, will be able to fight their own battles. In England I do not think *our* agitation can be appeased by the Reform Bill of this Parliament....

"Ever yours cordially,

"F. W. Newman."

The following letter concerns Vaccination almost entirely. Newman's views with respect to vaccination were very clearly set forth in Vol. III of his *Miscellanies*. They come under the heading of an article called "Barbarisms of Civilisation." [Footnote: Published in the *Contemporary Review* of June, 1879.] Newman owns to having no medical knowledge of the risks or non–risks of vaccination, but from what he considers to be the rational point of view he objects to it most strongly. He protests that Government Vaccinators have "for many years obtained a large part of what they called *lymph* ... (*pus*, or matter, is the only right word) by inoculating calves or bullocks with small–pox. The result in the animals they are pleased to call *cow–pox*, and when the poisonous matter is transferred back to human infants they assume that it will not produce small–pox! But while the doctrine is orthodox in London, the Local Government in Dublin allows no such dealing."

He adds: "Unless the *causes* of small–pox be removed (generally some impurity in the air or in the food), those causes will work mischief somehow. throw an eruptive disease back into the system is proverbially dangerous.... Moreover, what right has any physician to neglect the cures of small–pox, by which herbalists, hydropaths, and Turkish–bath keepers find it a most tractable disease?"

In a letter called "Compulsory Vaccination," published in 1884, he says: "To obviate it" (small–pox) "by extirpating its causes is good sense; to infuse a new disease without caring to extirpate the causes of the existing disease is a want of common sense." In the letter following, the "Harry" (Dr. Henry) is the boy who boarded with the Newmans, and left snail–shells stuck on a board when he left! He was well known in the world of science as Professor H. Alleyne Nicholson, of Aberdeen.

Memoir and Letters of Francis W. Newman

There is no date or address on this letter.

"My dear Nicholson,

"I have been pressed to make some reply to Dr. Henry's Vaccination pamphlet; but excused myself on the ground that it was not pleasant to me to be in public opposition to him, for he was son of an intimate friend of mine;... I have no special knowledge. I look on it from outside the medical art....

"Now in the contents of the pamphlet I read: 'Small–pox—never produced at present *de novo.*'...

"I make sure that it never *could* have spread, unless the conditions had in all the other places been highly congenial.... Predisposing causes cannot long accumulate and fester, without curdling into vital action. The *provisional assumption* with me concerning smallpox, is, that wherever its predisposing causes exist, there the disease will not long be absent. In new foci it may meet new influences which modify its aspect, so that medical men do not recognize it; but that signifies not....

"Now, what is Dr. Henry's proof?...

"Is there so much as one disease, the origin of which has been recorded scientifically? What he calls 'the primitive origin' of small–pox has not been recorded to us scientifically: yet he does not on that account doubt that it did once arise 'spontaneously.' I judge just in the same way, when it breaks out now in an English country village. What does the 'scientific record' mean? We cannot have a medical man in every room of every house at every moment examining what is under the shirt and shift, with microscope in hand, to see the disease come of *itself,*... Dr. Henry goes on to say, 'and it APPEARS to have spread solely by infection or contagion.' It *appears!* This is so modest, that the reader fancies he may grant it. But the next words are: 'TWO CONCLUSIONS FOLLOW from this,' etc. etc. In short, he has forgotten that it is only 'it appears,' and fancies that it was c indisputably certain and manifest.' ... After all; if unhealthy conditions are among the prerequisites of small–pox, we have only to remove the unhealthy conditions, and shall not need vaccination (if it were ever so safe): and if you do not remove unhealthy conditions, you are sure of other diseases quite as bad however you may modify the name."

144

Memoir and Letters of Francis W. Newman

Letters from 1872 to 1882 (*to Dr Nicholson*).

The first letter of this series is dated 26th December, 1872, from Weston– super–Mare, and is concerned chiefly with his wife's terrible fall, and also with the movement of the peasants under the initiative of Joseph Arch.

The name of Joseph Arch is too well known to need more than a few words in explanation of the reason why he came to help forward this movement as he did. He was born in Warwickshire in the year 1826, and was essentially one of those who, having determined to rise from the ranks—*rose*. He educated himself during the time while he was working as farm–labourer. Those who have read Father Benson's *Sentimentalists*, and also Robert Louis Stevenson's book on the same subject, will not fail to understand how complete and full is the education which comes to a man through both doors—that of physical labour, and that of mental as well. Joseph Arch started in 1872 the National Agricultural Labourers' Union. Soon he had freed the peasantry from many of their former disabilities. Later he went to Canada to find out as much as he could about emigration and labour questions. In 1885–6 he stood for the N.W. Division of Norfolk.

"*26th Dec.*, 1872.

"My dear Nicholson,

    * * * * *

"Did I, or did I not, tell you of my wife's mishap from a terrible fall downstairs? Her right hand will be for a long while stiff from having been tied for nine weeks with a splint on the inside, no finger being allowed to move. This, I am assured, is hospital practice; but it is vehemently condemned by others, and in her case, at least, I believe it was wrong. Whether she will ever recover her *thumb*, I am not sure; for I fear it is still dislocated at the base. She necessarily gives us a great deal to do; I have to act as her amanuensis, besides oiling, shampooing, etc.

"Knowing as I do how you sympathize with rustics and disapprove our existing Land Laws, I make sure that with me you are delighted by the movement of the peasants under the initiative of Joseph Arch to claim access to freehold land by purchase or equivalent payments. I never dared to hope such an initiative from the peasants themselves, but I always foresaw that a destruction of slavery in the U.S. would give to the States such a desire to people their territories and the South, with English immigrants, that our peasants, as soon as they became more wideawake, would have the game in their own hands, and neither farmers nor landlords could resist.... I now should not wonder to live to see ... household suffrage extended to the peasantry—and as results, coming some earlier, all soon, overthrow of the existing Drink Traffic, of Contagious Diseases Act, Army Reform on a vast scale, Female Equality with Men in the Eye of the Law, overthrow of Landlords' predominance.... I wonder whether abolition of Foreign Embassies must precede a serious grapple with the National Debt. I doubt whether any nominally free State ever had such an Augean Stable left to it by forty years' eminently active legislation. "In corruptissima Republica plurimae leges," sounds like it. Without carving England and Ireland into States, I do not think the work can be got through: if indeed we are to avoid new wars with Ireland and India, which may God avert!...

"Your constant friend,

"F. W. Newman."

I quote next from a note written three years later, which ascribes his health to the Triple alliance of his three "Anti's"—anti–alcohol, anti– tobacco, and anti–flesh food.

* * * * *

"How many a pleasant year has run its course since I first visited you at Penrith! It was the summer of 1842, I think, that we ascended High Street together, a company of seventeen.

"It is my fancy that I could walk as well now: yet I believe it would make me lazy for a week after. Moderate exertions are surely best when one is past seventy, yet my spirits are inexhaustible, and my sense of health perfect. Seriously I attribute this to the TRIPLE ABSTINENCE [from alcohol, from narcotic (tobacco), and from flesh meat]....

"Your affectionate friend,

"F. W. Newman."

The same year he states in a letter to Dr. Nicholson that the Vegetarian Society is that in which he feels most active interest, "though I am a Good Templar and am earnest in nearly all the *Women's* Questions." And in another, written in August, "I here, as usual" (at Ventnor), "get the luxury of fine fruit at this season (and the unusual luxury of mushrooms), but I do protest that their demand of 4s. a pound for grapes is enough to frighten Cato the elder. [Footnote: Marcus Portius Cato, born at Tusculum 234 B.C., passed his childhood on his father's farm. In later years he wrote several works on husbandry, its rules, etc. When he was elected Censor in 184 he made great efforts to check national luxury and to urge a return to the simpler life of his Roman ancestors. He was very strict and despotic as regards contract prices paid by the State, and constantly altered those for food, carriages, slaves, dress, etc.] The price of lodgings at Shanklin and here is much higher than two years back. It seems to me that everything is going up, here, in America, on the Continent, and in India; yet I do not see how to impute it to the increased supply of gold. I think that the working classes are everywhere demanding and getting a larger share of the total which is produced....

"Believe me your true friend,

"F. W. Newman."

Four years elapse between this letter and the next from which I shall quote. During this interval Newman's wife died (16th July, 1876), and was mourned long and sincerely. He was now seventy–one years of age, and had, as his letters show, begun already to feel lack of power and health. It was evident to himself towards the end of the eighteen months which followed her death that he should not be able to live alone, and yet there was no relation he could ask to come and be with him.

In December, 1879, the following letters were written by Newman to Dr. Nicholson concerning his second marriage to Miss Williams, who had for many years lived with his first wife, and been very devoted in her care and attention to her.

"*29th Dec.*, 1879.

"My dear Nicholson,

"I felt very warmly the kindness of your letter which congratulated me on my remarriage, and I have often desired to write to you that you might feel how unchanged is my regard for you, though circumstances do not at all carry me so far north as your dwelling. I may briefly add, that a year's experience quite justifies my expectation. The marriage was not in my estimate an experiment, which might succeed or fail.... That my wife's health is not robust, I certainly grieve, but she is nineteen years my junior. Our love and trust has only increased month by month.... This black edge" (of the note paper) "is for my only surviving sister, whose death is just announced to me. She was my fondest object of boyish love, and it is impossible not to grieve. On the other hand, I had long expected it, and did not at all think she would survive *last* winter.... I believe she was loved and respected by *everyone* who knew her, as truly she deserved to be. I feel good consolation in this.... For three years our public doings have been to me so mournful and dreadful—with no power anywhere to stay the madness of the Court and Ministry,—that I have been made unwilling to write about them. Retribution for such deeds seemed to me certain, inevitable: it seems to be coming more speedily than I had expected. Stormy controversies must in any case be here encountered. But ever since 1856 (I might date from the day when Lord Dalhousie went to India—1848?) we seem to have been storing up wrath and vengeance against ourselves,—worse and worse at home as well as abroad, since the death of Peel. I never admired Peel: he had to trim to the Tories: but I now see how moderate Peel kept them, and in comparison how wise Peel was.

"So many are the eminently good men and women in England that I am certain we must have a nobler future: but that may be separated from the present time by a terrible struggle....

"I am your affectionate friend,

"F. W. Newman."

In briefly reviewing the year 1881 in its effects on nation and Government, it is necessary to cast one's thoughts back to the time when Lord Beaconsfield took office in 1874, in order to grasp the drift of Newman's next letter. In 1874 the former became Prime Minister for the second time. He had not been long in office before he made an end of Church patronage in Scotland. The next year he was carrying forward his design of procuring part ownership for England of the Suez Canal. He did not attach sufficient importance to the Bulgarian atrocities to set going any British interference. This in itself is an act which can find no defence. He declared Turkey must be upheld as a stronghold against the aggression of Russia. In the year 1878, Beaconsfield and Lord Salisbury attended the Berlin Congress. This at once raised the former to the highest political importance, but it undid all the splendid work done by the English army, which had, at the order of a blundering, mistaken Government, been sent to obtain for England, through means of the Crimean War, a victory rendered completely null and void a short time later by the doings of this Congress at Berlin.

Then followed the Afghan and Zulu Wars and subsequent troubles and upheavals: trade depression in Ireland; and finally, in 1880, came the General Election, which restored the Liberal party to power.

"*1st Oct.*, 1881.

"My dear Nicholson,

"I was glad to get your letter, but frightened when I found it open (the gum wholly fresh) and no photograph in it. [Footnote: I believe the photo given in this volume, of Dr. Nicholson, to be the one referred to here.] I feared it was taken out. But next day came the real thing. It is excellent. The slight excess of black in the left eye is perhaps quite natural. In a three–quarter face the light does not fall alike on both eyes, and we do not in real life compare a friend's two eyes (they move too quick); we see only one at a time. [Footnote: Francis Newman expressed once his theory that in the case of a photograph being taken of a man, unconsciously to himself, the expression of the portrait will in some curious manner change as his character changes.] The photo pleasantly renews my old memories....

"*Immediate* politics sicken *me* as well as you. I do not (with a zealous friend) groan over 1881 as unrelieved gloom, completed by the murder of an amiable and innocent President: but I deliberately conclude we are launched in a season of TRANSITION that *must* have its sadness just as has a war: and it is wise to look on beyond the troubled years.... The course of change may largely depend on events in India which not one Englishman in a thousand dreams of. In 1881, thus far, I rejoice in the incipient elevation of Greece, and the probable deliverance of Armenia. I think the great Powers *will not* quarrel over the carcase of Turkey: and though Frenchmen may justly make outcry against French ambition in North Africa, yet as an Englishman and a European I do not regret it. As *I* see no power but Russia who can impart improved rule to Armenia and Persia, so no one but France can give it in North Africa. My *immediate* interest in the politics of the High Powers is to see them combine against the Slave Trade, in Turkey, and *in the Pacific*. In domestic Politics I care *most* for the social and moral questions, which are painful, pressing, and disgracefully delayed. But all will come; and the great question of Landed Tenure will aid the best influences....

"I am your affectionate old friend,

"F. W. Newman."

On 26th Nov., 1881, Newman caused some copies of the following letter to be printed and sent round to his friends, etc.:—

"My dear ——,

"Friends are always greedy of details concerning sudden illness. This is my excuse for sending a printed circular.

"In short, my general health continues as excellent as usual; but I have received a sharp warning, which I would gladly be able to call a mere fright. After many days of close and continuous writing, I found myself suddenly disabled in my right hand. I could not interpret it as merely muscular. There was no inability of motion or grasping, but want of delicacy in feeling, which made my pen slip round in my fingers. I was forced to conclude the *brain* involved.

"Therefore it seemed possible that I was only at the beginning of real paralysis. Prudence absolutely required me to back out of two engagements. This illness, such as it is, has not come on in a day, and demands time for cure. Some ten days of cessation have somewhat (but very imperfectly) restored my power of writing; but I must not undertake any tasks at present. My sole remedy has been to keep the arm warm. It is still somewhat weak. I wished, if this affection were temporary, to say nothing about it; but that has proved impossible.

"I am, yours as ever,

"Francis W. Newman."

* * * * *

There are many allusions to this trouble of the arm in later letters. Indeed, it is impossible not to see how very much it has crippled his handwriting; he mentions once or twice that he finds it very difficult to keep his hand steady.

In May, 1882, he writes to Dr. Nicholson concerning the news of the moment—the murder of Lord Henry Cavendish and Mr. Burke, at Phoenix Park. It will be remembered that it happened at the end of all the obstructive tactics used by Parnell and his Home Rule Party, which was organized to prevent coercion being used, and also to force on England the compulsion of legislating promptly for Ireland the measures demanded by the Nationalists. It was not until 1886 Gladstone brought before Parliament a measure which would give a Statutory Parliament to Ireland. Later, after the rejection of the bill on its second reading, Gladstone appealed to the country, and when the General Election brought back a Conservative majority, he was defeated.

Lord Frederick Cavendish became in 1882 Chief Secretary for Ireland, in succession to Mr. Forster. On 6th May he and Mr. Burke (his unpopular subordinate) were stabbed in Phoenix Park.

The allusion to Newman's study of the Libyan language occurs in the letter following, as it has done in more than one of the others about this time. The Numidians were descended from the race from which the modern Berbers are drawn. Their name was drawn from the Greek word Nomades—Land of Nomads; and was given to tribes in Northern Africa by the Romans.

"*8th May*, 1882.

* * * * *

"To−day we have heard with horror of the murder of Lord Frederick Cavendish, and with grief, if with once or twice that he finds it very difficult to keep his hand steady.

In May, 1882, he writes to Dr. Nicholson concerning the news of the moment—the murder of Lord Henry Cavendish and Mr. Burke, at Phoenix Park. It will be remembered that it happened at the end of all the obstructive tactics used by Parnell and his Home Rule Party, which was organized to prevent coercion being used, and also to force on England the compulsion of legislating promptly for Ireland the measures demanded by the Nationalists. It was not until 1886 Gladstone brought before Parliament a measure which would give a Statutory Parliament to Ireland. Later, after the rejection of the bill on its second reading, Gladstone appealed to the country, and when the General Election brought back a Conservative majority, he was defeated.

Lord Frederick Cavendish became in 1882 Chief Secretary for Ireland, in succession to Mr. Forster. On 6th May he and Mr. Burke (his unpopular subordinate) were stabbed in Phoenix Park.

The allusion to Newman's study of the Libyan language occurs in the letter following, as it has done in more than one of the others about this time. The Numidians were descended from the race from which the modern Berbers are drawn. Their name was drawn from the Greek word *Nomades*—Land of Nomads; and was given to tribes in Northern Africa by the Romans.

"*8th May*, 1882.

* * * * *

"To–day we have heard with horror of the murder of Lord Frederick Cavendish, and with grief, if with less horror, of Mr. Burke's. I felt persuaded from the first that the assassins would aim only at Mr. Burke, who has long been regarded as the perverter of every Viceroy and Secretary; but in mere self–defence they also killed his companion, perhaps not even knowing who he was. Lord Frederick Cavendish was almost unknown to the Irish, and cannot have been hated by them as Mr. Forster was.

"My second thought on this grievous affair is, that it is likely to call out so sincere a disavowal from collective Ireland, and from the most extreme of Irish politicians, that it may help to reconcile Irish patriots and the Liberal Ministry. To have a common grief is a moral cement. Also it seems to compel Mr. Gladstone to send as Irish Secretary an *Irishman*, and one publicly esteemed as Irish patriot, as well as a sincere friend to the

English connection; and from what I have heard before this event, Mr. Shaw seems to be a very likely man.

"Meanwhile, sad to say, Mr. Gladstone entrenches himself, and *blocks up* business by the Rules of Procedure.

"Well, Ireland is taking a leaf out of Nihilism. It is bad enough, yet not so bad as with the poor Czar....

"Yours cordially in old esteem,

"F. W. Newman."

"On Saturday I corrected the last proofs of my essay towards a Numidian dictionary. Yesterday a friend sent me a scrap from Paris, in which Renan avows that until a Numidian dictionary is compiled they cannot begin to decipher inscriptions in the *Canaries!* I fancy the Canary language is a wide step off."

Each succeeding year after 1882 Newman complains from time to time, in his letters to his friends, of increasing infirmities and physical disabilities, which made travelling often exceedingly trying for his head, and rendered him more and more dependent on his wife. He had for a long time suffered a great deal from his eyes, and consequently during the last few years of his life writing letters became a physical weariness. He was also subject to a sudden loss of brain power, when he found himself completely unable at times to speak consecutively.

[Illustration: ANNA SWANWICK FROM A PORTRAIT PAINTED BY MISS V. BRUCE]

CHAPTER X. LETTERS WRITTEN TO MISS ANNA SWANWICK (BETWEEN 1871 AND 1887)

Anna Swanwick was one of the most remarkable women of her age—one of the most intellectual, one of the most thoughtful as regards the social educational movements of her time, which was the early part of the last century. Yet there is a passage in a lecture delivered by her at Bedford College which reveals only too clearly the straitened and limited means at the disposal of girls in those days who wished to climb the stairs of that Higher Education so easy to men, but then so very difficult of access for women. She says:—

"In my young days, though I attended what was considered the best girls' school in Liverpool, the education there given was so meagre that I felt like the Peri excluded from Paradise, and I often longed to assume the costume of a boy in order to learn Latin, Greek, and mathematics, which were then regarded as essential to a liberal education for boys, but were not thought of for girls. To give some idea of the educational meagreness alluded to above, I may mention the fact that during my schooldays I never remember to have seen a map, while all my knowledge of geography was derived from passages learnt by rote." I quote this from one of the most delightful memoirs I have come across for a long time: *Anna Swanwick; a Memoir and Recollections*, by Miss Mary Brace. [Footnote: Published by Fisher Unwin.]

But no "educational meagreness" can keep the feet of some climbers off the educational ladder. It may be with slow, "sad steps" they "climb the sky" of the higher education. Nevertheless the effort is doggedly made. For in all great men, as in all great women, there is something call it genius, call it what you like—which *forces* its way through, be the impediments what they may.

Anna Swanwick, to whom the following letters were written at various intervals, was well known for her philanthropic and educational work among the poorer classes, and also for her earnest endeavours for the larger development of women's work and education. A large part of her own education in Greek and Hebrew was carried forward at Berlin. In 1830 Bedford College was opened. Miss Bruce tells us that Francis Newman and Augustus de Morgan, Dr. Carpenter, and other famous lecturers were among the first to lecture there. I imagine it was here that the friendship of forty years between Anna Swanwick and Francis Newman began. The former was specially impressed with Newman's method of teaching mathematics. I quote her words from Miss Bruce's *Memoir* :—

"I remember being particularly impressed by F. W. Newman's teaching of mathematics, including geometry and algebra; he saw at a glance if one of his pupils in algebra was not able to follow his calculations, which were often very elaborate; on such occasions, instead of endeavouring to explain the difficulty to a single pupil, thus keeping the entire class waiting, he would interest them all by placing the subject in an entirely new light, which was possible only to one who had a complete mastery of his subject—one who, looking down from a mental height, could see the various paths by which the higher eminence could be reached."

I cannot but mention here the supreme service Anna Swanwick was able to render Newman at the end of his life. It was in the last letter which he wrote to her, when he was ninety–two, that these words occur. After stating that he wished "once again definitely to take the name of Christian," he adds: "I close by my now sufficient definition of a Christian, c one who in heart and steadily is a disciple of Jesus in upholding the prayer called the Lord's Prayer as the highest and purest in any known national religion.' I think J. M. will approve this. [Footnote: James Martineau.] ... My new idea is perhaps with you very old.... Asked what is a Christian, I reply, one who earnestly uses in word and substance the traditional Prayer of Jesus, older than any Gospel—this supplants all creeds." This letter was written shortly before his death.

Since I have been writing this memoir I had a letter from Mr. William Tallack, who quoted these words of Mr. Garrett Horder with respect to Francis Newman's final return to the Christian Faith. This fact had been published in a paper in 1903.

"Not more than three or four years before Dr. Martineau's death I was sitting in an omnibus at Oxford Circus, when Dr. Martineau, accompanied by his daughter, got in, and took seats by my side. After I had expressed my pleasure at seeing them, he said, c I think you ought to know that the other day I had a letter from Frank Newman, saying that when he died he wished it to be known, that he died in the Christian Faith.'"

To my mind no memoir would be complete with that knowledge left out— Newman's return to his former Faith.

The first letter in the collection before me concerns one of Newman's brothers. Perhaps most of us can count a "Charles Robert" in our environment. Someone whose "worm i' the bud" of their character has so completely spoilt its early flower on account of the "one ruinous vice" of "censoriousness," of perpetual nagging, and fault–finding developed to such a pitch that it has eaten out at last the fair heart of human forbearance and kindness which is the birthright of everyone. Such a person makes the true, free development of others in his proximity a harder task than God intended it to be, for this reason: that the best character cannot do itself justice if it is aware that all its sayings and doings are capped promptly by wrong constructions placed there by "the chiel amang" them "takin'" unfavourable "notes."

Such a one was Charles Robert Newman. At the date at which this letter was written his own family had found him so "impossible" that for thirty or forty years no intercourse had taken place between them.

To Miss Anna Swanwick from Frank Newman.

"45 Bedford Gardens, W.

"*Tuesday, 4th July*, 1871.

"My dear Anna,

"... I look forward with hope that after my whole life has been a constant preparation for doing—as yet very little—for the good of those who have had fewer advantages than myself, I may perhaps be able in my very ripe years to contribute something more; especially by aid of the noble women who from all quarters spring up to the succour of their own sex and of the public welfare: I trust I shall not permit *any* literary tastes or fancies to withdraw my energies from this and similar causes.... But every one of us who is to do anything worthy must forget self, and, above all, must not cast self–complacent glances on what he is, or does, or has done; and, in truth, I have so deep a dissatisfaction with what I am and have been, that my poor consolation is to think how much worse I might have been.... I must add you evidently do not know that I have *two* brothers. The eldest, Dr. J. H. N.; the second, Charles Robert N., three years older than myself, of whom we do not speak, because he is as unfit for society as if insane. He is a Cynic Philosopher in modern dress, having many virtues, but one ruinous vice, that of perpetual censoriousness, by which he alienates every friend as soon as made, or in the making, by which he ejected himself from all posts of usefulness. ... He has lived now more than thirty years in retirement and idleness. His moral ruin was from Robert Owen's *Socialism and Atheistic Philosophy*; but he presently began his rebukes on Robert Owen himself. His sole pleasure in company seems to be in noting down material for ingenious, impertinent, and insolent fault– finding; hence no one can safely admit him. He formally renounced his mother, brothers, and sisters about forty years ago, and wrote to other persons requesting them not to count him a Newman ... because we were religious and he was an Atheist. He had *all the same dear sweet influences of home as all of us*; yet how unamiable and useless has he become! still loving to snarl most at the hands that feed him. Is not this an admonition not to attribute too much to the single cause of home Influences, however precious? I shall be happy to attend to your *Aeschylus*. Lovingly yours,

"F. W. Newman."

"Weston–super–Mare, "*30th July*, 1880.

"My dear Anna,

"... I am made very melancholy these two days by the news from Afghanistan, not that anything comes to me as new: I have dreaded it all along, ever since I discerned that the Gladstone ministry would not act on the moral principles which Mr. Grant Duff definitely professed, which, indeed, Mr. Gladstone so emphatically avowed in his book on *Church and State*, and in every grave utterance. Ever since Sir Stafford Northcote so boldly taunted the (then) Opposition, in the words: 'You call our policy *crime*; but will you dare to pledge yourselves to reverse it if you come into power? No, you will not dare.' And none of the Opposition said frankly, 'We *will* reverse it'; it was clear to me that they had not the moral courage. Accordingly I warned friends who asked my judgment, that it is *in the Russo–Turkish affairs* the Liberals (so called) would reverse *the policy, but in Afghanistan and S. Africa* they would act precisely as Lord Beaconsfield would act; would accept the positions which they had condemned; would appear to the natives as continuing the same course of wicked aggression; would do justice only *so far as compelled*, and *no sooner*; which is exactly what Lord Beaconsfield was sure to do.... We now see that a new war opens upon us both in Afghanistan and, it is to be feared, from the Basutos with the Liberal party in power, and their great leader to bear the main responsibility!! It is a frightful outlook.... We had only to say frankly to the Afghan chiefs: 'We always opposed the war as unjust: we bitterly lament it: we cannot restore the dead or heal the crippled, but *we will repay you whatever sum of money a Russian arbitrator may award to you against us.* (!) We will withdraw from your country in peace as fast as we can, and leave you masters in your own land.'"

It will be remembered that so far back as 1838, Sir James Outram [Footnote: Named by his great friend, George Giberne (later on Judge in the Bombay Presidency), the "Bayard of India."] did great services in the first Afghan War. It was thought by many that had he remained in the Ghilzee country many of our disasters might not have occurred. But Lord Ellenborough—one of the many mistakes placed by our Government in authority in India during a critical time—never recognized in any way his services.

"It is certain they would have seen this to be sincere, and would have been delighted to get rid of us without more bloodshed.... It is pretended that it would be *cruel* to leave Afghanistan without first securing to it a stable government, when obviously we are without moral power there to add stability. Our presence makes enmity among them.... Alas! once more I find Mr. Gladstone fail of daring to act according to his own moral principles. He ought not to have accepted office.... It makes me very sad for what must come upon England, and perhaps on all English settlers in S. Africa, to say nothing of India and Anglo–Indians.

"I am, yours ever affectionately,

"F. W. N."

The next letter is dated 31st Dec., 1880, and treats mostly of agriculture in the fens, in connection with a writer on the subject in some current paper.

"He" (the writer) "says that if a general move were made in the fens to stamp out the weeds (which would require an immense expenditure of money in wages), 'very different results would be obtained from what we now see.' No doubt they would. But what then? The landlord would raise the rent, and the farmers would have spent their capital without remuneration. *Nothing but a security against the rise of rent* can encourage the farmers to make sacrifices. He justly says ... that fruit might be more profitable. But if a farmer plant a fruit tree, it becomes his landlord's property at once, though it may need thirteen or thirty years to come to its fullest value.... The writer treats a *lowering* of rent as out of the question. Yet from 1847 up to about 1876 it was constantly *rising*. Now, forsooth! to go back is *impossible!!!* And why, because *recent buyers have bought at so high a price* that they only get three per cent. They are to be protected from losing, and that, though many have bought at a fancy price to indulge other tastes than properly agricultural. Mr. Pennington [Footnote: An old friend of Newman's.] told me he had farms under his own management and despaired of not losing by them, unless he could drive down the need of *paying wages*. This is what the farmers find. Up to 1875 rents kept rising, and wages rose too, yet prices rising, the peasants were not much better off. In 1873 the peasants claimed more still, and the farmers could not give it. They are ground between two millstones—higher rents and higher wages. This seems to me a fundamental refutation of the peculiarly English system. *Fixity of rent is the first necessity.* The landlord must not pocket the fruit of the tenants' labour."

The following letter has to do almost entirely with politics, and with English misrule of Ireland.

It will be remembered that from 1880, when Gladstone came into office, until 1885, when his Prime Ministership ended, wars were the order of the day constantly—wars in the Transvaal; war in Afghanistan; war in Egypt, and General Gordon left to die in Khartoum. Besides all these, that which came upon us constantly, the care of countries nearer at hand over which we tried experiments.

"Weston–super–Mare. "Sunday night, *20th Feb.*, 1881.

"My dear Anna,

"Many thanks for your kind interest in the approval of my writings.

"I have come to a pause in another matter. My Libyan dictionary is as complete as I can make it.... What next? I ask myself; for *to be idle is soon to be miserable.* I do not quite say with Clough, ' *Qui laborat, orat*' No! An eminent vivisector may be immensely laborious. We must choose our labour well, for then it may help us to pray *better*. But Coleridge is surely nearer the truth: 'He prayeth well who *loveth* well.' I put it, Qui *inferiora* recte diligit, Superiorem bene venerabitur.

"But I turn to your question, What do I think of the Coercion Bill? It is hard to say little, and painful to speak plainly. I immensely admire *very much* in Mr. Gladstone; so do you: of possible leaders he is the best—at present! and it is a bitter disappointment to find him a reed that pierces the hand when one leans on it. I fear you will not like me to say, what I say with pain, that only in European affairs do I find him commendable. In regard to our unjust wars he has simply *betrayed and deluded* the electors who enthusiastically aided him to power.... He has gone wholly wrong towards Ireland, equally as towards Afghanistan, India, and South Africa.... He knows as well as John Bright that Ireland is not only chronically injured by English institutions, but that Ireland has every reason to distrust promises.

"Those of William III in the pacification were violated; so were those of Mr. Pitt in 1801.... The very least that could soothe the Irish and give them hope is a clear enunciation *what* measures of relief Mr. Gladstone is resolved *to propose*. But he is incurably averse to definite statements, and seems as anxious as a Palmerston might be to reserve a power of shuffling out.... He tells the Boers of the Transvaal that if they will submit unconditionally, they shall meet 'generous' treatment. If the injured Basutos submit, their case will be *carefully considered*.... Nothing was to me more obvious than that as soon as he saw a beginning of unruly conduct in Ireland, he should have pledged himself to clearly defined measures, and have insisted on the existing law against lawlessness. But 'Boycotting' is *not* lawlessness. Lynch–law against oppressive landlords or their agents cannot be put down by intensifying national hatred.... Has the Coercion been wisely directed and reasonably guarded from abuse? I am sorry to say, flatly and plainly, No; and that Mr. Gladstone himself, as well as Mr. Forster, seems to have gone more and more to the wrong as the Bill moved on.... Mr. Forster's tone has been simply ferocious, out of Parliament as well as in, and Mr. Gladstone has borrowed a spice of ferocity.... To imprison (for instance) Mr. Parnell, and *not tell him why*, may cause an exasperation in Ireland, followed by much bloodshed.... Meanwhile, Ireland is made more and more hostile, and foreign nations more and more condemn us.... It seems to be forgotten that we have an army locked up at Candahar. *That a severe spring may be its ruin*, deficient as it was known to be long ago in fodder and fuel, and lately of provisions also. Cannon are of little use when horses are starved. And what may not happen in India, injured and irritated as it is, if that army were lost!... John Stuart Mill wrote that if we got into civil war with Ireland about Landed Tenure, no Government would pity us, and 'all the Garibaldis in the world' would be against us....

"Your affectionate friend,

"F. W. Newman."

The following letter concerns the Transvaal war, and is dated March 2nd, 1881:—

* * * * *

"Since Mr. Gladstone cannot have *changed his judgment* concerning the Beaconsfield policy in Afghanistan, in India, or in South Africa, the only inference is that (from one reason or other which I may or may not know) *he is not strong enough to carry out his own convictions of right*. If he was not strong enough to give back the Transvaal to the Boers, though he pronounced the annexation all but insanity, when he entered office, and *had a power of stipulating* on what terms alone he would be Premier, much less is he strong enough now. Not Tories only, but Whigs (to judge by their past) and the whole mass of our honest fighters, and certainly the Court, will find it an unendurable humiliation to do justice *by compulsion of the Boers*. Their atrocious doctrine is, that before we confess that we have done them wrong, we must first murder enough of them to show that we are the stronger. It is awful to attribute sentiment so wicked to the Premier, or to John Bright and the rising Radical element of the Ministry; but the melancholy fact is that they act before the public *as if* this were their doctrine.... The Coercion Bill and its errors are past and irrecoverable.... How will it now aid us to hold up to the public Mr. Gladstone's irrecoverable mistakes? That is what I cannot make out. He has destroyed public confidence in all possible successors to the Premiership, if confidence could be placed in any. I know not one who could be trusted to INSIST on stopping war and wasting no more blood. Yet the longer this war lasts, the greater the danger (1) that all the Dutch in Orange State, in Natal, in Cape Colony will unite against us; (2) that an attack on us in retreat from Candahar, where Mr. Gladstone has 'insanely' continued war, if moderately successful, may make even yet new 'vengeance' of Afghans seem 'necessary to our prestige'—such are the immoral principles dominant among Whigs as well as Tories; (3) any such embroilments may animate Ireland to insurrectionary defiance; (4) further Afghan fighting may lead to Indian revolt.... The nation has found that no possible Ministry will make common justice its rule. Penny newspapers make us widely different now from thirty or forty years ago. The masses *abhor war*, and will only sanction it when we seem forced to it in defence of public freedom. ... The internal quiet of France has stript Republicanism of terrors to our moneyed classes. Not the thing, but the transition to it is feared: with good reason, yet perhaps not rightly in an intelligent people.

"Some sudden change of events may put off Republicanism yet for thirty years; but great disasters may precipitate it.... We, the people, can do nothing at present that I see except avow with Lord John Russell (1853–4), 'God prosper the Right' which now means 'May we be defeated whenever we are in the wrong.' This is the only *patriotic* prayer.

"F. W. N."

Again, in October, Newman is reviewing Gladstone's political character, and regretting that it has not fulfilled its first high promise.

* * * * *

"We must make the best we can of all our public men, and eminently of Mr. Gladstone, and be thankful for all we get from him. Yet I cannot help, when I remember his undoubtedly sincere religion and moral professions, expecting from him *a higher morality* than from Palmerston, Wellington, or Peel. Peel was a valuable minister, and better every five years. I counted and count his loss a great one. Yet his first question in determining action or speech was, "How many votes will support me?" a topic reasonable in *all minor questions*, but not where essentially Right or Wrong are concerned. I grieve if you rightly attribute to Mr. Gladstone that he would have arrested Mr. Parnell earlier, only that he did not think the English public *ripe* for approving it. The public is now *irritated* by Mr. P.'s conduct. If it is against law, he ought to be prosecuted by law, informed of his offence, and allowed to defend himself.... The whole idea of *lessening crime* by passing an Act to take away the cardinal liberty of speech enjoyed by Englishmen (and M.P.'s) and deprive them not only of Jury, but of *Judge* and *Accuser*, while REFUSING to prohibit evictions in the interval between the passing of the Violence Bill (coercive of guilt it is not) and the passing of the Conciliation and Justice Bill, is to me amazing.... I rather believe the fact is that he" (Gladstone) "carried his Coercion Bill against the scruples and grave fears of all the most valuable part of his Cabinet. Instead of earning gratitude from Ireland, he has intensely irritated both the landlords and the opposite party, and certainly has not diminished crime, nor aided towards punishing it.

"I attribute it all to the fact that he has not understood that when pressed into the highest post by the enthusiasm of the country, he was bound by *honour* and common sense to carry out *his own avowed policy*, not that of weak friends and bitter opponents. The attempt to *count votes beforehand* is fatal where great moral issues are involved."

And again, in November:—

"Have we yet the measure of what we are to suffer from the continuance of the Afghan war? I believe a million and a half per month does not exceed the cost—that is, about fourteen millions *since Mr. Gladstone came into power*; but if the winter continue severe, the whole army may be lost, in spite of our bravery and military science. We seem to forget how the Russian winter ruined Napoleon, and in the case of the Transvaal how much our armies suffered in the war against our American colonists from the vastness of distances, and the skill of shooting almost universal to the colonists.

"I regard Mr. Gladstone as the best Premier by far now possible to us.... There is no shadow of responsibility left in a cabinet if we do not impute all its errors to its *Head*; and I regard it as a terrible fact, pregnant with possible revolution, that *he has betrayed the Electors*. The country hushed its many and various desires of domestic reform for one overwhelming claim, PEACE. They bore him into power on that firm belief. Instead of peace we have war—war which may spread like a conflagration. His clear duty was (and John Bright's too) *to refuse to take office* except on the condition of instantly reversing all the wickedness and insanity which he denounced when out of office. He and he only could have stayed these plagues. We are now hated for our acts, and despised for our affectation of Justice and Philanthropy.

* * * * *

"I am thoroughly aware that my judgment of Mr. Gladstone may be wrong, and to myself it is so painful that I expect a majority of his supporters will differ from it. But when I say he has increased—immensely increased—ALL HIS DIFFICULTIES, I marvel how you can deduce from my judgment that I *underrate* his difficulties.... If Ireland be in chronic revolt, and India seize the opportunity, few Englishmen are likely to suffer less from it than I. Probably Mr. Gladstone, by the fear lest the Tories now seek to ride back into power on the shoulders of Ireland, will resolutely make *household suffrage for the counties* his main effort.

"But there the Lords can checkmate him."

Before quoting from the next letter before me, written to Anna Swanwick in February, 1884, which treats of the best method of teaching languages, ancient and modern, that practice should precede the scientific study in this matter; and that the "popular side should go first," I think a quotation from Newman's article (*Miscellanies*, Vol. V) on

Memoir and Letters of Francis W. Newman

Modern Latin as a Basis of Instruction, would fitly come in here. The article makes a great point of popularizing the study of Latin. That it should practically be made an interesting subject not devoid of romance and imagination. He condemns the old fashion (still, alas! in vogue in many schools) of committing to memory an enormous amount of matter quite unworthy of being retained in the mind. He urges the need of a "Latin novel"—a Latin comedy; one that would set alight the imagination of young scholars.

In Miss Bruce's *Memoir and Recollections* of Anna Swanwick, there is mention of the fact that the latter often mentioned the insight she herself obtained in the intricacies of the Greek language through help given her by Frank Newman. She also quotes his words with regard to geometry, showing that the same need in teaching it prevailed as with the study of Greek. That the imagination must be stimulated. A sense of beauty must be cultivated. That the whole secret lay in the *way* a thing was presented to the mind of the student. For unless the sense of beauty and symmetry had been aroused in him, he would of necessity find far more difficulty in retaining the, so to speak, statistical Blue–book of the groundwork and rules of any science. Newman himself was an adept at putting a subject in an entirely new light, when some pupil failed, perhaps, to follow his calculations or explanations. In relation to the teaching of Greek, the following words of Miss Swanwick's (in the *Memoir* to which I have just referred) show how thoroughly she and Newman were in accord.

"Deeply interested as I was in the study of Greek, and intense as was the pleasure of its acquisition, I yet hesitate to recommend it as a part of the curriculum of boys and girls, unless it can be taken later, and with more concentrated determination to master the extremely difficult grammar, than is usually given to school lessons.... It is to be remembered, moreover, that in the literature of Greece and Rome there are no words adapted expressly for the young. The ancient classics, written by adults for adults, are beyond the intelligence of immature minds, whilst in regard to the moral lessons to be drawn from them, the superiority, in my opinion, is vastly in favour of more modern writers."

Anna Swanwick's original desire to learn Greek was (Miss Bruce tells us in the former's own words) "to be able to read the New Testament in the original."

I quote now from Newman's article:—

"Children can learn two languages, or even three at once; and this, if these are spoken to them by different individuals, without confusion and without being less able to learn other things. Memory is aided because imagination connects the words with a person, a scene, or events; and, little by little, the utility of speech calls forth active efforts in the learner.... In general the old method was one of repetition: *it dealt immensely in committing Latin to memory*.... Nothing is easier to boys than such learning, even when the thing learned is uninteresting... yet... means should be taken of making it interesting and instructive and rhythmical.... It seems to me that we want what I may call a Latin novel or romance; that is, a pleasing tale of fiction, which shall convey numerous Latin words, which do not easily find a place in poetry, history, or philosophy.... If anyone had genius to produce, in Terentian style, Latin comedies worthy of engaging the minds and hearts of youth (for I can never read a play of Terence to a young class without the heartache), I should regard this as a valuable contribution." [Footnote: Mr. Darbishire says in a letter to which I have had access: "One of his" (Newman's) "special endeavours was to accustom his students to deal with Greek as a spoken language, as he and we did in reading Greek plays."]

To return to the letter.

"Weston–super–Mare, "*16th Feb.*, 1884.

"My dear Friend,

"The late Professor George Long (my predecessor in University College), editor of the *Penny Cyclopaedia* was originally professor of Greek and a student of Sanskrit. He maintained that German, studied as it ought to be, prepared the mind for other work as effectively as could Greek, and, as Dr. W. B. Hodgson (and I too) independently alleged, that the study of *modern* languages and learning to *talk* them ought to *precede* the study of Greek. To make Greek the basis of an entire school and force it on all is with me cruelty as well as folly. Five out of six women and men would not learn it enough to *retain* or *use* it. If you place ancient languages and all that cannot be learned by *talking* at the END, only those will study who have a special object, and these will duly *use* them. I think that is the only wise and *just* way. Further, I think it a grave mistake to teach the scientific *side* of any language first, and try to proceed through science to practice. The popular side should go first. Greeks talked rightly before Protagoras, but Protagoras first taught that Greek had three genders.... *After* a full acquaintance with the substance of a language, its laws and relationships come naturally and profitably. In a dead language we are *forced* to bring on the science earlier: that is the reason for deferring such study till a riper age; and best if delayed until *after* learning several *modern* languages (by talking, if possible), the more different from one another the *better*. English, German or Russian or Latin, and Arabic would be three very different in kind.

"Our English Professor Latham used to talk much error, in my judgment, of the supreme value to the intellect of studying FORM. This word was to include the 'accidence' of language with the fewest possible words; algebra with the least possible arithmetic ... Logic without real proposition.... Now, in my belief, and that of *De Morgan* and the late Professor Boole, nothing so ruins the mind as to accustom it to think that it knows something when it can attach no definite ideas to the symbols over which it chatters."

To—day, what educational strides should we not make if we could but bring our present systems of teaching into line with these of Newman's!

It will be remembered that in March, 1886, Gladstone caused great dissension in his own party by bringing in his measure for giving Ireland a statutory parliament. The bill was rejected at its second reading, and when Gladstone made his appeal to the country, the general election showed he had lost its confidence. He had based his belief that Ireland was ripe for some measure of Home Rule, on account of the fact that the election under the new Reform Bill had proved that out of 103 Irish members 87 were Nationalists.

"*5th May*, 1885

"My dear Anna,

  * * * * *

"The Irish question, as now presented, is in a very sad imbroglio. After our monstrous errors of policy and the infliction on Ireland of miseries and degradation unparalleled in Europe, to expect to bring things right without humiliation and without risks of what cannot be foreseen, seems to me conceit and ignorance. Evildoers *must* have humiliation, *must* have risks, when they try to go right. Opponents will always be able to argue, as did Alcibiades to the Athenians: 'We hold our supremacy as a despotism; therefore it is no longer *safe* for us to play the part of virtue.' In so far, I may seem to favour Mr.

Gladstone's move; and I think I do rejoice *that it has been made*. Probably those are right who say, 'Henceforth it becomes impossible to go back into the old groove.' I do not believe that a Parliament elected on new lines will endure it.

"But neither would the Democratic Parliament in any case have endured it. A new civil war against Ireland seems morally impossible. Therefore Mr. Gladstone is *ruining* a measure which might have been good, by his preposterous dealing with it. Lord Hartington said (as indeed did John Bright) the very truth, that the Liberal Party cannot so disown its own traditions, and its wisest principles, as to allow an *individual*, however justly honoured, to concoct *secretly from his old and trusted comrades*, a vast, complicated, and far–reaching settlement and make himself sole initiator of it (as *I* have kept saying, reduce Parliament to a *machine for saying only Yes and No*).... It is a vile degradation of Parliament. But that is only a small part of the infinite blunder. He pretends that everything has been tried and has failed, *except* what he now proposes.... In 1880 no one forced him to bring in an Irish measure: he chose to do it, *and did it in the worst possible way,* by treating the Irish members as ENEMIES, and refusing to consult them. [The Scotch members have *never* been so treated on Scotch questions.]

"Down to last September Mr. Gladstone declared that the Irish members were men, who, by a conspiracy of *rapine*, were seeking to *dismember* the empire. He carried '(?)' against Ireland during his unparalleled supremacy, acts of despotism unequalled in this country, and that, though they *had no tendency to lessen crime*; and he joined them with *imprisonment against Mr. Parnell*. Only his monstrous incompetency to see right and wrong, made his well–intentioned measure all but fruitless. Peel and Wellington did mischief, long since deplored, in teaching the Irish that England cared nothing for justice, but very much indeed for the danger of a new civil war; but now Mr. Gladstone has been teaching them still more effectually. In September last he denounced Parnell and his friends as bent on dismembering the empire, deplored the danger of consulting them, begged for votes to strengthen him *against* them; but as soon as the country, from various and very just discontent with his WARLIKE POLICY, and his utter neglect of our moral needs, showed in many of the boroughs their deep dissatisfaction, and he found Mr. Parnell *twice as strong* as in the Old Parliament ... he gave notice that he was ready to capitulate to Mr. Parnell. And he *did* virtually capitulate; Mr. Parnell *understood* him, and defeated Lord Salisbury, and Mr. Gladstone in accepting the power *to which Mr. Parnell invited him,* insulted all his trusting comrades by keeping them in total ignorance of his scheme, while he concocted it by consultation with the very men whom just before

167

he had *maligned* as conspiring to *break up* the empire.

"Such conduct from a Tory minister sounds to me more extreme than anything I ever read of in English history; and from a pretended *Liberal* leader would have seemed incredible, if predicted. I suppose he was *predestined (vir fatalis) to break up his Party.*

"I shall indeed rejoice and praise God if Mr. Gladstone's wonderful folly do break down this ... *system of legislation.*—There's a long yarn for you!!

"Ever your affectionate

"F. W. Newman."

In the next letter, in November of the same year, Newman complains of temporary paralysis in his left–hand fingers and stiffness in that arm "as though it had a muscular twist."

The actual putting on of an overcoat now becomes no slight undertaking, and he finds that reading now tires his eyes much more than does writing. He touches on the Burmese war, "which seems likely to be even worse than the Egyptian and Sudanese iniquity in its results to us." And he adds, "We have now without any just cause of war, or even the pretence of any, invaded this province, which is subject and tributary to China, and lawlessly act the marauder upon it, claiming it as ours, and treating the patriots who oppose us as rebels and robbers. The Emperor of China now finds our frontier, if we succeed, pushed up to his own, and, whenever convenient to him, he can send in his armies against us, especially if India were to revolt."

In October, 1886, matters in Bulgaria were at their highest tide. At last, after all her efforts, since 1356, at independence from the hated power of Greece, when "Almost" she and Servia were "persuaded" to form a great Slavonic State together, she seemed near attainment of her constantly prolonged efforts.

In 1872 the Bulgarian Church was again able to break her fetters, which she abhorred, which bound her to Greece. Then, in 1876, the atrocities committed by the Turkish inhabitants of Bulgaria took place. The Porte, when besought by the Constantinople Conference to make concessions, refused point–blank. Then Russia stepped in and declared war, and proposed themselves to make a Bulgarian State. England and Austria promptly refused to lend themselves to this scheme, and a Berlin Congress was summoned. The Berlin Treaty in 1878 arranged the limits and administrative autonomy of this State, and the Bulgarians chose Prince Alexander of Battenberg, cousin of the Grand Duke of Hesse, and he became in 1879 Alexander I of Bulgaria. Eventually the recognition of him by the Porte as Governor– General of Eastern Roumelia followed. In 1886 Russia made herself felt unexpectedly. Alexander was kidnapped by order of the Czar and carried to Russia.

The upshot of it all was that, though he returned to Bulgaria, yet he felt it was in vain to struggle against Russian animosities, and so abdicated.

The letter following shows Newman to be in failing health and under doctor's treatment:—

"Weston–super–Mare, "*7th October,* 1886.

"My dear Anna,

"... My brief London visit which ought to have come off is forbidden positively, and I doubt not wisely, by medical command, *not* because I am ill, *but* because I had formidable threatening of illness, like a black cloud which after all does not come down. The threat consisted in my left hand losing all sense and power. This is now the sixth day. On the third I regained power to button, though clumsily, and to use my fork. Of course I am ordered to use my *brain* as little as possible, and in future to change my habits. I must leave off all letters and other writing much earlier in the evening. But frequent short walks I hold salutary to my brain; and my feet have not failed me.

"... You ask what I think of the Bulgarian outrage.... In the present instance the one thing primarily to be desired, and eminently difficult to attain, was cohesion of the little Powers. As of old, Sparta and Athens could not coalesce, and therefore after weakening one another they ill– resisted Philip, and were overpowered by Alexander armed from Macedonia and Thrace, and under–propt by gold from Asia; so now the little States— Servia, Bulgaria, Roumania, Greece—each envied the other, perhaps was ready for hostility, but all looked up to Russia with more than fear.

"But this atrocious kidnapping of a reigning Prince has given just *the external compression which was wanted* to make the little States desire union, and the greater Powers to think that such union is for European benefit. Not only has it reconciled Servia and Bulgaria, late in actual war, but it has elicited public outcry in Roumania for federation with these two States. Whether Greece can lay aside her jealous enmity against Bulgaria is not yet clear. Her ambition is to acquire Macedonia and Constantinople ... perhaps ... Albania.

"... To me it seems a wonder that the Greek statesmen do not see that Constantinople is too critical a spot for the European Powers to yield up to any secondary State. If it is to be under European protection, Greece would find her power in Constantinople merely nominal....

"The brutality of the Czar not only drives the little Powers to desire union, but makes the great Powers ashamed of it, and it seems, though reluctantly, they will oppose him.

"*This is the first time that a Hungarian statesman has initiated European movement.* If in Europe they are forced to displease Russia, so much the more will they wish to keep Russia in better humour by not thwarting her projects in Armenia, which projects I believe to be just, philanthropic, and necessary under the circumstances; since the inability of the Sultan to rescue the Armenians from marauders has been proved, and *no* Power but Russia can do the needful work....

"It is to be feared that Germany cannot add any real strength to control Russia, while Russia knows that the insane vanity of French politicians is preparing a war of vengeance against Germany. Until the masses of the people have a practical constitutional plebiscite to *veto* war *beforehand,* it seems as though horrors which seem dead and obsolete must rise anew. *Perhaps* this is the lesson which the populations all have to learn. The earliest great triumph which the old plebeians of Rome won was the constitutional principle that wars could not be made without previous sanction of the popular assembly. England, alas! has not yet even demanded this obvious and just veto. The men whose trade is war, whose honours and wealth can only be won by war, will make it by hook or by crook, while their fatal and immoral trade is honoured.

"Affectionately yours,

Memoir and Letters of Francis W. Newman

"F. W. Newman."

In April, 1887, the Irish question was again to the fore, and part of the letter from which I quote shows clearly that Newman was in favour of some form of Local Government for Ireland, though not of the same kind as was being pressed forward by Mr. Parnell, who had urged on his countrymen agrarian agitation and boycotting as the screw which was to force the hand of the Home Government.

"My opinion is unchanged (1) that Grattan's Parliament was foolishly, mischievously, and immorally subverted by English double–dealing; (2) that in one hundred years things are so changed in Ireland and *in Rome* that we cannot go back to that crisis and heal old wounds by reinstating Grattan's work without making new wounds; (3) I deeply blame Orangemen in Belfast as (apparently) bent on promoting animosity, and on convincing us that they will rather rush into civil war than endure a Parliament in Dublin supreme over all Ireland: but however much this may be suspected as the bluster and cunning of a minority in Ulster, to ignore it totally may be unjust as well as unwise. And besides, I think that Ireland needs the practice of Local Government, varying locally, before that of a Central Irish Parliament. This forbids my desiring a complete triumph to Mr. Parnell.

"You are aware that I have long desired Provincial Chambers for all three kingdoms, and can see nothing to forbid them now for Ireland if Mr. Gladstone were to take that side. If he did it would be carried against Mr. Parnell by a vast majority of votes. No mere political measure can cure famine and rackrent or insecure tenure; but if the agrarian evil be appeased, no hatred of England on the part of Irish leaders will suffice to make Ireland discontented. If Mr. Gladstone fixedly opposes, if he says 'Honour compels me'—his Midlothian defence of the Egyptian war!—I should not the less say he had made a wrongful treaty. But 'a fac is a fac': *someone* hitherto makes this settlement impossible. If now the Tories miscarry, apparently Gladstone will come in again, and not Oedipus can tell us whether he will dissolve Parliament.

"It is supposed that he will; and Mr. W. S. Caine, whose prediction in this matter I cannot underrate, warns Mr. Gladstone that to dissolve *again* will bring on him redoubled failure,—an immense lessening of supporters.

"The new voters, at the last election, had not had time to learn a thousand things. After such a transformation of the constituencies, I not only *expect*—I *desire*—the break–up of the Liberal Party. Little by little they have adopted the Tory idea of 'follow your leader': never think for yourself. In the Parliament, in the Newspapers, in Arguments of Foreign War, at the Hustings, they treat it as 'Treason to the Party' not to do whatever the Premier says they *must* do, or he will resign and wreck the party.... I see only one sunbeam through the clouds ever since the fatal Egyptian war; and that is the recent Peace–Union of *Germany, Austria–Hungary and Italy*. I look on it as the inauguration of the future European Confederacy which is to forbid European wars, and become a forcible mediator. Under its shelter Roumania, Servia, and Bulgaria seem likely to consolidate a union of defence; and as soon as all the Powers understand that the Triple Alliance is based on permanent interests, the Alliance will not need to keep their armaments on foot; to *train* them, as the generations grow up, will suffice. The royalties everywhere will struggle for actual armies: the burdened peoples will murmur.

"Meanwhile we need long patience, I suppose, while Irish rent wastes to smaller and smaller worth; and one new election will suddenly precipitate the struggle. *I* do not fear that any Irish success will make Irishmen desire the burden of undertaking their own military and naval defence.

"Affectionately yours,

"F. W. Newman."

* * * * *

As regards Newman's opinions on one of the national questions which so closely concern us to–day—the Drink Traffic—they are very clearly and definitely stated in an article he wrote in the year 1877, and which appeared in *Fraser's Magazine, in re* Sir Wilfrid Lawson's Bill.

Here again decentralization was the key–note, as he firmly believed, of the remedy.

"The palace–like jails which now disgrace our civilization, and cause expenses so vast, are chiefly the fruit of this pernicious trade.... What shadow of reason is there for doubting that such sales as are necessary... will be far more sagaciously managed by a Local Board which the ratepayers elect *for this sole purpose*, than either by magistrates... or by an *irresponsible* and *multitudinous* Committee of Parliament? Finally, a Board elected for this one duty is immeasurably better than the Town Councils, who are distracted by an immensity of other business....

"Such a Board should have full power to frame its own restrictions, so as to prevent the fraud of wine merchants or chemists degenerating into spirit shops....

"To secure sufficient responsibility, no Board should be numerous: *five* or *seven* persons may be a full maximum, and no Board should have a vast constituency. Therefore our greatest towns ought to be divided into areas with suitable numbers, and have Boards separately independent. With a few such precautions, the system of elective Licensing Boards, which can impose despotically their own conditions on the licences, but without power to bind their successors in the next year, appears to be a complete solution of the problem...."

He adds, that to Sir Wilfrid Lawson "is due more largely than to any other public man the arousing of the nation" in the matter of the Drink Traffic, "To him our thanks and our honour will be equally paid, though the name of another mover be on the victorious Bill"—whatever it may be.

"Noble efforts for a good cause are never thrown away, are never ineffectual, even when the success does not come in the exact form for which its champion was contending. It may hereafter be said: 'Other men sowed—we reap the fruit of their labours.'"

I quote now from the letter to Anna Swanwick, in which he refers to this question in 1887:—

"Unless at a very early day the causes of Un–Employ be removed, we must calculate on frightful disorder. Evidently two measures are indispensable.

"1. To stop our land from going out of cultivation.

"2. To stop the demoralizing waste of 135 millions per annum on pernicious drink.

"Only a most stringent change of law, perhaps very difficult to pass, can effect the *former* and when passed, the good effect cannot be instantaneous. The *second* topic has been before the nation for thirty– four years; could be passed, if there were a *will* in *either* ministry, in a single fortnight, and when passed, the benefit would be sensible in a single year. Yet these topics are indefinitely postponed. The Tories do not even talk of them. *Some* 'Liberals' round Mr. Gladstone are eager for the stopping of Drink Bars, but the eloquent leader *talks* (in general) rightly, but never *acts*.

"Alas! He showed his heart in bringing a Bill to enact that every Railway Train should have (at least?) one travelling carriage with a Drink Bar. When it is told, people will not believe it."

The final letter from Francis Newman to Anna Swanwick, from the collection so kindly lent me by Miss Bruce, is dated 17th April, 1897, "15 Arundel Crescent, Weston–super–Mare."

It is not written by himself. By that time he was too feeble to be able to write, and of course it was only a few months before his death. This letter was written in response to one from Anna Swanwick. To me, I must frankly own, it breathes of the past tragedy, of those doubts and fears by which Newman's religious life had been beset. Even now, notwithstanding his statements to his two lifelong friends, Martineau and Anna Swanwick, that he wished it to be known that he died in the Christian faith, the uncertainty by which, according to the following letter, he was very evidently governed as regards the question of immortality, suggests a submissive mind indeed, but one devoid of the splendid force of conviction as regards his faith in "the life of the world to come."

Anna Swanwick always declared, we are told, that his was a "deeply religious nature," yet throughout the greater part of his life he was unable to take hold of the dogmas of Holy Scriptures. He was always trying to make a "new" religion, compounded of all the best parts of the faiths professed in various parts of the world. Yet even were this done it might interest, but could never become, like the Christian Religion, once for all delivered—a faith to be *sure* of, a faith Divinely inspired, not man–made.

"My dear Friend,

"I have read your letter this morning with deep interest and thanks. I do not intend to oppose it at all, but to add what it now seems to need. First, that I have always dreaded to involve another mind in my own doubts and uncertainties; only when I saw death not far off I thought it cowardly towards one who has shown me so much love to leave you ignorant of my last creed. For this reason alone did I send you my inability to maintain popular immortality.

"Next, it is not amiss to let you know the talk which passed between me and the Rev. James Taylor—Martineau's co–partner. He asked me my own belief concerning known immortality, and I replied that the Most High never asked my consent for bringing me into this world, yet I thanked Him for it, and tried to glorify Him. In like manner He never asked my leave to put me after my death in this world into any new world, and if He thought fit to do it I am not likely to murmur at His will. But not knowing His will, nor what power of resistance He allows me, I do not attempt to foresee the future. I seem to remember J. J. Taylor's remark, that he thought I went as far as anyone could be expected to go. And now, my dear Anna, I still wait to know how far I am straying from the man whom you and I are expecting something from—Dr. Martineau.

"Accept this kind remark, and be sure that I can use, and do use, concerning you, what a certain Psalmist says of the Most High: 'I will praise Him as long as I have any power to praise in my soul.'

"Yours while I exist "(You will not ask more of my weakness),

"F. W. Newman."

One wonders—but that wonder remains unsatisfied—what "that something" was which he and Anna Swanwick were then "expecting" from Martineau. Probably it was some statement as regards religion which Newman longed for from the man who had been permitted to help him now in his old age (when he distrusted more and more his own old judgments and former convictions) once more on to the old paths, led by that "kindly Light amid the encircling gloom," which now was fast closing in upon him.

CHAPTER XI. THE STORY OF TWO PATRIOTS

England possesses, as a rule, a memory of decidedly insular proportions and proclivities. On the tablets of our country's memory are chalked up many names which have figured in the history of her own concerns, or at any rate in concerns with which she has some connection. Perhaps it will be said that this is inevitable. Perhaps it will be said that this way Patriotism lies. Perhaps it will be said that our interests as English citizens and citizenesses are bound to be local, or we could not impress the seal of our empire upon other nations' memories.

And if it *is* said, it is no doubt in great measure true. It is inevitable that we remember, in sharp unblurred outlines, the names and deeds of our own great men. It is this way that the soil of Patriotism is kept well manured for fresh crops of doughty deeds. We *are* bound to impress our individuality, as a nation, upon other countries; for if we did not, we could never exist for any length of time as an empire at all.

But when all this is owned up to, there still remains another great necessity which can never with safety be disregarded. And this is the cultivation of our—so to speak—*foreign* memory. We cannot afford to pamper our insularity. It is true it must exist, but it is equally true that English interests can never be—at least, *ought* never to be—the sum total of our mental investments. Patriotism is a fine thing. It is an eminently inspiring thing. But it is also a thing that needs to take walks abroad to keep itself in good mental health. There is a certain sort of cosmopolitanism without which no nation's life can be complete—nay, without which it cannot go on at all.

It is the cosmopolitanism of recognizing greatness outside our own borders. The cosmopolitanism of owning that there are as good fish in foreign seas as ever there were in the English Channel. The cosmopolitanism of a human brotherhood, whether it hails from the Sandwich Islands, from France, from Finland, or from Hungary; which recognizes as a salient truth, big with vital issues, that, after all is said and done, it is not the soil which matters, but the man whose feet are upon it now, at this present day, though by birth he may own natal allegiance to a far distant shore.

There are two names to-day which are practically forgotten by modern England. Yet it is only half a century ago that the men who owned them were making a gallant stir for patriotism's sake.

How many Englishmen to-day remember the story of Kossuth and Pulszky? Yet fifty years ago their names sounded loudly enough in the political arena. Fifty years ago they had struck the drum of fame with a boom which reverberated through many a European country.

Yet here is a curious instance of the uncertainty which attends a nation's memory in regard to foreign heroes. Some quite unaccountable factor seems to rule their choice of whose achievements shall be nailed to the door of their memories, like British trophies of old, and which shall be completely forgotten. Garibaldi and Kossuth were patriots of the same decade—one of Italy, the other of Hungary. Yet to-day in England the "red shirt" of the Italian patriot still casts a flaming glow on the English memory, while the struggle of Kossuth for his country is almost dead to us, as far as our remembrance of it is concerned.

Nevertheless in the history of his country, what Kossuth achieved for her of independence and freedom was in no way less fine than Garibaldi's exploits.

In Francis Newman's *Reminiscences of Two Wars and Two Exiles*, the story of the Hungarian reformer and *patriot* stands out clearly before us. He gives as his reason for writing it that when, in 1851, Kossuth and Pulszky, his brother agitator, came to England, he himself became their close friend. He says: "When ... Kossuth and Pulszky quitted England in 1860, Pulszky told me they were glad to leave behind in *me* one Englishman who knew all their secrets and could be trusted to expound them." He goes on, however, to say that he was never able to be of so much service to them as Mr. Toulmin Smith, "a constitutional lawyer ... and a zealot for Hungary."

1848 was the year when the affairs of Hungary were at their most crucial point. For long the situation had been growing more and more strained between Austria and Hungary. Austria had been trying her hardest to force Hungary into entire subservience to herself—to force her to give up her separate individuality as a nation and become fused into the Austrian empire. But Hungary made a gallant stand against all these attempts which aimed at destroying her independence. She had always been a constitutional monarchy, with power of electing her own kings. Austria had always practically been considered to be a "foreigner" as far as Hungarian laws and offices were concerned.

The London Hungarian Committee in 1849 quoted Article X, by Leopold II, of the House of Hapsburg, in 1790, which definitely stated that "Hungary with her appanages is a free kingdom, and in regard to her whole legal form of government (including all the tribunals) independent; that is, entangled with no other kingdom or people, but having her own peculiar consistence and constitution; accordingly to be governed by her legitimately crowned king after her peculiar laws and customs."

This statute, however, was no sooner made than fresh attempts were made to nullify it. Hungary's needs, as a country, were many. Her taxation required alteration; her peasants had still feudal burdens to bear, instead of being freehold proprietors of land. Religious toleration was not enforced, and free trade was an unknown quantity, for Austria insisted on the produce of Hungary being sent only to her market. Fresh roads and bridges and agricultural improvements were imperatively necessary, but the need was passed by, by Austria.

To every nation, as to every individual, when the hour of worst need strikes, the hand of the man or woman who brings rescue is upon the latch of the door. In the present instance Kossuth was in readiness to redeem his country from the yoke of Austria.

In March, 1848, the Opposition in the Hungarian Diet, with Kossuth at their head, carried a vote "that the Constitution of Hungary could never be free from the machinations of the Austrian Cabinet until Constitutional Government was established in the foreign possessions of the Crown, so as to restore the legal status of the period at which the Diet freely conferred the royalty on the House of Hapsburg." This vote paralysed the Austrian authorities.... The Hungarian Diet immediately claimed for itself also a responsible ministry.

Prompt measures were now taken by the Hungarians to restore the old status of the country, and laws were made which conferred upon the peasants freeholds of land and all other reforms for which they had for so long been agitating.

The London Hungarian Committee, to whose paper I have before referred, tells us that before the French Revolution had broken out this Bill had passed both Houses. "The Austrian Cabinet, seeing their overwhelming unanimity, felt that resistance was impossible"; consequently this Reform Bill of April, 1848, was considered by all Hungarian patriots as their Magna Charta.

Nevertheless it was their fate very shortly after to appreciate the truth of this hard fact, that it is one thing to make a Charter and another thing to keep it. Austria had many ways up her sleeve of breaking the spirit of the letter. First she saw to it that Hungary had no properly equipped home regiments for her defence, and next she dissolved the Hungarian Diet, and again tried to fuse Hungary into the Austrian Empire. Then at last the Hungarians determined at once, by force, to end the contemptible, practical joke which

Austria was engaged in playing off upon their country. They gathered an army together, but their utmost efforts could only raise one not half the size of that of their opponents, and consequently the result of the battle was defeat for themselves. Later on, when Kossuth had managed to collect more arms and men, battles on a much larger scale were fought; and after the Austrians had been defeated more than a dozen times, the whole of their armies were driven ignominiously out of Hungary. It was after this series of victories that Kossuth was made his country's governor, and the whole nation declared as one man that the House of Hapsburg had for ever forfeited any claim to the Crown.

It was now that, had England attempted mediation for Hungary (according to Francis Newman), "we should have saved Austria from the yoke of Russia, and have at least *put off* the Crimean war," because, when Russia had come to the assistance of Austria in her final difficulties with Hungary, after she had been driven out of that country, "if England and France had not fought it, nothing short of an equivalent war must have been fought against Russia by other Powers ... because the security of *all Europe* is endangered by the virtual vassalage of Austria to Russia... for Austria is now so abhorred in Hungary that she cannot keep her conquest except by Russian aid." [Footnote: *Reminiscences of Two Wars and Two Exiles.*]

In 1848 Kossuth's envoy, Pulszky, was sent to England, and, quite ignorant of the wheels within wheels which hampered the political movements of Lord Palmerston, was amazed that he himself found a repulse awaiting him at the English Minister's hands. Lord Palmerston asserted that the rights or wrongs of Hungary were practically a dead letter to England, who had never thought of that country as existing apart from Austria. He considered "a strong Austria was a European necessity"; but notwithstanding all he said then and later, the impression made itself felt on men's minds that there was a "power behind the throne" in all his speeches, and none knew what that hidden power was. To−day we all know that it was the foreign counsellorhood of Baron Stockmar, who advised Prince Albert in those days. As Newman says: "It is now open to believe that Stockmar and his Austrian policy ... sometimes drove Palmerston to despair, and our diplomacy into heartlessness."

[Illustration: LOUIS KOSSUTH]

This elucidation of the whole puzzle throws fresh light on that attitude of Lord Palmerston which so completely mystified Kossuth.

"I cannot understand," he said, "what is the policy of Palmerston's *heart*. He talks one way, yet acts another way—always against the interests and just rights of Hungary."

Kossuth's next step was to take refuge in Turkey, and here he at once set to work to learn the language, and succeeded so well that he wrote a grammar, which was afterwards used in the Turkish schools. It was said to have been due to Lord Palmerston, by the way, that the Sultan refused to give him up to Austria and Russia. But at any rate the Sultan seemed to owe the decision which guided this refusal in large measure to his own loyalty to those who had sought shelter with him during civil war. At any rate, Kossuth reported that he certainly said, "I will accept war rather than give up the Hungarian fugitives." Eventually an American ship conveyed Kossuth out of Turkey, and he landed at Marseilles. Of course, by then the monarchy had been overthrown in France, and Louis Napoleon–with whom Kossuth was later on to be closely connected—was President.

In October, 1851, Kossuth crossed to England. Newman tells us that though "he was enthusiastically received by the whole nation," yet that "he was slandered, feared, despised, and disliked by those esteemed highest and noblest in England." But, at any rate, he was given a hearty welcome in America, for he did not stay long in England when he saw that those in authority did not warmly espouse his cause.

It is necessary here to remember that in 1851 Louis Napoleon had stepped on to the top of the Republic, whom he had previously served as its President, and had made himself Emperor of the French. It is necessary also to remember that there was a very general sense of alarm throughout England as to his plans regarding an invasion. He was thought to be collecting a fleet destined to attack us. But, later, it was proved that we had been exciting and disturbing ourselves quite unnecessarily. Louis Napoleon wanted something of us, it is true. But that something was alliance.

By this time Kossuth was back in England. One day, Francis Newman says, "Kossuth called suddenly on me with an English Blue–book in his hand, and abruptly said: 'We foreigners look to you to explain your own Blue–books. Please to tell me what does this strange sentence mean?' I read carefully these words from the despatches of the Western Powers to the admirals of their fleets in Constantinople: c You must clearly understand that you are not sent to fight against the Emperor of Russia, but to save the Sultan from *religious enthusiasm and fatal auxiliaries*'! He pointed out these last words.... 'Religious enthusiasm* is the diplomatic phrase for Turkish patriotism; *fatal auxiliaries* mean

Hungarians.... Because Austria dreads lest exiled Hungarians fight in the Turkish ranks, and the object of the Western Powers is to please Austria and not to aid Turkey.... They are angry with the Turks for defending themselves against Russia.'" [Footnote: Reminiscences of Two Wars and Two Exiles.]

[Illustration: This certificate is dated the year after Kossuth's first visit to England, and is in possession of Edward G. Sieveking, Esq. of the firm of Sieveking, Podmore, and Wright, Gracechurch Street, E.C.]

In 1848–9 the Whigs and Tories in England mistook the whole meaning of the disturbances which were going forward abroad. Macaulay (whom Newman quotes) distinctly asserts that in Hungary and Italy "kings were fighting in the cause of civilization, and nationalities were rising to destroy it in the cause of anarchy."

Comment on this is, of course, quite needless when one remembers how misinformed were the English ministers as to the nature of the struggle for liberty which was then going forward in both countries, and how treacherously and cruelly the people had been treated by those in authority over them: and what efforts had been made constantly against their rights as citizens. In 1854 Kossuth was again doing his best to rouse interest on behalf of his country in England. He called on Newman to enquire what would be the best and quickest way of collecting subscriptions. He wanted for immediate national use L5000. Newman referred him to a printer who "was a Zealot for Hungary," and who would supply him with the names of the richest men who had "spoken vigorously for Hungary."

Kossuth proceeded to write out a circular to be sent to these Englishmen, asking for subscriptions. A little later Newman found out that the result of this fishing in English waters was L400, and he had wanted L5000 to enable him to carry out his projects for Hungary!

The following letter from Francis Newman to Professor Martineau (about whose friendship with him I shall have more to say later) is dated November, 1854, and concerns his opinions *in re* the Crimean War:—

"As to the war, while it is always thought rash to have any strong military convictions, I have always believed that if they would go straight to Sebastopol early in the season they would take it with little difficulty. We have been juggled partly by Austria, partly by the too great age of our military men, partly by clashing counsels of allies. The fortification of Gallipoli I regarded as stupid infatuation: our old military men said it was necessary for *safety!* We lost all our time while Russia had her hands full on the Danube, we let in Austria to hinder the Turks pursuing the retreat, we delayed ten weeks longer to make preparation, and landed, leaving all our preparations behind. This *delay* has been the mischief.... The climate is now my fear, not the enemy. But I look on all this as a part of the providential or fatal necessity which determines that war shall not be decided by regular armies. If we *will* do things in a 'slow and sure' way, Russia will beat us, for she cares nothing for the lives of her men; to us it is agony. But to yield is to make her omnipotent. I expect, therefore, that the harder we fight, and the poorer our success, the more will Austria show Russian sympathies, and the more will the Western Powers be forced to call up Poland and Hungary.... I suppose nothing but severe suffering and vain effort will reconcile Louis Napoleon or the English aristocracy to the revolution in Europe, which alone can permanently cripple Russia.

"Ever yours affectionately,

"F. W. Newman."

And in August, 1855, he wrote again:—

"I do not think you see truly the *treachery* of our Government (I cannot use a weaker word), nor know truly what Kossuth has always demanded. To my first question, 'Do you expect us to drive Austria into hostility?' he replied (probably in November, 1853), 'Certainly not; but I claim that you shall not *try to hinder* our fighting our just and necessary battle against Austria.' This is the turning point. We did try to hinder it, hoping thereby to seduce Austria to our side. To whisper to Austria the words 'H. P. I.' would not have been to stir up those countries to insurrection, but to *compel Austria not to threaten Turkey with her armies*. Our Government encouraged her in it, and aided her to occupy the Principalities, forcing the Sultan to take pliable Ministers.... We reap the bitter fruit, as Kossuth from the beginning told us we should. I, however, still hope that we shall regain a morally right position, and that if we fare the worse Hungary may be the better; for *then* Austria might have been neutral, now she will be our enemy."

Kossuth suffered greatly in his political aims and endeavours from lack of funds. Indeed, from his first journey to England until he finally gave up coming over here, he was terribly hampered by want of money. Newman, too, was out of pocket owing to his efforts to push forward the Hungarian cause. I have before me now a letter from Kossuth written in January, 1854, from 21 Alpha Road, Regent's Park, to E. Sieveking and Son, members of my family, who were keenly interested in Hungarian politics, and who transacted many business arrangements for Kossuth from time to time while he was in England. The letter is on behalf of a friend of his, a Mr. Ernest Poenisch, and is written in German:—

"Honoured Sir,

"Would you not do me the kindness to give a favourable reference about the honourability [*sic*] of Mr. Ernest G. Poenisch if anyone should happen to make enquiries of you about him?

"Mr. Ernest Poenisch is a merchant in the city, a German by birth, and was a merchant of importance, and as he often has commercial business of importance to look after for me, you will be doing to me myself, a kindness if you would give him a good reference in a general way, should opportunity occur.

"Renewing my request to you, I sign myself, "Respectfully yours,

"L. Kossuth. "To E. Sieveking and Son."

In June, 1855, Francis Newman writes to Dr. Martineau, in answer to a letter from him:—

"I do not write in support of the oppressed nations *because* 'I have confidence in the stability and morality of a continental democracy,' but because the *foreign* kings who now trample nations down *neither have nor pretend to have* any right but that of armies; it is a pure avowed robber– rule, essentially in morals, and all will extol the nations as patriotic whenever they throw it off. ... Certainly I maintain that Hungary and Poland are nations; so in fact is Italy: but Austria is only a Court and Army, not a nation. We have had public relations with Hungary as a nation; we violated our duty to Hungary in 1848–9; and complain we are still allowing Austria to get the benefit of our wrong. So

183

also to Poland, I feel we have grossly neglected our duty, and still neglect it.... We know that Hungary (Poland, Italy) is in the right; but though called on to say so, we will not say it; nor even mediate, *for* it will lead to republicanism. Again, I call it immoral to argue: 'We know that Austria is giving Turkey just cause of war; but we must *not allow* the Sultan to resent it by declaring war; *for* it will give the nationalities an opportunity of throwing off the Austrian yoke.'... Then, my dear friend, do you forget that I approved of the *French*, and disapproved of the *Austrian* alliance?... Not to ally with Louis Napoleon is not to join him *against the French nation*; while to ally with Francis Joseph was to join him *against the French nation*, which his armies are trampling down. Again, we did not catch Louis Napoleon engaged in a scheme with Nicholas (Emperor of Russia) to dismember Turkey, and bribe Louis Napoleon to join us by the promise or hint that he should still get his slice of Turkey. We *have* done this to Austria, and have used our severe pressure on the Turkish Government to get Austria admitted into the Principalities.... I fear this summer will be as deadly to our army as the winter was; my only comfort will be, that I shall make sure that Austria will the clearer show her true colours.

"Hoping you are all well, I am,

"Ever yours affectionately,

"F. W. Newman."

[Illustration: FACSIMILE OF LETTER FROM KOSSUTH TO MESSRS. SIEVEKING JANUARY, 1854]

"Hungary and Poland are nations; so in fact is Italy: but Austria is only a Court and Army, not a nation." Here is practically the gist of the whole matter, as far as Francis Newman is concerned. Throughout all his writings one comes again and again upon this note. "The People! The People!" is his ever–recurring thought. What are "the People" suffering; what are *their* needs, their wrongs which call for justice? The People is the living nation; the Court and the Army may be inevitable adjuncts of a nation's being, as things at present are constituted; but they are artificial adjuncts; the People are the very life essence of the Nation, its real motive power. Let their voice be heard, and the soul of empire at once springs into being.

In the next letter from Newman to Martineau, 9th June, 1856, from which I shall quote, it is shown that our Colonial Office was enraged against Kossuth because he had "mischievously *hindered* the Austrian Government from getting troops to put down Italian insurrection." Newman goes on to show how the treachery of Austria in her dealing with other nations was a potent fact, and he adds, "Hungary was bound" (according to Kossuth's views) "to assist Austria against foreign attack, and therefore against the *King of Sardinia*; but in the interval, before this could come to any practical result, the intrigues of the Austrian Court with the Serbs were brought to light; Austrian officers with the Emperor–King's commission in their pockets were made prisoners from among the Serb ranks, and the internal danger of Hungary, as well as the treachery of the Court, made it simply impossible to carry out, or wish to carry out, the Protocol. But Kossuth was still the King's Minister, and could not say this openly. Unless he would have taken the first step to civil war, he was bound to throw a thin veil over it in public speech and action. The measure which he then promoted was ... that no Hungarian soldier should leave the country until the internal rebellion was thoroughly subdued. That no Hungarian regiments should fight against Italians until the Italians had had from Austria the offer of national institutions and freedom under the Austrian Crown, putting them on a par with the Hungarians."

Nothing could have been fairer than these conditions, and this was very shortly recognized when it became known that Latour and the Court were employing all their energies for long after this date in stirring up the Serb rebellion. Yet they were shameless enough to complain of Kossuth having incited the Hungarians to revolt. Writing the next day to Dr. Martineau, Newman openly avows his belief that "every nation in the world is grasping and unjust in its foreign policy in exact proportion to its power, *England not being at all an exception.*" The italics are my own. Have we not proof positive of this before our very eyes to–day? We cannot look at India and say "no," for by our charter of 1833 we bound ourselves over to hold India only until the education, which we had made possible for them, should enable the Indians to take a share in the government of their own country. But when we look at the India of to–day, we cannot but plead guilty to not having kept that charter honestly before our eyes. There is but *one* office to which natives are admitted on equal terms with Englishmen to–day!

To go back to the letter:—

"England has no great European army, and cannot *covet* and subdue any portion of the European continent. That is no great credit; but in Asia, where she is strong and her neighbours weak, she is as grasping and unjust as Russia, Austria, France, or the U.S.... Lord Palmerston had never heard (or pretended never to have heard) of the peace of Satmar, and that England was mediator of it between Austria and Hungary. I think it is not mere knowledge, but higher morality, which is the first need of policy on *both* sides the Atlantic."

It is now that Louis Napoleon comes on the scene as regards the beginnings of his connection with Kossuth. Newman says that it was in 1856 that the closer friendship between Napoleon and Cavour (Sardinian Minister) had begun. Not very long after it was borne in on the mind of Cavour that Kossuth would be an invaluable ally in the plans of future conquest which they were then preparing.

Louis knowing that Kossuth was in sore need of funds for his political enterprises, sent a messenger to him to intimate that he would join forces with him; that *he* would supply him financially with all he would require in the way of ready cash. Kossuth was not averse from receiving in good part Napoleon's advances, though he offered temporary resistance. He saw clearly that if France were to help Italy, Austria would be weakened, Newman tells us that when Napoleon announced in 1858 that he was about to marry Clotilde, daughter of the King of Sardinia, Kossuth at once said to him: "I have always resisted Napoleon's overtures, but I expect now that I shall be forced to visit him in Paris, because I now see that he is resolved upon war against Austria. This Piedmontese marriage is evidently his pledge also to Italians that he means to drive Austria out of Italy."

Then, in 1859, a few inimical words which Napoleon spoke to the Austrian ambassador showed very clearly to what quarter the political wind in France had veered. "War was felt to be intended, and Russia was no longer a support to Austria behind."

In March, or a little later, Kossuth and Pulszky were invited to Paris, and were met, very cordially, at the station by Prince Napoleon, cousin to the Emperor. Later, Louis Napoleon himself spoke with them, and said very frankly that he had never had any special idea of assisting Hungary, but that in case he could not settle affairs in Italy, as regarded his war with Austria, and he should find himself obliged to send his army into Croatia, he wanted advice with respect to many details regarding this province, which he knew that Kossuth could give him. Newman was the recipient of Kossuth's communications concerning this secret interview with Napoleon. And he told him that besides needing his advice about Croatia, he wanted him (knowing he had influence in England) "to drive Lord Derby out of office." I quote Napoleon's words as recorded by Newman.

"The French army is very formidable; but I cannot pretend that in it I have such superiority to Austria that I may expect easy or certain success. My only clear superiority is on the sea. As Louis Philippe before, so have I from the first carefully nursed my fleet. Hereby I override Austria in the Adriatic—a most critical advantage.... I cannot be sure but that without declaring war, or giving warning, he (Lord Derby) may all at once strike a blow which will annihilate my fleet, and then what could compensate me? If you can find any way of moving discontent against this ministry, I want you to cripple or eject him."

Newman adds that Kossuth did not tell him what reply he himself gave to all this.

Everyone knows the sequel to this. After Lord Derby had resigned in March, Lord Palmerston took office. In May the Austrians were defeated; and this defeat was followed by more disaster for them, and the end of the whole matter resolved itself into a peace between Francis Joseph and Louis Napoleon.

Then it was that the latter proclaimed freedom from Austrian supremacy to all Italy; and *now* came the end for which Kossuth had struggled, and longed, and waited. Napoleon despatched a messenger to him asking what demands Kossuth wished now to make. His prompt answer was delivered thus to the envoy:—

"Sir, I have two demands on your master: *First*, he must extract from the Emperor Francis Joseph an amnesty for every Hungarian or Croatian soldier who has taken military service under the King of Sardinia. *Secondly*, no man thus amnestied shall ever be pressed into the Austrian army."

A fortnight went by, and Kossuth heard nothing from the Emperor. Then, when at last the news came, it was almost too good to be true. Francis Joseph had agreed to both stipulations.

Memoir and Letters of Francis W. Newman

In August, 1860, Francis Newman, writing from Keswick, touches on the progress in success made by the Italian patriot, Garibaldi.

"I do not think you can be dissatisfied with Garibaldi's progress. Louis N. *could* have stopt [sic] him, and ruined his hopes for ever, by one word to Austria as soon as Garibaldi landed in Sicily. On the contrary, he has sternly forbidden Austria to meddle at all in Italy, and has allowed Cavour to proclaim in Parliament that L. N.'s greatest merit to Italy is *not* the great battle of Solferino, *but* his having avowed in his letter to the Pope *that priests shall no longer rule in Italy....* When Hungary is free, all views will change, and perhaps France also."

Kossuth and Pulszky, who had visited England constantly between the years 1851 and 1860, finally left our shores for good in the latter year, Kossuth for Italy, for he took no further share in politics, and Pulszky for Hungary, where he became Finance Minister to Francis Joseph's new constitutional monarchy.

Before finally leaving England, Kossuth gave to Newman his own "reading" of the real character of Louis Napoleon. He said: "Louis Napoleon is a man at whom, on account of his *coup d'etat*, [Footnote: Louis Napoleon's raid on the French citizens, in violation of his promises, in order to make himself supreme.] I shudder, and it may seem a duty to hate him. Yet I am bound to say, not only has he been wholly faithful to us, but every time I have been closeted with him I have come away with a higher opinion, not only of his talents and sagacity, *but also of his morals.*" The italics are mine. It seems difficult for the outsider to–day quite to sign to this point of view, when one remembers Louis Napoleon's deception and his broken honour and cruelty. There is a very enlightening and suggestive passage in one of Robert Louis Stevenson's books, "To travel happily is better than to arrive." In Kossuth's case the reverse was true. He travelled towards his goal unhappily, but he "arrived," and that was a reward which is not given to every patriot who gives his life to win his country's freedom.

In *Hungary in 1851*, by Charles Loring Brace, there are many keenly interesting details about Kossuth. Mr. Brace made a tour in Europe, chiefly on foot, during the spring of 1851, and met Kossuth in Pesth; his mother was then living there. "To say that Kossuth is beloved here seems hardly necessary after what I have seen. He is idolized. Every word and trait of his character is remembered with an indescribable affection ..."; but they all acknowledged, he added, that he did not possess the necessary gifts for a revolutionary leader. Still, he moved his countrymen in so stirring a manner that they would have followed him anywhere. "He 'agitated' the whole land, and there is not a Bauer in the villages or a Csikos (wild cattle driver) on the prairies, they say, who does not remember as the day of days the time when he listened to those thrilling tones ... as they spoke ... of the wrongs of their beloved Fatherland."

This is a short account by a journalist who knew him personally, and was present at the time, of the manner in which Kossuth was received in Scotland during his visit to Britain:—

"In travelling from Edinburgh to Perth, Kossuth was received at every station by vast crowds of people, including many ladies, with vociferous cheers and waving of hats and handkerchiefs. This was particularly the case at Stirling, where hundreds crowded up to the carriage in which he sat to grasp his hand."

One day it was suggested that Kossuth, Colonel Ibaz his aide–de–camp, and the journalist should go for a drive up Kinnoul Hill, near Perth. "We soon got into a rough country road winding among the farms. At one place the carriage came to a stand while a gate had to be opened to allow it to pass through. At this gate stood a tall, venerable–looking farmer, with long white hair and beard ... who might have served as a painter's model for an old Scottish Covenanter. He stood ready to open the gate.... He had, of course, heard of Kossuth's invitation to lecture in Perth, and at once divined that the carriage might contain his hero, as all visitors to Perth ascend the Hill of Kinnoul.... In a very deep and solemn voice he said ... 'I reckon that Loois Koshoot is in this carriage. Am I richt? Whuch is him?' Kossuth leaned forward and said in a very gracious manner, 'Yes, he is, good man. I am Louis Kossuth.' Whereupon the venerable man reverently took off his bonnet, came close up, grasped Kossuth's hand in both his own, and said, 'God bless you, sir, an' may He prosper you in your great waurk to free yer kintra frae the rod o' the oppressor. May He strengthen ye and croon ye wi' victory....'

"Colonel Ihaz was a bronzed, stern–looking officer, perhaps ten years older than his chief; yet with all his military stiffness and sternness he was quite capable of relaxing into ordinary human feelings and becoming quite a facetious old fellow under favourable conditions. He could speak very little English. He enjoyed the humour of some Scottish stories and anecdotes I told, and which Kossuth translated for him. He was greatly pleased and amused when I initiated him into the art and mystery of concocting a tumbler of whisky toddy as a proper and orthodox finish to the evening.... He thoroughly appreciated the beverage, smacking his lips ... and exclaiming with gusto, 'Toddo is goot. Toddo *very* goot.'" He mentions that Kossuth was keenly interested in Scottish ballads and stories, etc., and he actually learnt *one* ballad by heart, "which for thrilling passion, and power, and sweetness ... were never equalled by human voice. His appeals ... were addressed exceedingly often to the religious feelings of his hearers. In fact, this tendency of his is perhaps one great secret of his power over the people of Hungary—for the peasantry of that land, beyond that of almost any other, are remarkable for a simple, reverent piety."

When, after the deliverance of Hungary from the yoke of Austria, Kossuth was made Governor, Brace says that he considers he belonged, by reason of his talent for organization and finance, to the highest rank of statesmen. He had not "the unrelenting, tremendous force of a Cromwell or Napoleon, or the iron will of a Jackson...." But he has shown that a man "could be a military Dictator without staining his hands either in the blood of his rivals or of his friends."

"One of the privates in an Austrian regiment stationed in Vienna, himself a Hungarian, was overheard by his officer to say 'Eljen Kossuth!' He was ordered 'five–and–twenty' at once. It appears when a man is flogged in the Austrian army he is obliged by law to thank the officer. This the Hungarian refused to do. Another 'five–and–twenty' were given him. Still he refused. Again another flogging; and the Hungarian, as he rose, muttered his thanks with the words, 'My back belongs to the Emperor, but my heart to Kossuth.'"

In regard to Kossuth's manner of delivery in his great public speeches, Mr. Brace says: "His opening words, they say, were like Hungarian national airs, always low and plaintive in the utterance.... But gradually his face lighted up, his voice deepened and swelled with his feeling," and there came forth tones which thrilled his hearers with a strange rousing power.

CHAPTER XII. FOUR BARBARISMS OF CIVILIZATION

In every civilization there will always be found, sheltering under its wall, evil things not yet brought to book—not yet revealed in their true nature, but still dragging back the wheel of true progress and the betterment of humanity. Yet though they come "in such a questionable shape," it is often not until someone ahead of his or her age, pulls them into the open glare of another point of view, and thus shows up all their hidden moral leprosy, that the arrow of condemnation is driven full–tilt at them from the stretched bow of a Higher Criticism.

In Francis Newman's *Miscellanies*, Vol. III, four of these evil things are dragged by him into the open daylight of a mind far ahead of its age, and these four are: Cruelty to Animals; Degradation of Man, as brought about by the drink traffic; War, as the great throw–back to Civilization; Punishment as understood in England, and our own methods of reform as regards the treatment of misdemeanants.

To take the first of these—Cruelty to Animals. Of course there are three kinds: Legalized cruelty, cruelty caused by thoughtlessness, and cruelty caused in order to give pleasure to men and women. Of the first—well, of course this has to do with vivisection, said to be carried on for the advancement of science and for the sake of alleviating the sufferings of humanity.

As regards the first reason, men who know what they are talking about are pretty generally agreed that science has *not* largely benefited by vivisection. As regards the second, it is by no means sure that anything can be proved of direct use to mankind from discoveries made by doctors and scientists after operating on animals. "What sort of tenderness for man can we expect from surgeons who can thus teach by torture, or from students who can endure to listen?" Here Francis Newman puts his finger on a very significant factor in the case—that of the barbarizing, the deteriorating of the mind that cannot touch the black pitch of torture and not be defiled.

Everyone will remember the words of Lord Shaftesbury, one of the greatest men of his day: "I would rather be, before God, the poor victim in the torture–trough than the vivisector beside him." And it is this point also which is of importance in the vivisection question—not the point of view alone of the animal tortured, but as well the inevitable effect on the vivisector. For there are some things undeniably which, when done, do not leave the man who does them where he was before in the moral scale.

As Archdeacon Wilberforce says: "If all that is claimed by vivisectors were true—and I absolutely disbelieve it—the noblest attitude would be to refuse physical benefit obtained at the cost of secrets stolen from other lives by hideous torture." These words exactly express the attitude of all thoughtful men and women who feel the impossibility of accepting help at the cost of such torture to the lower creation by what the Archdeacon very aptly calls the "barbarities of science."

Well may Francis Newman say: "When we ask by what *right* a man tortures these innocent creatures, the only reply that can be given is, because we are more intelligent. If in the eye of God this is justifiable, then a just God might permit a devil to torture us in the cause of diabolic science.... To cut up a living horse day after day in order to practise students in dissection is a crime and abomination hardly less monstrous from his not having an immortal soul. An inevitable logic would in a couple of generations unteach all tenderness towards human suffering if such horrors are endured, and carry us back into greater heartlessness than that of the worst barbarians." The bill in 1876, of which the chief aim was to amend the law, to regulate better the doings of vivisectors, insisted on the fact that a licence from the Home Secretary was to be a *sine qua non* in the case of all who practised these experiments upon animals. But experience of the way in which this law works shows quite clearly that very inadequate inspection takes place, because in so many cases inspectors and vivisectors play into each other's hands.

Of the other kinds of cruelty, those caused by thoughtlessness and in order to minister to the pleasure of men and women are very many and very present to us. I use the word "thoughtlessness," but perhaps it would be nearer the truth to say lack of power to realize, for thoughtlessness can no longer be pleaded by those women who persist in wearing aigrettes, and other plumage of birds. The barbarous method has been too often described to them by which these aigrettes are procured: how the plumes are torn from the males of the small white heron; how, this appalling cruelty perpetrated, the birds are left to die on the shore. Women of fashion cannot but be aware how wholesale this savage slaughter of the innocents is; that each bird only contributes one-sixth of an ounce of aigrette plumes; that we are told that thousands of ounces of plumes are sold by one firm during the course of one season alone. It is not too much to say that each woman's bonnet in which these plumes (so barbarously procured) figure, is a veritable juggernaut car. It is not alone for fashion's sake that we perpetrate these barbarisms, however, for what can be said in defence of cruelties practised upon animals for the sake of man's stomach? Of the method in vogue now of stuffing capons by means of an instrument which forces food down their throats relentlessly in order to make them of great size and of tender flesh? or of calves being slowly bled to death that their flesh may be white? What of the horrors which precede the making of *pate de foie gras*? The name of these atrocities is legion, however, and it is useless to enumerate them here. Fashion loves to have it so, and the ordinary diner does not trouble his head about the terrible ordeal of the animal which has preceded the delicacy for himself. But, putting his dinner aside, the Englishman's sport is often not far removed from barbaric.

Look at coursing! What can be the nature that can take *pleasure* in seeing an absolutely defenceles animal let out in a confined space, with no chance of escape, no fair play at all, nothing in front of it but certain death whichever way it turns? What can be the nature which can *enjoy* the death–scream of the agonized hare as the dogs' fangs dig into the quivering flesh? Coursing is nothing more nor less than an absolutely degrading sport to the beholders.

There is no *sport*, in the right acceptation of the word, in it at all. At any rate, there is far more of the element of real sport in fox–hunting or in stag–hunting, especially in those districts where one is told that the stag practically enters into the spirit of the game, when, after a good run, it pauses, and is helped into the cart which is to take it into "home cover" again! Be that as it may, at least there is some fair play to the quarry. In coursing that is an unknown quantity.

"The accomplished Englishman shoots for sport. Sport, being a mental impulse or appetite, is insatiable, and therefore far more deadly than hunger.... A boast is made that ninety millions of rabbits are reared for the consumption of our nation. Ninety million rabbits sent out at large to nibble the young shoots of the growing crops—each of whom destroys and wastes ten times what a tame rabbit would eat in a hutch—are boasted of as an increase of our supplies! If twenty million of these reach the town markets, it is much; how many beside are cruelly massacred with no profit to man! and how many beside, with unhappy hares, foxes, rats, stoats, and weasels, are held for days and nights in lingering torture by horrible steel traps? All this goes on in the midst of refinement, without prohibition from men or remonstrance from women. It is a fruit of the modern English system of game preserving;... and the artificial love of sport which cruel Norman tradition has fostered in the stolid Anglo–Saxon race." [Footnote: "On Cruelty" (*Miscellanies*, III, by Francis W. Newman).] It is an unassailable truth that if you look for the last remains of barbarity in a civilized nation you will find them in their sports. But I confess that to me it is difficult to justify a *woman's* love of sport when it is combined—before her very eyes—with the suffering of an animal. Yet I heard only the other day of a woman who boasted that she had been among the few "in at the death" one day in fox– hunting, and that when the brush was given to her, her face was *spattered with the blood of the fox.*

To turn to another "barbarism of civilization"—the subject of the Drink Traffic.

Newman's words about this come with startling appositeness to–day, when we are all eager as regards the pros and cons of the new Licensing Act, and when all the publicans in the country are watching anxiously in fear of the ruin it may spell for themselves. Thirty years ago Francis Newman flung these words broadcast into the country:—

"Parliament ignominiously sits on the beer barrel. The thirty–three millions a year" (which was the revenue in 1877 derived from "complicity with distillers and brewers"), "are to every Ministry like the proverbial wolf which the woodsman holds by the ears. To keep him is difficult, to let him go is dangerous. Their position is becoming worse than embarrassing when the best *men* of every class, and *all the women* who see the public miseries, condemn the deadly policy of bartering national morality for payments to the exchequer.... The mode in which those in power fight to retain the public immoralities proclaims the quality of their motives. As one example out of several, see with what tenacity the Sunday sale of intoxicating drink in Ireland is kept up, after it is visible that Ireland disapproves, and after the English Parliament has voted with Ireland. *Trickery* is here the only right word; but *trickery* cannot in the long run support any cause. In this matter, as in several others, national indignation is ripening. Many old ways will have to be reversed, among which the treatment of the drink traffic has quite a leading place."

He then goes on to treat in detail of the pros and cons of Sir Wilfrid Lawson's Bill, and its principle of Popular Local Control; also of those of Mr. Joseph Cowen's Bill on the same subject, both belonging to the year in which he wrote his article on "Local Control of the Drink Traffic." And he proceeds to consider the two alternatives: the Permissive Popular Veto, and the Popular Control by an unfettered Licensing Board.

Later on Newman propounds his own opinion as to where the true remedy lies for the shocking state of public morality in connection with the drink traffic. Almost invariably his remedies for social evils are based on specialization. In this case he advises Licensing Boards in large towns. He urges that each Board should have full power to frame its own restrictions, that "no Board should be numerous: *five* or *seven* persons may be a full maximum"; that each Board should be elective, "without power to bind their successors in the next year." "What shadow of reason," he asks, "is there for doubting that such sales as are necessary and inevitable will be far more sagaciously managed by a Local Board, which the ratepayers elect *for this sole purpose*, than either by magistrates who are irresponsible and do not suffer sensibly from the public vice, or by an *irresponsible* or *multitudinous* Committee of Parliament? Finally, a Board elected for this one duty is immeasurably better than the Town Councils, who are distracted by an immensity of other business."

It is not difficult to see that his suggestion for a local Licensing Board has a great deal that might be said for it. His idea as regards a Ward– Mote to settle difficulties in local self–government in the same way would deal first hand with difficulties. In both cases these local boards would obviate the necessity for the despatching of endless little Private Bills to a Parliament which really has not time to deal effectually with them. Francis Newman certainly taught a truth which only gets more insistent as year succeeds year, that specialization is indeed the word of all others which holds within its letters in great measure "the healing of the nations," the simplifying of their puzzles.

As regards the rights and wrongs of making war, Newman asks, "Why does one murder make a villain, but the murder of thousands a hero?" And again, "Why do princes and statesmen, who would scorn to steal a shilling, make no difficulty in stealing a kingdom?"

Before calling this, as many an Englishman would not hesitate to do, a topsy–turvy morality, let us realize that sayings such as these really give us the true values of things as nothing else could. For there are more sins "in heaven and earth than are dreamt of" in a nation's classified immoralities. Stealing a shilling is a recognized immorality, and as such the law of the land punishes the thief. Stealing a kingdom, however, is one of those national achievements which men justify to themselves as a patriotic feat, or, it may be, a necessity of empire, and it is not classified among punishable offences at all. And then it is necessary to remember that many things that are indefensible when only a few do them, seem to become, by an extraordinary method of reasoning, regarded as allowable when so many people do them that a spurious public opinion and a decadent fashion is born, which shelters them and prevents the light of an unbiassed judgment from showing up their shortcomings in morality. One has only to read up old records of the eighteenth century to see how slavery flourished in England among otherwise honourable men, and how public opinion condoned, nay, justified it to realize that public opinion regarded as *vox populi*, is often many spiritual leagues away from being *vox Dei*.

Newman's point of view regarding war and extension of territory was not the popular one:—

"There are many who believe that the time will come when no weapons of war shall be forged, and universal peace shall reign.... We also believe that a time will come when men will look back in wonder and pity on our present barbarism; a time at which to begin a war—unless previously justified by the verdict of an impartial tribunal, bound in honour to overlook what is partially expedient to their own nation or party—will be esteemed a high and dreadful crime.

"The 'Governments' will never initiate such institutions until compelled by public opinion and by the inevitable pressure of circumstances, nor is any nation in the world yet ripe to put forth such pressure; otherwise it would not be difficult to devise a supreme court, or rather jury, which would put a totally new moral aspect on war." [Footnote: *Ethics of War*, Francis W. Newman.]

He goes on to say that a great many wars might have been avoided by us if we had been willing, which we are not, to submit to arbitration; and he urges that war should be "declared *in the Capital... with the formal assent of Lords and Commons.*"

Under the present system, as he points out, when war is declared against any country, it is not a necessity, as it was in the fourteenth century, that Parliament should be applied to for consent and approval when the King of England wished to make war. Later, Henry V asked Parliament what it would advise in "matters of foreign embroilment"; and when the King of France wanted to make peace with him, he would do nothing in the matter until his *Parliament* had told him "what will be most profitable and honourable to do in the matter."

But to–day, in arranging to make war or to make peace, it is the Cabinet— the two or three in the inner Chamber—who take all responsibility upon themselves. As often as not their decision is largely influenced by party questions—and the questions do *not* depend on the morality of the war, whether the reason for it is a just one or no. "It is the singular disgrace of modern England, [Footnote: *Deliberations before War*, Francis Newman, 1859.] to have allowed the solemn responsibility of war to be tampered with by the arbitrary judgment of executive officers; ... the nation permits war to be made, lives by the twenty thousand or fifty thousand to be sacrificed, provinces to be confiscated, and permanent empire over foreign subjects established, at the secret advice of a Cabinet, *all of one party, acting collectively for party objects*, no one outside knowing how each has voted." Yet "the whole nation is implicated in a war, when once it is undertaken, inasmuch as we all have the same national disgrace, if it is unjust; the same suffering, if it is tedious; the same loss, if it is expensive"; and all the time, "according to the current morality of Christendom, two nations may be engaged in deadly struggle, and *neither be in the wrong*."

Newman attributes this present method of deciding war or peace by means of the Cabinet, rather than the voice of the people as expressed by their representatives in assembled Parliament, to the "anomaly of the East Indian Empire." Then, when the Board of Control was formed in 1784, "the orders to make, or not to make war, went out direct from the Board of Control; that is, really, from the ministry in Downing Street. Two, or even one, resolute man had power to make war without check." The fatal war with Afghanistan in the eighteen–thirties which cost us so dear in the matter of men and fame, was settled in England by "secret orders of two or three *executive* officers of the Queen, without previous debate in Parliament." It is necessary to remember, when thinking of the barbarisms which war brought in its train, not a hundred years ago, that what Newman calls, very justly, "the atrocious system" of paying our soldiers and sailors *head–money* for the numbers killed by them, was only done away with about sixty years ago.

But it is impossible even to touch here upon the unthinkable miseries which are inevitably suffered by thousands of innocent men, women, and children whenever that Barbarism of Civilization, War, marches through a land. Apart from all the devastation that marks its advent, no one can know how indescribably far the real moral and industrial progress of civilization is retarded by even what we consider a *small* war. As Newman says: "No one can wonder at the rise and progress of an opinion that war is essentially an immoral state."

In connection with Punishments as understood in England, and Penal Reformation, [Footnote: *Corporal Punishments and Penal Reformation*, Francis Newman, 1865.] he owns that "it has hitherto been most difficult to discover what due punishment of felony will not demoralize the felon." And of course, undoubtedly, that *is* the crux of the whole matter. But there is no one in England to–day but will agree that some change in our prison system is imperatively needed. Only the other day a woman, thoroughly qualified to judge, declared that the inevitable effect of prison life on women was to make them lose their self–respect. It was a degradation and nothing else. Now a punishment practically loses its whole point if it is simply a lowering, without any building up; while apart from any other considerations, to herd, without due specialization, a number of criminals and misdemeanants (for that last is the true description of very many who are punished by this system of incarceration) tends, in many instances, to increase, by "evil communications," the numbers of those who are in for a first offence only, and would not, but for the enforced bad influence of others in prison, offend again. Newman's conclusion of the whole matter as regards prisons is irrefragable: "In order to *prevent* crime, the institutions which generate crime must be remodelled." He urges upon the nation's consideration that for a great many cases which now fill our prisons (thereby adding enormously to the national expenses) there is a very simple punishment, which has been condemned from many modern points of view as being degrading to the sufferers and brutalizing to the inflictors.

"The infliction of flogging," he argues, undeniably answers in these cases, both as a sharp and effectual punishment, and also as a deterrent from future misdoing. "To us it appears an obvious certainty, that whatever punishment is believed to be righteous—whether the whipping of a child, the shooting of a soldier, the constraint of the treadmill, or whatever else—is wholly free from the least tendency to brutalize the officers who inflict it." As to the wisdom of this statement, one would think, there could be no question. He quotes our old laws as regards the practising of public floggings, and adds, "We cannot hesitate to believe that all outrages on women ought to be punished by the severest whippings.... Dastardly offences against the weak and the weaker sex eminently call for this punishment; and in such offences may be included the seduction of a woman." That offences against the body should be visited by punishment *on* the body is beyond all doubt just. Had we been in the past, or were we at the present moment, as eager as we ought to be for defence, for justice, to be given to the citizeness as equally as to the citizen, there would not be so many wrongs done to the weaker sex as now is the case in England. Newman strongly condemns long sentences and transportation, not so much on account of the prisoner, (though for him the long term of "doing time" with other criminals exercises in most cases a distinct low moral tone upon himself) as on account of his wife and family, if he is married. These people are left without news of him, and without their legal means of subsistence during his absence. His wife often indeed, practically becomes a pauper.

"It is vain to talk of the evil of 'degrading' a criminal by flogging him, if we degrade him by penal labour, subjecting him to a very ignominious and tedious slavery. It is vain to say that whipping demoralizes, until we have a system of effective and severe punishment, clearly free from this danger.... A felon destined to long penal servitude cannot fulfil a father's duties, and no one is so weak as to imagine that his commands concerning his children deserve respect.

* * * * *

Legislation must deliberately study this problem, not wink at it." [Footnote: *Corporal Punishments and Penal Reformation.*]

Perhaps when it does, something more stringent will be determined on concerning our regulations as regards the marriage of criminals: those with insanity or inherited disease strongly marked on their family records; and those who have shown the tendency to the latter in their own persons.

CHAPTER XIII. SOME LEGISLATIVE REFORMS SUGGESTED BY LECTURE AND ARTICLE

Fifty years ago Newman was cutting and polishing his diamond scheme of legislative decentralization till its facets flashed to the lighted intellects of the world a thousand messages—a thousand clear–cut suggestions for the welfare of his country and the betterment of its legislation, as he firmly believed. He was never tired of urging it on the notice of his fellow men, never tired of pleading for it as a solution of many social difficulties, as a setting of many dislocations of our local systems. Perhaps there was no more earnest apostle of decentralization than was Francis Newman. But at the same time, to be fair to him, it should be said that, first, he threw light upon the old paths, and, secondly, showed where modern obstructions lay which seemed to him to hinder true progress. At all costs the fact must be kept well in view, he believed, that the paths were made for the men, not the men for the paths —a fact which is not always so well remembered as it should be to–day. Fifty years ago he published an article in *Fraser's Magazine* on "Functions of an Upper House of Parliament." Eight years later he gave a brilliant lecture [Footnote: In the Athenaeum, Manchester.] on "Reorganizations of English Institutions." In this last he touched only briefly upon the former subject because of a notice by the metaphysical railings of his lecture that he was "to keep to the path," and not speak trenchantly on the question of the Upper House, because it would not have found an appreciative audience there!

To begin, however, first upon the article which came out in 1867. He affirmed that the House of Lords does, by its veto, exercise a very powerful, though unseen, influence over the administration of the country. He insisted on the urgent need of its becoming "a real, supreme, judicial court for maintaining the rights of the princes of India, and an authoritative expounder of the treaties which have passed between us and them." It will be seen why this step is called for when we recall the fact that in 1833 the Home Government signed a treaty in which it was definitely agreed that the professions in India should be open to the natives—a promise which has never been kept.

Newman goes on to say, "Until India can have its own Parliament, it needs to find in England such protection as only our own Upper House can give it." He places before us the possibility of economizing the time—to-day so terribly overcrowded—of the House of Commons by letting domestic legislation, "which is in no immediate relation to executive necessities," proceed from the Upper House. That in that House it could be so adapted and so regulated, that when it came back finally to the House of Commons no otherwise inevitable delay need occur. Thus "the Commons would have for their chief business Bills connected with immediate administrative exigencies, *and private Bills would be cast upon local legislatures*" (a measure for which he was, as we know, constantly pleading). He reminds us that the Roman executive was successful and prompt in the methods at which they aimed, *because* "the Senate guided and controlled it, *prescribed the policy and required the execution.*"

In his "Reorganization of English Institutions" he insists very strongly on the great need of such a scheme of decentralization as the formation of Provincial Chambers—in other words, the dividing the country into local government centres which should send delegates, chosen delegates of tried men, "virtually its ambassadors to Parliament, with instructions and a proper salary, for a three years' term; but reserving the power to recall any delegate earlier by a two–thirds vote, and to replace him, like an ambassador, by a successor." Now, here comes in Newman's proposed drastic change—a change which, in the opinion of those of us who have seen at close focus the evils of our present system of canvassing for votes, could not be condemned as a change for the worse.

For each delegate sent up to Parliament "would be elected without candidacy and without expense ... confusion and intrigue would be lessened.... There would be no convulsive interruptions of public business." Many questions very naturally rise in our minds when we fairly face this plan. Newman feels so confident, besides, that it would "settle our harassing Irish difficulties."

The "old institutions of the shires are known only to students of ancient law," says Mr. Toulmin Smith, one of the greatest authorities of his country's old records, documents, etc. "They have been overridden by justices of the peace, county lieutenants, and other functionaries.... From this general decay of local institutions centralization has grown up."

From this "decay of local institutions," Newman points to what he designates as the "Trades' Union"—the Cabinet (the "Secret Diplomacy"), which has, he declares, superseded the old Privy Council.

"Since William III became king, parliaments of Scotland and Ireland have been annihilated, and no subsidiary organs have replaced them.... Our population is four times as great as William III knew it; yet the people are more than ever divorced from the soil and cramped into town...." Now, "Parliament is too busy for domestic local reforms; it has to control the action of the whole Executive Government, Central and Local.... It has sole right to direct public taxation.... It has to control the action of the ministry towards foreign Powers.... It has a similar function towards colonies ... and the Army and the Navy.... It is responsible for all India" (population then two hundred and forty millions).... "It is the only court of appeal to Indian princes who believe themselves wronged" (by the king's representatives).... "No other authority can repeal bad laws, or enact new laws for the general public." But were we to *return* to the "legislative courts of our shires," Newman protests, which existed before our present systems of Parliament, all the inevitable delays and congestions which now occur to prevent the dealing with and passing of imperatively necessary reforms would be done away with *in toto*.

Long ago Lord Russell said that for any great measure a ministry needs "a popular gale to carry the ship of State over the bar." "Hence all our reforms, working against a stiff current, sail over the bar fifty or one hundred years too late."

This, then, briefly stated, was Francis Newman's plan of dealing with the accumulation of business, etc., which beset the House of Commons as matters stand at present.

The whole of Great Britain, he urged, should be divided in provincial chambers for local legislation. He proposed ten for England, four for Ireland, two for Scotland, and one for Wales.

These local powers "must be to the central like planets round a sun.... All unforeseen business would fall to the central power, which in all cases would undertake: public defence, communications with foreign Powers, principal highways, shores and harbours, Crown lands, national money and weights, and national taxes.... Our impending Church and State question will be solved in this island, with least convulsion, if local variety of sentiment be allowed free play." [Footnote: Perhaps then we should be rid of the anomaly which allows a Prime Minister, of whatever religious denomination, to choose Bishops for the Anglican Church.] Newman proceeds thus to describe further his suggestions with regard to the working of the provincial courts: "Each electoral district to send one member to the Provincial Chamber; household franchise, of course, would be the rule, and I trust women householders would not be arbitrarily excluded." They would deal directly, and on the spot, with local pauperism in the provincial courts. That, in itself, would be one great gain. For pauperism cannot effectively be dealt with except by local legislation. Some system such as Ruskin's, with powerful local legislation, could not fail to end the trouble which is at the present moment making a tremendous drain on the pockets of the law–abiding citizen of this country, in that system of workhouses, which besides being subversive of the very idea of home–life amongst our poor, degrades the non–worker, and rankles as a lasting shame in the hearts of those whom misfortune alone has driven to that last resource of the unfortunate. Were one able to follow the example set us, among cities, by Leipsic (where the word pauperism is absolutely non– existent), we should have effectually turned the corner out of the ill– kept vagrant road into which Henry VIII first led us, when "pauperism" began to be a sore in the midst of England's healthy body of citizens. Now, it is a self–evident fact that "pauperism," which is a living drag on our social wheel, can *not* be dealt with other than by rigorous local government. Cases could then be dealt with personally; the whole area would not be too gigantic for this; but, of course, it is a moral impossibility to generalize in dealing with this subject.

After all, this is not, as Francis Newman insists, a new departure in any way. He points to other countries to show that as a fact, centralization has been gradually establishing itself in England, though in other times decentralization was a very potent force in our midst, and a success.

In 1875, Newman quotes the following countries as regards their local legislatures: "Look ... at Switzerland. Environed by ambitious neighbours far superior in power, her institutions have well stood the severe trial of time. She has her Central Diet and Ministry, vigorous enough; but also in her several cantons she has local legislatures, each with well–trained soldiers, simply because every man is bound to learn the use of arms, as Englishmen used to be; therefore they need no standing army.... Italy also has local legislatures which belonged to independent States—Sicily, Naples, Piedmont, Tuscany, and so on—besides her National Parliament.... In Hungary notoriously the national spirit has been maintained for three centuries and a half ... solely by the independent energy of the local institutions.... The seven united provinces of Holland similarly prove the vitality of freedom and good order when free local power is combined with a strong centre.... And on a far greater scale we have... an illustrious example in the United States—a mighty monarchy and a mighty republic.... The American Union started in that advanced stage. It is a cluster of some thirty–seven States, each with its own legislature, for all which, and for the outlying territories, the Federal Parliament also legislates. Contrast their condition with ours. Only of late has their population outrun ours. They have thirty–eight legislative systems: we have one only. Surely our system is a barbarous simplicity. France ... goes beyond us. Nay, our Indian centralization is worse still. No virtue, no wisdom in rulers can make up when the defect of organs lays on them enormous duties."

Finally, Newman urges for provincial chambers that they should be on the "scale of petty kingdoms," and not of mere town populations. "All parts and ranks of the local community are then forced to take interest in local concerns. Each province becomes a normal school for Parliament, and a ladder by which all high talent of poor men may rise."

SHOULD NOT THE CONSENT OF THE NATION BE OBTAINED BEFORE MAKING WAR?

This was a question constantly in Newman's mind. That, and the answer.

Memoir and Letters of Francis W. Newman

Everyone is doubtless aware that he wrote a very great deal upon the subject, and spoke a great deal also. In the third volume of the *Miscellanies* he has four or five articles on this great question. The first was printed in 1859, the second in 1860, the third 1871, and the fourth 1877. Then in "Europe of the Near Future" (1871) he treats it at greater scope, chiefly in regard to the Franco–German War. In "Deliberations before War" (1859) Newman takes the two points of view from which the question of war is as a rule regarded—the Moral and the International. The first considers if a war is a just one or no, and considers the prosecutor of an unjust war as neither more nor less than a robber. The International (or second) "looks only to the ostensible marks which make a war 'lawful'—that is to say, 'regular.'" As Newman very rightly says, however, there is a third point of view, which he calls the "National." I shall quote his words regarding this third view. "Inasmuch as the whole nation is implicated in a war, when once it is undertaken—inasmuch as we all have the same national disgrace if it is unjust, the same suffering if it is tedious, the same loss if it is expensive—it is an obvious principle of justice ... that every side of the nation should be heard to plead against it by its legitimate representatives."

I cannot forbear saying that at the present moment of writing this last is impossible, for those who often suffer most from a war—at any rate longest—are the women, and there is no legitimate representation for this large body of the community. Thus, even if the men of the nation could "plead against" a war, the women would have no voice.

Newman urges that there are many among us who firmly believe that a time is coming when no destructive weapons will be made, and "universal peace shall reign." He believes himself, he says, that "a time will come when men will look back in wonder and pity on our present barbarism, a time at which to begin a war—unless previously justified by the verdict of an impartial tribunal, bound in honour to overlook what is partially expedient to their own nation or party—will be esteemed a high and dreadful crime." These are strong words, but they are not too strong, for, looked at by any thoughtful man or woman, war is an anomaly. It proves nothing by reason; it simply acts by brute force, and by sheer superior strength the victor, at the sword's point, drives defeat down the throat of the defeated. But the arbitrary destruction of thousands of men on each side who slay each other at the word of command (often for no reason that concerns their own welfare, but only on account of some political quarrel), is, from the point of view of civilization, of morality, of humanity, without reasonable defence. It throws civilization, land development, education back incalculably. Indeed, when one regards the matter *au fond*, one sees that nothing could hinder the *true* civilization, the *true* humanity, more than does war. It *is* barbaric; there is no other word for it. It *is* the great flaw that runs throughout the whole garment of humanity.

Newman reminds us that it is only within very recent years "that the atrocious system of paying *head money* to soldiers and sailors for the numbers they kill, was abolished by us."

John Stuart Mill very rightly said "that our force ought to be as strong as possible for defence and as weak as might be for offence," only that it is so very difficult sometimes to tell which is which.

In the *Ethics of War*, Newman argues that "there is nothing more fundamental to civilized warfare than that no war shall be commenced without a previous statement of grievances, and demand of redress—a demand made to the Sovereign himself; and that *only after* he has refused redress, and when in consequence war has been solemnly declared, with its motives and aim, shall hostilities be begun. In dealing with great Powers we anxiously observe these forms.... But it is our Asiatic wars which have brought out the formidable fact that the Cabinets claim to discard the authority of Parliament altogether.... There is no more fundamental principle of freedom ... than that no nation shall be dragged into a war by its executive, against its will and judgment.... Nay, if even a majority of every class in the nation desired war, yet they have no right to enter into it without first hearing what the minority has to say on the other side. This is the essential meaning of deliberative institutions."

Mr. Toulmin Smith, whose weighty words bring to bear on the subject the witness of an England of medieval days, says that in the fourteenth century it was a positive rule that "*consent* of the Great Council, and afterwards *of the Parliament, was necessary* to a war or to a treaty." In his *Parliamentary Remembrances* he gives many precedents, both from the histories of England and Scotland, showing that no peace was made, no war was made, without Parliament being summoned. Henry V, he says, would not enter "matters of foreign embroilment" (war with France, for instance) without the consent of Parliament; and when the French king wished for peace, Henry replied that peace needed to "be allowed, accepted, and approved by the three Estates of each kingdom." The same process was gone through with regard to the French king and his Estates of France. Newman quotes Rome, whose citizens went through a long formality before making any war, the King and Senate "consulting the College of Heralds for erudite instructions as to minute ceremonies. For perhaps four centuries the discipline of the army was admirable; its decline began from the day when a general (Gen. Manlius) first took upon himself to make war at his own judgment, trusting to obtain a bill of indemnity."

Livy tries to force on us the belief that the Romans were never aggressive; that they only conquered the world in self–defence. And it is true that here would come in difficulties in the way of carrying out John Stuart Mill's *obiter dictum* as regards wars of defence and of offence, for many plausible reasons have been constantly brought forward for aggressive wars: to take one only, it is not always easy to say what is "defence" and what "offence." One may see some other country assuming a warlike attitude towards ourselves, and it might very possibly be allowed to come within the bounds of the word "defence" if we were prepared to strike the initial blow before our enemy—to all intents and purposes, save for the actual throwing of the glove—were fully prepared as to armaments, etc. It is well known how earnestly Richard Cobden, the Manchester Apostle of Free Trade, was one of the most prominent champions of peace; he who, for championing the cause of the Abolition of corn duties for the sake of his poorer countrymen, when he and others pushed forward the "Anti–Corn Law League" (which was passed in 1846), lost all his own private funds, and his business was ruined, simply because his time was *all* given not to his own affairs, but to the service of his country. Mr. Cobden, as Newman reminds us, "was entirely convinced that European wars could be stopped by a general agreement to abide by arbitration." Indeed, he prevailed on the Ministers of his day so far that, when the Russian War ended in 1856, "Lord Clarendon, in the name of England, initiated some important clauses, of which one avowed that the Powers who signed the treaty would never thenceforward undertake war without first attempting to stay and supersede it by arbitration. England, France, Russia, Sardinia, and Turkey all signed this treaty, yet in a very few years the solemn promise proved itself to be mere wind." He goes on say, "When passions are at work, superior might, not unarmed arbitration, is needed to control them."

Cobden always declared that no one need fear Russia's strength because of her climate, her vast wildernesses, her frozen seas, her great unwieldiness. It is seen, therefore, that the sort of arbitration planned out by Cobden did not work. It must, according to Newman, be an armed one. It is clear that it is not possible to agree *in toto* with the Quaker method of opposing war, and the most thoughtful Quakers will hardly urge it perhaps to–day. War, for defence of one's country, is a present necessity. What, then, are

Francis Newman's proposed remedies? For in the beginning of this chapter I stated that he, very definitely, had his answer to the great question as regards the nation: its veto or agreement, whenever war is proposed. First of all, before giving these however, let us look for a moment at the plan pursued in such case in modern England. This plan he always set himself against with all the force of personal conviction: "It is the singular disgrace of modern England to have allowed the solemn responsibility of war to be tampered with by the arbitrary judgment of executive officers: ... this same nation permits war to be made; lives by the twenty thousand or fifty thousand to be sacrificed ... at the secret advice of a Cabinet, *all of one party, acting collectively for party objects*, no one outside knowing how each has voted.... The orders to make or not to make war went out direct from the Board of Control—that is, really from the Ministry in Downing Street. Two, or even one resolute man had power to make war without check.... If Earl Grey is right, and a Cabinet must be a *party*, this is a decisive, irrefragable reason why a Cabinet must *never* exercise the function of deciding on Peace or War. The recent [Footnote: He is writing in 1859.] overthrow of the East India Company has swept away all the shams which have hidden from England that the Ministry in Downing Street worked the Indian puppet.... Parliament should claim that public debate shall precede all voluntary hostilities, small or great ... to protest in the most solemn way that henceforth no blow in war shall be struck until the voice of Parliament has permitted and commanded it."

Then, in Newman's article "On the War Power," he goes on to say: "In regard to the difficulties as regards arbitration, and also as regards the voice of the people being made a *sine qua non*, whenever a proposal for war emanates from the powers that be: When an evil is undeniable, serious, unjust in principle ... (referring to secret diplomacy), a remedy must exist. Where there is a will there is a way: nay, many ways."

Then he declares that these (following) measures have commended themselves to him. The full discussion in Parliament by representatives of the people; the determination that nothing shall be settled by secret diplomacy as regards war until the whole matter has been thoroughly threshed out. In more than a few ways, *Vox populi, vox Dei* is still true.

Next he puts before us the advisability of an *armed* arbitration.

"If we look to a great central European Power as having for one of its functions to repress wars and enforce arbitration, it is evident that a large increase of force is necessary beyond all that is at present in prospect. If wars voluntarily taken up for noble objects must be sustained out of spare energy, much more does the place of that Power which is to forbid wars require a great superfluity of energy. To be able to do this within the limits of a great federation is in itself a mighty achievement." [Footnote: Europe in the Near Future, F. W. Newman.] And again: "Apparently the only way in which European wars can be suppressed is by the successive agglomeration of free men, living under and retaining their separate institutions, into powers which have no interest in war, but much interest in peace; until unions reach such a magnitude as to be able to forbid wars of cupidity, and offer a high tribunal for the redress of international grievances.... If all parts of a mighty union have their proportionate weight in questions of war and peace, no partial and vicious expediency can actuate them in common. Justice alone is the universal good which can unite their desires and efforts, or make them collectively willing to undergo sacrifice.... The wider the federation, the more benign its aspect on the whole world without, especially if the populations absorbed into it are heterogeneous in character, in pursuit, and in cultivation.... A federation resting on strict justice, conceding local freedom, but suppressing local wars and uniting its military force for national defence, is economic of military expenditure in time of peace in proportion to the magnitude of the populations federated."

CHAPTER XIV. DECENTRALIZATION AND LAND REFORM

"If law be centralized, it always lingers far behind men's needs." This *obiter dictum* of Francis Newman's, spoken nearly sixty years ago, strikes one as more true to–day even than when he originally gave voice to it. For if there is one thing truer than another, it is that half the wrongs to which we are heir to–day, are due to centralization. This may be due in part, no doubt, to the enormous increase of population; but certainly one overwhelming reason is that class with class has lost in very great measure all sense of cooperation, all sense of sympathy, all sense of their real intimate connection and relationship with each other. Instead of provincial legislature, we have our one parliamentary centre, instead of treating our own local matters ourselves, we hale them up before a central bureaucracy—a bureaucracy already so overcrowded with business that it is absolutely and practically unable to deal with all the questions which come up for settlement. So that instead of imperative local matters being dealt with first hand, private bill after private bill swarms through the doors of Parliament, and it becomes a veritable impossibility to go into detail with respect to the pros and cons which they bear upon their pages, much less grasp the whole drift of the question with justice in its entirety.

Far wiser was the old system of provincial legislature, in which the people were really represented, a system in which personality counted for much and men were brought into familiar and friendly relations with each other, not kept apart by the rubicon of red–tapeism, and liable to have the door of the Closure slammed in their faces at some critical juncture of discussion, and the subject shelved. It is true that since Francis Newman's day we may have made some effort after local councils, but it is also true that these local councils do not really bring class and class together. Each class is by no means adequately represented in them, nor is it the council's object that this should be the case. To compare the England of to–day—the agricultural England, at any rate—with the England of the past, brings all true thinkers to the same conclusion, that class demarcations are as insistent, as absolute as ever they were, even in the culminating early Victorian days. [Footnote: "We must mainly refer our practical evils to the *demoralization* of the State which the restoration of the Stuarts caused.... Then began the estrangement of the Commonalty from the Church of the aristocracy."—Francis Newman.] One has but to go abroad to be convinced how "classy" we are as a nation, for class prejudices and insularity are produced by provincial England, and indigenous to the soil, and alas! this crop never fails. There are, unfortunately, no lean years. There are, it is true, plenty of organizations in which the more fortunate class tries to ameliorate the lot of the less fortunate one, plenty of organizations in which the more cultured class tries—often devotes its whole life to this trying—to make better conditions for the less cultured one, and all honour and praise is due to self–denying work of the kind, but it is not enough. The truest, purest Christian socialism [Footnote: I use the word in its truest ancient sense.] requires that helper and helped meet on absolutely equal ground; that there is banished that indescribable stalking figure which follows close in the wake of most meetings between rich and poor in England, the Gentleman–hood (or Lady–hood, for I have seen that often quite as insistently in evidence) of the class which, so to speak, "*stoops* to conquer," the limitations of the less fortunate classes, in its work for the people.

I remember coming across the word "gentleman" interpreted in a far different sense in an old fifteenth–century book. Many words change their meaning with time, but this word has changed from its fifteenth–century interpretation more than any. The sentence ran thus: "Jesus Christ was the first Gentleman." Anything further from the original conception of its meaning as set forward in this sentence than our English idea of what is meant to–day by "gentleman" it would be difficult to find. For He went among the people as one of themselves, was born among them, and was educated as they were. There was no hint of patronage, no suggestion of any social demarcation. He Who was the world's Redeemer was yet a Socialist [Footnote: I cannot but add here that, in my opinion, the much– abused word "Socialist" has changed in character in the same way as the word "gentleman," and the modern interpretation is very far from being the true, admirable, original thing signified.] in the highest and best sense of the term.

We have come far since those days, but we have not come beyond the need to deprive birth and riches of some of that arbitrary power by which they have assumed more authority than is their due in the matter of legislation, influence, disposal of land, and economic local conditions in the provinces.

As regards decentralized government and the "immense importance of local liberties," I cannot do better than quote first from the preface written by Francis Newman to his lectures on *Political Economy*, when he issued them in a printed form in 1851:—

"Of the immense importance of local liberties, and their actual deficiencies among us, I became fully convinced during six years' residence in Manchester; but it is only from Mr. Toulmin Smith's works (the most important political work, as to me appears, which the nineteenth century has produced in England) that I have learnt the immense resources of the Common Law of England, and that nothing but the arbitrary encroachments of Parliament at this moment hinders a vigorous local legislation and local government under the fullest local freedom which can be desired."

The lectures themselves, notably the twelfth, are in my opinion a counsel of perfection which we should do well to follow to–day in very many respects. For instance, he urges very strongly that "every town in England, and every county, ought to have the feelings of a little State, *as in fact it once had*" [the italics are my own]. "Our own history for many centuries shows that this is quite consistent with the existence of a central power—a Crown Parliament—*for all purposes truly national*; and if the action of the central power were strictly limited to such things, the provinces would, now more than ever, have abundant room for high ambition." He shows how all organization has been lost in large provincial towns, even though meetings are held from time to time, and men *seem* to come together for counsel and combination of ideas; the only really fixed "moral union" being that narrow tie of family life which does but make a number of separate entities in the big whole of citizenship. There is no corporate union which makes each citizen the charge, to all intents and purposes, of his neighbour. Each family holds together. It rises and falls by itself. It holds to its heart no innate real sense of responsibility of a wider citizenship. That is lost—undeniably lost.

[Illustration: TOULMIN SMITH ENLARGEMENT FROM A PHOTO. BY KIND PERMISSION OF MISS TOULMIN SMITH]

The question arises naturally: When was this splendid link of "Each for All" broken and mislaid? For nothing is more imperatively necessary among the ranks of workers to–day.

Mr. Toulmin Smith tells us: "The link which has been broken and mislaid was the "English Guild" (or "gild," as seems the more correct spelling). He tells us—and it is generally conceded that he is our great authority on this subject—that as a system of practical and universal institutions, a English Guilds are older than any kings of England." [Footnote: "They were associations of those living in the same neighbourhood, who remembered that they had, as neighbours, common obligations."] And as another authority on medieval life—Dom Gasquet—says: "The oldest of our ancient laws—those, for example, of Alfred, of Athelstan, and Ina—assume the existence of guilds to some one of which, as a matter of course, everyone was supposed to belong."

There were of course trade (or handicraft) associations and social guilds. Dom Gasquet describes thus their object: "Broadly speaking, they were the benefit societies and the provident associations of the Middle Ages. They undertook towards their members the duties now frequently performed by burial clubs, by hospitals, by almshouses, and by guardians of the poor." [Footnote: "Poor laws had no existence in medieval England, yet the peasants did not fear and die of starvation in old age. The Romans had no poor laws ... until the destruction of small freehold."—Francis Newman.] "Not infrequently they are found acting for the public good of the community in the mending of roads and in the repair of bridges.... The very reason of their existence was to afford mutual aid." [Footnote: Parish Life of Medieval England.] They were in very deed, as Mr. Toulmin Smith describes them, institutions of "local self–help." And everyone who knows anything of the subject is aware that they "obviated pauperism, assisted in steadying the price of labour, and formed a permanent centre." Also it has been proved that they acted as the lever which effectually made citizenship more together as a whole, bound together by common need and common responsibilities.

This sense of oneness of interest of "Each for All," then, we have unfortunately as a nation lost. And with the loss have gone many of the people's rights and privileges both with regard to local self–government, local liberties, and co–operation.

Now the question arises how are we to recover what was so necessary to the public well–being? And Francis Newman is ready with an answer.

"To recognize little states in our towns and countries would be the first step of organization; I believe it would be an easy one.... If each town had full power to tax itself for public purposes, a thousand civilizing ameliorations would be introduced.... If local institutions had been kept up in energy, the unhealthy buildings which now exist could never have arisen; there is at present an Augean stable to cleanse.... Look at the sellers in the street, look at the cab–drivers and their horses on a rainy day; what can be more barbarous than their exposure?... Nothing surely is more obvious than that in a city where thirty or forty thousand persons live all day under the sky, having no power to shelter themselves, there ought to be numerous covered piazzas, market–places, and sheds for cabriolets. By such means, to save the poor from rheumatism and inflammations, would be cheaper than to raise their wages, if that were possible, and would confer far more direct benefit on them than the removing of taxes."

Here is indeed the mind of a modern Hercules in its strong, rational suggestions as to how this particular "stable" must be swept out. It is a striking illustration of how far we have come since the days of the medieval guilds, this lack of grasp on our part of the particular needs of particular sections of the community. For were our local self–government in working order and thoroughly representative, it is not to be thought of for a moment that such a lack of shelters and proper appliances for the labouring man and woman would be in such evidence amongst us as now is the case. For look at England as she is, in respect of unsettled, rainy and stormy weather: her spells of wintry weather, her spring changes: one day warm, and the next, constant spells of snow, sleet, and bitter driving gusts of wind. Where do the loafers of our streets go? Where do the unemployed, hanging about at the street corner in search of a job, go during some pelting shower which drenches whoever remains to face it in less than three minutes? The centre of the street, and the streaming pavements clear almost at once, but where does the "man in the street"— the woman—the child go? Certainly they do not go into a shelter put up by Government for their protection, as a rule. There are, in provincial towns, no shelters sufficiently large to accommodate them.

I have often talked to the inspectors—to take a case in point—of provincial trams. These men have to wait, to stand about at corners of streets or cross roads great part of the day. Many of them suffer in no small degree from this constant standing about in all weathers.

Then again, there is no provision made for the drivers of the trams. It would be quite possible to provide seats for them, as is often done in motor buses, but the same reason holds good for this not having been thought of, as is in evidence with regard to the lack of street shelters.

There is not sufficient co–operation in the local government. When the guilds died out, no local arrangements took their place. In other words, the local government, of whatever nature it is, is not sufficiently representative. The men who work upon the road, day in day out, have not sufficient opportunity of saying, in open meeting of their fellow citizens, where their particular trade shoe pinches. It is, as old Sir Thomas More said very truly, the matter of the rich legislating for the poor, which is at fault.

Here, then, is the remedy suggested by Francis Newman: "The stated meeting of a number of people in a *Ward–mote* would make their faces familiar to one another, and give to the richer orders a distinct acquaintance with a definite portion of the vast community. Out of this ... meeting for discussion of practical business in a *Ward–mote* ... would rise numerous other relations."

Here men would meet—men drawn from every class—and could voice their complaints, their difficulties, their desire for improved conditions of work. Only in this way could local government become really a help to its neighbourhood. Only in this way could men consult on the best way of improving economic conditions, frame their own amelioration of existing laws, and send them up to the Imperial Parliament for consent or veto.

Then it would probably follow that some measure of land reform would be the natural result of such local government. Perhaps it is over the land that the Plough of Reform needs most urgently to be driven. More than eight centuries ago the first idea of parks began in this country. Then it was that in the selfish desire for private property the dwellings of the people were swept away to make room for those of game for royal sport. Later this method was adopted by Henry VIII's baronial retainers, who ejected the tenants from their estates for the sake of trade profit— profit to be gained by exporting wool from the large sheep farms into which they made their private estates.

But the system of large tracts of land in a small country, such as our own, being bought up for private property, and made into parks or game preserves, is of course at the root of very many economic evils which have largely helped to cause pauperism and unhealthy conditions of life for the agricultural labourer. If rich men may add, without the law stepping in to limit amount, land to land as their pocket makes it possible, it follows, as a matter of course, that more of the rustic population must move into the towns: and that more and more crowding and over–competition are the result later on.

Newman—the man who was always boldest where there was a cause that needed fighting for, or fellow citizens who were powerless to right their own wrongs, and who required someone to voice them—spoke out his views on this subject, unhesitatingly. "That a man should be able to buy up large tracts of land, and make himself the owner of them—to keep them in or out of culture as he pleases—to close or open roads, and dictate where houses should be built ... this is no natural right, but is an artificial creation of arbitrary law; law made by legislation for personal convenience ... certainly not for the benefit of the nation.... I find it stated that in 1845 the Royal Commission estimated that, since 1710, above seven millions of acres had been appropriated by Private Acts of Parliament." (This was because of the enormous extension of claims made by lords of the manors.) "It is certain that wild land was not imagined to be a property in old days. The moors and bogs, and hillsides and seacoast imposed on the baron the duty of maintaining the King's peace against marauders, but yielded to him no revenue.... Supplies open to all ought never to have been made private property.... Vast private estates are pernicious in every country which permits them. It was notorious to the Romans under the early emperors how ruinous they had been to Italy.... There they wrought out, among other evils, emptiness of population, and extinction of agriculture." He represents that it was really due to the break–up of the feudal system in the Tudor times which was responsible for the "chronic pauperism" and multitude of "sturdy beggars" of later centuries. And the reason is a very patent one. If more and more land is swamped in private enterprise, private revenue, it is a *sine qua non* that peasant proprietorship must get less and less. There is not, in effect, enough land to go round. Newman points out that, as regards land cultivation, we are behind France, Spain, Italy, Germany, and Hungary; that a hundred years ago there were far more small freeholds in England than is now the case; that England is a "marked exception in Europe in the land tenure." "We know not whither beside England to look for a nation of peasants living by wages, and divorced from all rights in the crops which they raise."

214

As Henry Fawcett said long ago, these wages of English labourers will not allow of the least provision to be made either for the sickness or the feebleness of old age. They have, at the close of a life of hard toil, nothing but the workhouse to live in, the road to beg in or sell in that out–at–elbow, trade, the modern "chapman's."

Look at the average labourer of our own day. He has, as Newman clearly points out, "more than enough to do in rearing a family, and has no better prospect in his declining years than rheumatism and the poorhouse, perhaps with separation from his wife, or at least a miserable dole of out–door relief." [Footnote: We have gone some way since these words were written in our Old Age Pensions.] Here he puts his finger on the very spot where one thoughtless cruelty of bureaucratic legislation is most shown. For many faithful servants of the State come in their last extremity to this destiny. This irony of legislation shone out lately in its true colours when it was discovered that, of over a thousand survivors of the Indian Mutiny, a large proportion, who were invited to the demi–centenary celebration dinner, came out of workhouses where they, who had served their country so well in the days of their youth, had been forced to spend their old age.

There is no doubt that Francis Newman's remedy for the economic evils of the people is the right one. To develop rural industry, to come back to the land, is the hope for England's future. "It is essential to the public welfare to multiply to the utmost the proportion of actual cultivators or farmers who have a firm tenure of the soil by paying a quit–rent to the State.... The soil of England ought to be the very best investment for rich and poor, pouring out wealth to incessant industry, and securing to every labourer the fruit of his own toils."

And in this way, he urges, can this suggestion be carried to its definite conclusion. The revival of small freeholds, the re–institution of peasant proprietorships, are the ways out of the block at the end of the way where there is at present a deadlock in regard to the peasants' individual advancement. It is well known how admirably this system has worked in France, where millions of peasants have profited by the law in favour of small freeholds, and its regulation that such land shall always be divided equally among the children of the landholder. It is well known how largely Indian revenue was drawn from the rent paid by small cultivators in the Dekkan. It may be taken as an invariable consequence that the measure which really profits the citizen profits the State too.

I remember seeing among some old papers dating back to the early quarter of the nineteenth century, an account showing that tobacco planting was really started somewhere in the Midlands by two or three Englishmen, and it was found that the soil was thoroughly adapted to the culture of tobacco. Indeed, the venture proved a complete success. Then the Government of that day, fearing later consequences to the import trade, promptly intervened and put a stop to the home cultivation. But the fact remains that it had been proved, by a definite experience, that there *was* an opening for this industry in England.

It was suggested to me only the other day how many more cider–growing districts, for instance, might be with advantage started in the provinces. For the truth of the matter, when we look at it fairly and squarely, is that the home country can give rural work to many more of her inhabitants than she is allowed to do at present; that, as Newman was always suggesting in his lectures, the labourer should be given an interest in the land; that he should be encouraged in trying to make a crop as good as possible by adopting some modification of the Metayer Culture; that he should have *rights* in the land; be associated in the profit accruing to his overlord; that if the wages of a farm labourer were small, yet that he should be given, perhaps, one–twentieth of the produce; and that he should be encouraged to invest what saving might be possible to him in the farm or trade. Newman was not in favour of the Savings Bank, as we understand it in this country. He thought that associated profit and investment of savings in the employer's land or trade would work far better in the long run, and lead to keener fellowship between labourer and master.

To–day his plan, as it seems to many, stands very good chance of success, if given a fair trial among the right sort of Englishmen. I am aware that these last four words sound vague, but I have a very clear idea of what they mean myself! Newman thought that if a co–operative society began by buying a moderate–sized farm, and divided it into "portions of six to ten acres, they might find either among their own members or among other tradesmen known and trusted among them, persons rich enough to provide seed and stock, and thus to live through the first year on such holdings, and willing (later) to occupy them for themselves or for their sons. The beginning is the great difficulty.... The first thing of all is to show, on however small a scale, that such a cultivation can succeed.... If once peasants see peasant proprietors they will have new motive for saving."

CHAPTER XV. VEGETARIANISM

The London Vegetarian Society was founded in 1847. When Newman joined it, therefore, it was, so to speak, in its childhood. It will easily be understood, therefore, that much amazement was excited (as is shown by the following letters), by his fellow guests at some large dinner parties at which he was present, when Newman withstood valiantly the long siege of savoury dishes at his elbow; and it seemed as if, though present in body, he was absent in appetite. This amazement was scarcely lessened when, after passing seventeen dishes, at length he threw the gates of his personal fortress open before some small omelet (prepared specially for him by the cook), and that, practically, formed his entire dinner!

To Newman's mind the theory of Vegetarianism was proved. He published some *Essays on Diet*; and was always an exponent of its rational claims on mankind.

Since the days when he wrote up the subject, many people have come over to his way of thinking, and the way is made easy for those who wish to follow its *obiter dicta* for health.

But it is quite as keenly a subject for debate now as formerly among a large proportion of men, though perhaps few among anti–vegetarians would dispute the point that there are, and must be, certain conditions involved by anti–vegetarianism which can hardly be evaded, or defended. One of these conditions, of course, is that it is not always possible to detect some diseases in flesh sold for food: and that these diseases are communicable to man; another, the degrading spectacle of the slaughter– house; another, the presence in our midst of the butcher's shop, with all its revolting display: [Footnote: I have not forgotten that M. Zola contended that the atmosphere of a butcher's shop conduced to the best and most healthy complexions of those who served in it!] another, as Mr. Josiah Oldfield points out to us, that "horticulture ... would employ an enormously greater amount of labour than does stock–raising, and so tend to afford a counter current to the present downward drift, and to congested labour centres." Mr. Oldfield urges also that "all elements for perfect nutrition in assimilable forms are found in a proper vegetarian dietary."

I have not opportunity for finding out in what years Newman took up this practical dietary of vegetarianism for himself, but I think it must have been towards the latter end of his life. Mention will be found in the Reminiscences contributed by Mrs. Bainsmith, the sculptor, relating to his bringing across occasionally, when she and her father and mother lived just opposite the Professor's house at Weston–super–Mare, some particularly delicious vegetarian dish (concocted by his own cook), which he had thought his friends could not fail to appreciate.

The following letters have been kindly sent me for reproduction by Mr. F. P. Doremus in connection with Newman's views on Vegetarianism:—

To Mr. F. P. Doremus from Professor Newman.

"*21st Sept.*, 1883.

"Dear Sir,

* * * * *

"I *deliberately prefer* the rule of our Society and by preference adhere to it. But I have never interpreted it as severely as I find some to do. On some occasions, in early years, when I could get no proper vegetarian food, I have eaten some small bit of ham fat (as I remember on *one* occasion) to aid dry potato from sticking in my throat. I do not interpret our rule as forbidding *exceptional* action *under stress of difficulty*. But when I found what a fuss was made about this, and saw that many people took the opportunity of *inferring* that a simple act implied a habit, I saw that it was unwise to give anyone a handle of attack....

"I can only say that I interpret our rules conscientiously, and obey them according to my interpretation faithfully. I do not see in our profession any vow or engagement comparable to that about *never tasting* intoxicating drink. If my wife, who is not a professed vegetarian (though in practice she is all but one), asks me to taste a bit of flesh and see... whether it is good, I find nothing in our rules to forbid my gratifying her *curiosity*. In that case I do not take it *as diet* to nourish me nor to gratify me. My words of adhesion simply declared that I had abstained from such *food* for half a year, and *I intended to abstain in the future*. Of course this forbids my *habit* or any *intention* to the contrary; but I deprecate interpreting this as a vow or as a trap and a superstition. One who feels and believes as I do the vast superiority of our vegetarian food, never can desire, unless perhaps in some abnormal state of illness, the inferior food....

"Faithfully yours,

"F. W. Newman."

"*1st Oct.*, 1883.

"Dear Sir,

"... On reading yours anew after some ten days or less, I think I ought to notice what you say of an unknown publisher.

"I cannot remember that for twenty years I have ever eaten in the company of any well–known publisher (anyone known to *me* as a publisher) except Mr. Nicolas Trubner *before* I joined the Vegetarians, and *one other* more recently. The latter was in the house of a lady friend who always anxiously humoured me by providing a *special dish* for me.

"Her cook was not skilful in *our* cookery, but did her best. I remember distinctly who was present on this occasion with this respected publisher. It was a luncheon with meats. I ate at the same table, and it may very easily have escaped his notice that a different dish was handed to me.

* * * * *

"I have several times sat at this friend's table with a large number of guests. I remember once counting that seventeen dishes were handed to me. I dined on my own food to the great marvel of those near me....

"I have always maintained that the main reason for proclaiming any *rule* of diet is, that the outsiders may be afforded facts to aid their own judgment; and that our engagement has no other element of obligation than that we shall not vitiate the materials of such judgment.

"Therefore also I have advocated several grades—for instance, an engagement allowing of *fish* as food (which many will take who will not go our length), and another in which absence from home (where one cannot arrange the cookery) is an exemption. I rejoice also in the Daniclete rule. Provided that it is KNOWN what is the diet, we give valuable information."

"*14th Oct.*, 1883.

* * * * *

"I knew that the publisher to whom you referred could only be Mr. Kegan Paul, who met me some few years back at luncheon in the house of my friends the Miss Swanwicks: that until *you told* me his name, I thought it better not to write to him. But thereupon I wrote and explained to him that my friend Miss Anna Swanwick knew perfectly that I could not accept their hospitality (as I have habitually done for a week or more at a time) if they expected me to partake of any food inconsistent with the rules of our Society. I long ago furnished her with some of our recipes, and she *showed her cook* always to make a *special* dish for me. At one of their dinner parties I remember the amazement of guests at my passing *all* the dishes, as at first it seemed, until my own little dish came. I told Mr. Kegan Paul that *he must have mistaken* what was in my plate (perhaps crumb omelette *browned over*—which I remember the cook was apt to give me) for some fish of which he and others were partaking. I have no doubt that this was the whole matter...."

"I am sincerely yours,

"F. W. Newman."

The closing letter in this series is evidently an answer to some questions from Mr. Doremus as regards Newman's portrait, and as regards the incidents of his life.

"My life has been eminently uneventful." When one remembers in how many questions of social reform, of theology, of written matter, Newman had been concerned, this short sentence strikes one's eyes strangely enough. For what is an "event"? Surely it does not mean only something which is a carnal happening: a material outbreak in some form or other which occurs before our eyes? Surely there are far greater spiritual "events" than physical ones? And of *this* kind of event Newman's life had been full. Originality of thought, of conception, of aim, is the Event which takes precedence of all other. And these events were strewn like Millet's "Sower" from side to side of his path: to take the true Latin significance of the word, they *came out* from him.

"*31st July*, 1884.

"Dear Sir,

"Your letter has been forwarded to me from home to this place [Keswick].... Messrs. Elliot and Fry (Baker Street, Portman Square), recently by pressure induced me to let them take my photograph. In fact they took four, in different positions, all judged excellent, all of cabinet size. Each, I believe, costs 2/–. I have none at my disposal. With or without my leave, anyone can publish them in any magazine. Now, as to my biography—my life has been eminently uneventful. There is nothing to tell but my studies, my successive posts as a teacher, and the list of books, etc., from my pen, *unless one add* the effects of study on my CREED, which more than one among you might desire *not* to make prominent in the *Food Reformer*.

　　* * * * *

"Can I assent to the request that I will myself write something? Others might wish to know in how many *Antis* I have been and am engaged!! Certainly more than you will care to make known will go into two pages of your magazine.

"I am, sincerely yours,

"F. W. Newman."

Two letters to Dr. Nicholson from Newman I think may be given here: one in April, 1875, and one in June, 1881, as both bear strongly on the vegetarian question:—

"25 *April*, 1875.

"My dear Nicholson,

"How time flies! Bearded men, active in moral and political questions, tell me they know nothing of the Austro–Hungarian events, because they happened when they were children.

"One of them asked me to give a lecture on Austria and Hungary of the Past, as he was curious and totally ignorant.... We are overrun with every kind of meeting, and the public are sated....

* * * * *

"Happily every day is too short for me, and I cannot have time on my hands.... I do not know whether you have attended the movement against vivisection, which is becoming lively. It has long been a dire horror to me. I rejoice to see that Sir W. Thomson, [Footnote: Sir William Thomson, born 1843, was late President of the Royal College of Surgeons, Ireland; Exam. in Surgery, Queen's University and Royal College of Surgeons, Ireland.] and other scientific men, desire a severe restriction to be put on it. I agree heartily with those who say we have no more RIGHT to torture a dog than to torture a man; but I fear that to move at present with Mr. Jesse for the total prohibition will only give to the worst practices a longer lease of life.

"Our vegetarianism is becoming more active with the pressure from the high price of butcher's meat. Not that we make many entire conversions, but plentiful well–wishers and half–converts, and a great increase in the belief that *too much* flesh meat is eaten, and that the doctors are much to blame for having pressed it as they press wine and ale, calling it 'generous' food. At the same time it is remarkable that the argument against slaughter–houses and for tenderness to tame animals plays a more decisive part, especially with women, than economic and sanitary arguments.... I am ever in experiment on something. At present it is on cacao butter and vegetable oils. We esteem the cacao butter for *savoury dishes* very highly. Messrs. Cadbury sell it 'to me and my friends' for 1s. a lb. In pastry and sweets the chocolate smell offends most people; but my wife likes it. It is too hard to spread on cold meat.

* * * * *

"The gardens are becoming sprightly. I have not had success with new vegetables, viz. German peas, celery, turnips, Belgian red dwarf beans. The drought last summer was bad.

No *warm rain* in spring last year.

"Ever yours heartily,

"F. W. Newman."

The following is quoted from the second letter I mentioned:—

"I send to you a Penny Vegetarian Cookery Book herewith. Surely I was a Vegetarian when I last was with you? I began the practice in 1867. But let me recite: (1) At breakfast and the third meal I need nothing but what all fleshmeaters provide. (2) At dinner the utmost that I need is *one* Vegetarian dish, which may be a soup. (3) If it so happen that you have any *really solid* sweet puddings that alone will suffice. (4) For the *one* Vegetarian dish good *brown* bread and butter is an acceptable substitute, or rather fulfilment. But I confess I am desirous of propagating everywhere a knowledge of our peculiar dishes, which teach how to turn to best account the manifold and abundant store of leaves, roots, and grains, besides pulse.

"My wife is fully able to impart practical knowledge: to please me, and see that others please me, she has given great attention to Vegetarian cookery for many years back...."

CHAPTER XVI. NATIVE REPRESENTATION IN INDIAN GOVERNMENT

It is rare indeed that an Englishman looks at India as Francis Newman looked at it. Fifty years ago—probably longer—he put his finger on exactly the spot which to-day is the crux which most puzzles and baffles politicians. In social and intellectual questions his were the clear– sighted, far–focussed eyes that reached beyond the measures of most men's minds. He saw clearly, fifty years ago, that India was drawing ever closer and closer to an inevitable terminus. That she was beginning to recognize —every year more definitely—her ultimate destination: was beginning to realize, too, that her foreign rulers were aware also of that terminus, but were not very anxious that she should reach it. Nay, were practically rather jogging her elbow to prevent her becoming so conscious of the direction in which the tide of affairs was drifting.

Nevertheless it is becoming more and more patent to everyone who really studies the question impartially that things are not what they were fifty or sixty years ago; that a critical juncture is drawing ever nearer and nearer—a juncture which inevitably will mean great changes for the governed and the governors.

Even the slow–moving East does move appreciably in half a century, when centres of education are doing their best to train Indians in European ideas of civilization, in European ideas of government, and of the authority which learning gives. We cannot expect to educate and yet leave those we educate exactly where we find them; for with education comes invariably, inevitably, the growth of ideas planted by it—their growth, and no less invariable fruition. To show someone all that is to be gained by reaching forward, and then to expect him not to reach, but to remain quiescent, is the act of a fool.

We have, as a nation, so taken it for granted that India is our own to do as we like with, that it is perhaps not a pleasant reminder which faces us as we cast our thoughts back to the initial steps taken by ourselves in the days which preceded the formation of the Honourable East India Company. It bids us realize that at first, as Francis Newman says in his *Dangerous Glory of India*, "neither king, statesmen, nor people ever deliberately planned from the beginning or desired such an empire. It began as a set of mercantile establishments which took up private arms for mere self–defence.... The Honourable East India Company was glad to legitimate its position by accepting from the Grand Mogul the subordinate position of a rent–collector; indeed, from the beginning to the end of its political career it was animated by a consistent and unswerving disapproval of aggression and fresh conquest."

Since that time, however, the English dominion spread rapidly. Since that time we became more and more aware of what a splendid field lay ready for occupation by our surplus population. Since that time we have moved forward through a vast country that formerly, through lack of European ways of civilization and co–operation, practically lay at our feet. It is true that we have done much—very much for India. It is impossible for anyone to deny that. We have brought to her doors European civilization; modern points of view; the miracles of new discoveries in science; inventions for making the wheels of life move easier; opportunities for cultivating and selling her land's produce, and for its quick transport. We have lifted her up—yes, but here is where the mental shoe pinches—we have insisted on preventing her from reaching her full stature. We have trained her sons to be able to work side by side with ourselves in various official duties;

and then when they are desirous—as is indeed only the inevitable consequence of their education—of entering the lists side by side with Englishmen, they find there is no crossing the rubicon which officially divides the two nations.

It is true that many Anglo–Indians stand aghast at this idea that they should cross it, but it is only those who are unaware that, as a general rule, education and environment combined come out as top dog over heredity in most instances in which it plays a part. It is only those who, when they go out to India, take, as it were, England with them, and fail to recognize how far Indian points of view and power of dealing with things have progressed. It is only those who have forgotten—if indeed they ever truly realized it—that it is a point of honour that such a proceeding should be carried out, if we, as Englishmen, remember all that the notable charter of 1833 bound us to do.

For the charter of 1833 [Footnote: During Lord Grey's ministry.] definitely promised that native Indian subjects of the English Government were to be admitted on equal terms with English subjects *to every office of State*, except that of governor–general or commander–in–chief. Not only that, but the solemn proclamation of the late Queen was issued in 1858, pledging the word of Sovereign and Parliament that the "sole aim of British rule in India was the welfare of the Indian people, and that no distinction would be made between Indians and Europeans in the government of the country, on the grounds of race, or creed, or colour."

As Francis Newman says very clearly, it is a "task which we have voluntarily assumed–to rule India, which means" (the italics are his) " *to defend it from itself in infancy, to train it into manhood....* It presupposes that the people gradually get more and more power until, like a son who comes of age, the parental control is discontinued.... We cannot take the last steps first, nor can we abruptly and recklessly resign our post...."

The Hon. M. G. K. Gokhale, in a keenly interesting paper read before the East India Association in the summer of 1906, states very definitely the point of view of educated Indians as regards our unfulfilled pledges of nearly eighty years since. He says: "Until a few years ago, whatever might have been thought of the pace at which we were going, there was no general disposition to doubt the intention of the rulers to redeem their plighted word. To–day, however, the position is no longer the same.... There is no doubt that the old faith of the people in the character and ideals of British rule has been more than shaken.... Half a century of Western education, and a century of common laws, common administration, common grievances, common disabilities, have not failed to produce their natural effect even in India.... Whatever a certain school of officials in India may say, the bulk of educated Indians have never in the past desired a severance of the British connection.... "But, he adds: "It is a critical juncture in the relations between England and India.... The educated classes in India ... want their country to be a prosperous, self– governing, integral part of the Empire, like the colonies, and not a mere poverty–stricken bureaucratically–held possession of that Empire."

Fifty years ago Francis Newman was urging with all the force in his power —and no one in his day was more farsighted in detecting just that social reform which would make more and more insistent demand for a hearing, as decade followed decade—that it was to our own interest as a nation, as well as the only honourable course open to us, to open up public offices in India to the educated native. It need not, he showed, be done otherwise than with caution, and gradually "many variations" were "imaginable; many different ways might succeed, if only the *right end in view*" was "steadily held up, namely, to introduce, fully and frankly, *into true equality with ourselves*" [Footnote: To "exclude natives from all high office," Sir Charles Napier said once emphatically, "is what debases a nation."] (again the italics are his) "as quickly as possible, and as many as possible, of the native Indians whose loyalty could be counted on.... Lord Grey and his coadjutors, in renewing the charter of 1833, understood most clearly that nothing but an abundance of black faces in the highest judicature, and intelligent Indians of good station in the high police, could administer India uprightly.... Every year that we delay evils become more inveterate and hatred accumulates. To train India into governing herself, until English advice is superfluous, would be to both countries a lasting benefit, to us a lasting glory."

Now, what are the "evils" which "every year become more inveterate" in our method of government in India? Perhaps one of the most palpable is the strongly centralized bureaucracy. Another, is the constant change of men in chief office every five years. Another, is that all competitive examinations are held in London. Mr. Gokhale very rightly urges that it is a great deal to require of an Indian that he should have to come all the way to England for these examinations *on the chance* of passing, and suggests their being held simultaneously in India and in England. Another, is that the field of law is the only officialdom open to the Indian, yet that there he is found capable of rising to the highest post. Another, that we have not pushed forward the education of the masses as far as we reasonably might if we had worked hand in hand with the educated classes. Mr. Gokhale tells us that to–day seven children out of eight are growing up in ignorance, and four villages out of five are as yet without a school–house.

There are other drawbacks to this system of foreign bureaucracy, which can only be briefly touched on here, but certainly Newman was right when he condemned that mistaken, high–handed measure of the autocratic East India Company—their destruction of all the local treasuries, and the manner in which these funds were diverted into the central treasury. Thus, as he pointed out very clearly, no moneys were left for the repair of roads, bridges, and tanks, etc. As he remarks, "In comparison with this monster evil, all other delinquencies seem to fade away."

As everyone probably is aware, Newman lost no opportunity in pressing home on the minds of his countrymen that it is decentralization that is so urgently needed; and that not alone in India, but in our own country as well. Repeatedly he urged that if Government is administered from one central bureaucracy, it follows inevitably that the business to be dealt with bulks so enormously that it is literally impossible to deal, in detail and with complete understanding, with the rights and wrongs of citizens at a distance in the provinces and remote parts of a big empire. Consequently, he was always trying to show how far more successfully local self–government—a local ward–mote, for instance—would deal with provincial matters in England. That every town should be, as it were, a little State, with all classes represented in it, and matters dealt with locally should only come up to the Central Parliament for veto or for sanction. In the same way he recommended strongly that in India every facility should be given to "voluntary (limited liability) companies to execute roads, works of irrigation, etc...." That country districts should be given local treasuries, as well as towns.

In "English institutions and their most necessary reforms," Newman declares and reiterates that this lack of local treasuries is a "hideous blunder," and adds, "every coin in every province is liable to be spent in some war." He urges other changes, which have come to pass in some measure, such as a Viceroy, a "prince of the blood royal," sent out to "receive their occasional homage." But there again lack of cooperation with the natives, lack of real understanding between us and them, have, as everyone is aware, worked havoc when a man [Footnote: It is impossible to forget in this connection what the *Tribune* called our "Curzonian statescraft" in the recent past.] without the necessary insight and sympathy into the people's points of view and ways of thought has been sent to posts of supreme authority.

There have been men of splendid capabilities for understanding and sympathizing with these points of view, men such as Sir James Outram, the Bayard of India; Sir John Malcolm, Lord Elphinstone, Sir George Russell Clerk, Lord Lawrence, Ovans, and many others, who helped forward the better understanding between England and India very greatly; and of these, Outram suffered grievous misrepresentations at the hands of his Government, Clerk was put aside, and Ovans had to stand his trial in England for an absolutely unjustifiable charge.

Whenever the question of co–operation and sympathy comes up, as from time to time it does, between Englishmen and Indians, whether it is fifty or sixty years ago, in Newman's day or now in the year of grace 1909, with a few honourable exceptions, the answer is identically the same. It is practically an unknown quantity. The East and West have not really met. Still the ranks of the service are absorbed by Englishmen; still, as all educated Indians protest, the "true centre of gravity for India is in London"; still India is unrepresented in the Viceroy's Executive Councils, and in Customs, Post, Survey, Telegraph, Excise, etc., and also in the Commissioned ranks of the Army; still, because district administration is to all intents and purposes not in existence, there is no compulsory education for boys *and* girls, though most educated Indians are very strongly in favour of it.

It is not, it cannot be, because our eyes, as a nation, have been shut to the fact of what the faults of our own administration have been in years gone by. If no one else had trumpeted them abroad, at least one man spoke out the whole truth and nothing but the truth about it in the last century: Francis, the great Social Reformer—Francis Newman, who was no time–server, no prophesier of smooth things; but, as much as in him lay, desired more than anything else to lay the whole unvarnished truth before his fellow men, things that concerned the weaker members of the community. In lecture after lecture he turned things to the "rightabout–face" which had hitherto been done *sub rosa* in India. He did in effect pull down the very rose tree which had acted as such an efficient shelter. His bull's– eye lantern always cast an uncompromising glare upon those sometimes very "shady" doings of our countrymen which characterized their treatment of natives in the early Victorian era, and—occasionally perhaps, even since.

No one has forgotten, for instance, the words of Mr. Halliday, Lieutenant– Governor of Bengal, when he described our police as a curse to India in 1854.

Newman reminded his countrymen that in 1852 a petition had been sent to the House of Commons from Lower Bengal, "among other grievous complaints," which "stated that by reason of the hardships inflicted on witnesses, the population" were averse from testifying to the ill–doings and tyranny of these police.

Again, as regarded the courts of law in India, Newman reminded us of the revelations contained in that volume by the Hon. Mr. Shore concerning our Government (the book which was withdrawn 1844).

It was there stated definitely that, until the days of Lord William Bentinck, Persian was the only language used in these courts. Consequently, as neither judge, nor clerk, nor litigating party, nor person accused, nor his witnesses understood it, it constantly happened that the case was a veritable *reductio ad absurdum*. No one knew what was happening until at last the man—if it was a case of murder—was shown that the case had gone against him by being shown the gallows!

It is true *nous avons change tout cela*, in these days, and the vernacular tongue is used instead, but now it is the judge who doesn't always know accurately what is going on, for he cannot always understand what the witnesses are saying! As Newman says very shrewdly: "If self– confident, he trusts his own impressions; if timid, he leans on the judgment of his native clerk; if formal and pedantic, he believes all clear and coherent statements. His weaknesses are watched, and it is soon understood whether he is to be better managed by fees to the clerk, or by the forging of critical evidence, in cases for which it is worth while. Very scandalous accounts have been printed in great detail ... and one thing is clear, that those Englishmen who have looked keenly into the matter and dare to speak freely, believe justice to have a far worse chance in such tribunals than before native judges."

Francis Newman tells us that his own eyes were opened to the prevailing state of things in those days, by "a very intelligent, and widely informed indigo–planter." He told him that when he first began indigo–planting, his partner had given this emphatic rule of conduct: "Never enter the Company's Courts!" And to his own amazed question as to what course of action was to be pursued when a difficulty arose, he clearly and openly explained. "If a native failed to pay us our dues, we never sued him, but simply publicly seized some of his goods, sold them by auction, deducted our claim from the proceeds, and handed over to him the balance." There is something almost humorous in this travesty of an *amende honorable* for so highhanded a measure!

One may in very deed be thankful that since the day of all these happenings, Indians *have*, as Mr. Gokhale tells us, "climbed in the field of law, to the very top of the tree," and can now deal out first–hand justice to their fellow countrymen.

I think I cannot give a fitter close to this chapter than by quoting Newman's suggestions as to measures of urgent importance with regard to our Indian Empire, which were made a little over forty years ago.

"The establishment of an Imperial Court in India to judge all causes.... The mark of a 'tyrant' (according to the Old Greeks) was his defence by a foreign body–guard: *we* bear that mark of illegitimate sway at present.

"To make India loyal, to save the yearly sacrifice of health or life to 10,000 young men, now the miserable victims of our army system, is so urgent an interest, that I put this topic foremost. Too much importance can hardly be given to it. Each soldier is said to cost us L100; hence the pecuniary expense also is vast. But until we restrain ourselves from aggression, all attempts permanently to improve our millions at home must be fruitless.... Our task is to rear India into political manhood, train it to English institutions, and rejoice when it can govern itself without our aid."

CHAPTER XVII. VOTES FOR WOMEN

There is always a large percentage of people who range themselves on the side of the majority in regard to any question of the day. They range themselves there not because of any principle involved, but simply and solely because they consider this mode of action expedient. And they feel far safer, far happier, taking the flabby, muscleless arm of Expediency than in venturing into unknown difficulties behind the uncompromisingly stiff figure of Principle. But there are others–thank God for them!—who hate the shifty, cunning eye of Expediency far too much to have anything to do with him. These others would far rather be in the minority in championing some good cause than with the "expedient" majority.

These others are the pioneers of civilization. Sometimes—to–day we have many cases in point as regards the social crusade of brave women against taxation without representation—they are martyrs as well as pioneers. But the splendid spirit of knight–errantry, which shone so vividly with the fire of enthusiasm in medieval days, is still abroad in our midst to–day. A few militant personalities fight for a great cause, a great principle— the raising of a better moral tone amongst us, the betterment of the lives of their fellows. Newman was one of these. His sword was always in the thickest of the fight when it was a fight against some social injustice to his fellow citizens. Forty years ago and more he spoke out in championship of woman's rights. So long ago as 1867 he led the movement which tilted at social wrongs, social injustices dealt out to the sex. It is a movement which has taken, as I said, more than half a century to make its way to the position it holds to–day. It has been opposed bitterly almost every inch of the way by men who love expediency, and turn their backs on the principle of the thing; which is fair play for women. Nevertheless, England is a country which prides herself on her keen sense of justice and freedom.

If Newman had done nothing else, his work for this movement would be unforgettable; his words were so outspoken, his way of dealing with the subject so broad–minded. In one of his articles he urged the following on his fellow men:—"Readers of History, and Lawyers, are aware that women's wrongs are an ancient and terribly persistent fact.... Why has our law been so unjust to women?—Because women never had a voice in the making of it, and men as a class *have not realized the oppression of women as a class*" (the italics are my own). "Men have deep in their hearts the idea that women *ought* to be their legal inferiors; that neither the persons of women nor their property ought to remain their own; that marriage is not a free union on equal terms; and that the law ought to favour the stronger sex against the weaker. It is remarkable that our law is more unjust to women than that of the great historically despotic nations, and in some important respects less favourable than that of the Turks. All these things point out that *equality of the sexes in respect to the Parliamentary Franchise* is essential to justice. The conscience of men is opening to the truth...." "Readers of newspapers cannot be ignorant of the miseries endured by wives from brutal husbands. In ordinary decorous families, sons at lavish expense are trained to self–support. The *daughters* in one class have nothing spent on their education; in another, are educated as elegant ornaments of a drawing–room, where they live in luxury for a parent's delight; yet when he dies, and their youth is spent, they are often turned adrift into comparative poverty, incompetent for self–help. When complaint is made of this, the ascendant sex graciously tells them, 'they ought to marry,' and this in a country where women are counted by the hundred thousand more numerous than men; where also men do not universally accept the state of marriage. Meanwhile, the law is made as if to dissuade the woman from such a remedy. If she dare to adopt it, it instantly strips her of all her property, great or little; [Footnote: Since then some amendment of the wrong has been done by the "Married Women's Property Act."] and if she earn anything, authorizes her husband to seize it by force. In the Marriage Service, the husband, as if in mockery, says, 'With all my worldly goods I thee endow': while the law allows him to gamble away her whole fortune the day after the marriage, or to live in riotous indulgence on *her* money, and give to her the barest necessaries of life.... He may maliciously refuse her the sight of her own children.... And if to gain one sight of them she return to his house for two days, the law holds her to have 'condoned' all his offences however flagrant."

Mr. Haweis many years ago said a very significant thing. He said that the best—if the rarest—men had always a good share of the woman nature in themselves. Francis Newman was one of these men. He understood the woman's point of view without any telling. He knew instinctively, intuitively, the mental cramp, the moral inability to rise to her full stature, which is induced by man's perpetual effort to fit her into a measured mould prepared by himself. He knew that if "a man's reach must exceed his grasp, or what's a heaven for?" what a hell faced the woman who could not even *reach* forward to fulfil all the many aims which she was conscious were stirring within her, longing for attainment. He had seen women, his countrywomen, shake the bars behind which they faced their world for the very passion of revolt against these man–set limits, which kept them in on every side. He knew that, of all hard fates, perhaps few are more bitter than to feel the power and ability within you to do some work as well as another does it, and yet to have no freedom to use that power. To be forced, by man–made laws, to wrap up your talent in the napkin of legal red–tapeism, when everything within you, perhaps, urges you to turn it to good account.

Let us look for one moment at some of the legal disabilities of women to– day. Perhaps some of us are hardly aware to what an almost incredible distance they reach.

Mr. Henry Schloesser, barrister–at–law of the Inner Temple, [Footnote: In his pamphlet published by the Women's Social and Political Union.] very explicitly explains how they affect women. "At Common Law the father is entitled against the mother to the custody of the children, and this right he could only forfeit by gross misconduct; so also he was entitled to prescribe their mode of education.... He remains *prima facie* the guardian of his children, *to the exclusion of the mother*" [the italics are my own]. "Alone of the learned professions, the medical is open to women...." (She constantly proves her aptitude to take the same honours as man as regards the others, but he still growls over his share and keeps *her* out.) "A husband is not bound at Common Law to cohabit with or maintain his wife."

These facts show luridly against the sky of woman's world, but perhaps few men know what purgatorial fires they light in many a woman's heart to–day. They show that man's injustice to her does not only concern her in public life, but even in the home life (to which he would fain limit her energies); she has practically no legal status at all. She has not even a right to her own children in the eye of the law. Quite recently a judge decided that "a woman is not a parent in the eye of the law," and therefore powerless in things relating to her children. She is excluded from the guardianship of them. Yet so curiously irrational is this same English law that, should any woman wronged by a man become mother to an illegitimate child, upon her falls the whole onus of its maintenance until it is sixteen years old. The man gets off scot–free; for the world which condones an offence (which is shared by both) in the case of the man, condemns it in the *woman*.

Thus, as Mr. Thomas Johnston [Footnote: *The Case for Woman's Suffrage*, by Thomas Johnston. Published by the Women's Social and Political Union.] very clearly puts it: "Where there is any stigma or blame, the woman bears it alone.... Under the law of England to–day a man can secure divorce by simply proving the unfaithfulness of his wife. But the wife, in order to obtain a divorce from her husband for the same unfaithfulness, must, in addition, prove cruelty or desertion." This in itself is very one–sided law, and certainly indefensible.

Francis Newman describes this law in no measured terms. He declares in his article on "Marriage Laws" (1867) that what undeniably needs reform in our country's government is "the extravagant power given by our law to a husband.... The exclusive right attributed to him over the children is unjust and pernicious. His rights over his wife's person [Footnote: According to English law, as evidenced in a recent case, the wife is *not* "a person" at all; presumably, therefore, she is simply his chattel!] are extreme and monstrous.... We need a single short, sweeping enactment that, *notwithstanding anything to the contrary in past statutes, no woman henceforth shall by marriage change her legal status or lose any part of her rights over property....*

* * * * *

"We implore all true and genuine Conservatives not to delay and use half– measures, but to do justice to the sex in good time. He who tries to uphold injustice is the true and efficient revolutionist, while he thinks he is Conservative."

He goes on to touch thus on what is perhaps the most cruel injustice of all—that the law permits a man to deprive his wife of the children, who, before God, are as equally hers as his:—

"Not only with regard to *property*, also in regard to *children*, the law is unjust to women. The mother has to undergo much in bringing a child to maturity—the agony of childbirth... the countless cares of tending and watching by night and day. The child becomes the darling of her heart, the image of her dreams, the great centre of her thoughts and hopes; and after all her toils, the law permits a husband to take the child permanently out of her sight, and (if he choose) to put it under the charge of an enemy ... who will fill its mind with falsehoods and teach it to hate and despise its mother. Such things are not possibilities merely and dreams; they are stern realities, and the law gives her no redress."

When one thinks of all that these words mean, one is face to face with the almost unthinkable fact that the case of the woman in England is unjust beyond description, and for this reason, that, as Newman says, "Men, who alone make the laws, make them with but little account of woman." At home with her children she is defenceless. She has no power over them, and her husband is not bound to "maintain" her, notwithstanding the sentence, which English law has made absolutely meaningless, of his marriage vow to her: "With all my worldly goods I thee endow."

In the world, if she have no husband or be unmarried, she is not a "person" in a legal sense; and during election time her house is described, in canvassing for votes, as having "no occupier"! In the world, too, she is unable to obtain a fair wage for her work. She may do the work as well as man, but nevertheless, in most cases, her pay is less. Mr. Johnston tells us that the average male worker's wage has been calculated to be about 18s., but the average woman worker's wage is only about 7s. And when women find out these many injustices suffered at home and in the world by their sex, as Miss Christabel Pankhurst says, they are absolutely unable to right these wrongs, for "women have no political power."

Here is the pivot round which the wrongs of women revolve—her lack of legal status, her voicelessness as regards the laws of her country, the country which is so openly irrational as to count her a "person" when it wants to get a tax out of her, but refuses to do so at any other time when she has something to ask of it in return!

Once the parliamentary vote is given to women, the same results would follow in England as have followed elsewhere. Wages and hours of labour are made just for women, as in many respects they have been now made for men. The laws of divorce are the same. Mothers are made joint guardians of their children with their fathers. The age of protection for girls is raised to 18. [Footnote: At the present moment, by the English law, a girl can contract a valid marriage at twelve years of age; a boy at fourteen. (See *Legal Status of Women*, by H. H. Schloesser.)] In New South Wales, after the women were given the vote, Dr. Mackellar brought in a bill to deal with the protection of illegitimate children, which has answered admirably; while in New Zealand and Australia the Wages Board, which the women's vote helped to pass, has raised in both countries the wages of women from 5s. to l6s. per week for the same amount of work done. And in other respects it has abolished sweating—that crucial question of crucial questions in England to–day.

There is another point, too, amongst many others, in which the vote helped the national life in Australia in the giving of old age pensions. Perhaps had women the vote here in England, the shameful system in which old men and women are separated in the last years of their life, as the workhouses ordain, would be altered. And this is a question which demands immediate attention—*immediate* attention; for more than L26,000,000 are paid by taxpayers each year to be spent in great part on our wretched system of poor laws.

Francis Newman was strongly against poor laws administered as they are in England to–day, as, indeed, is every thoughtful man. He was also strongly of opinion that there should be women on juries in some cases. And indeed it is a fact that women magistrates, as well as women jurors, are most certainly a *sine qua non* in those cases where, at the present moment, owing to juries being composed of men only, common justice for the unrepresented Englishwoman in relation with the other sex is not, in a great proportion of cases, rendered her. But even were women made eligible for these offices, it would be no new thing, for in Mary Tudor's reign there were two women appointed justices of the peace; and, of course, always there has been a provision in law for "a jury of matrons" in certain cases.

Indeed, when one goes far enough back in research into most questions, the invariable lesson, is taught us, which we are always so reluctant, in our cocksureness of the "antiquity" of our present–day conditions of life, to learn, and we find that our arrangements very often are *not* "as it was in the beginning," but only mushroom growths of a decade or two. As Mrs. Wolstenholme Elmy very justly says in her recent pamphlet on "Woman's Franchise," women possessed voting rights from time immemorial, and the year 1832 was the year when they were dispossessed of many ancient rights by the Reform Act passed in that year.

As regards other disabilities of women, Francis Newman wrote very fully and very strongly upon them, and it is impossible to leave them unmentioned here. In 1869 he wrote: "There is one important matter which young men need specially to be taught, viz. that at no time of life is any man ... exempt from the essential duty of curbing animal impulses.... Nothing so paralyzes his force of Will as to be told that some men have from God the gift of continence, and *others have it not*. This doctrine is disastrously prominent in the Anglican marriage service, and is borrowed from St. Paul. But that great and deep–hearted apostle was unmarried and without personal experience. He writes, not as one revealing supernatural communications, *but as imparting his best wisdom....* A general and just inference is, that a firm self–restraint is necessary and salutary for every man."

It is impossible to write more strongly and clearly of the wickedness of women's ancestral personal rights being swept away than does Newman in articles published in the fourth volume of his *Miscellanies*. He does not disguise the shameful state of the law as it affects woman to–day, and as it is carried out by Government—that law which makes wrongdoing so easy and unpunishable for man, and so hard and unjust to woman. The unjustifiableness of certain laws was shown up with no uncertain pen by him. He was himself convinced of their iniquity; and once convinced, he stood forward as a modern John the Baptist, spared no one, and passionately accused his countrymen of the injustice, immorality, and cruelty of their making one law for men and another for women. He inveighed against the world's point of view of this subject: and this not once, nor twice, but constantly; and urged with all his might that these wrongs to his countrywomen should be righted. Nevertheless his articles, many of them, are forgotten. The dust of neglect is lying thick upon them on many an unused shelf to–day. His voice has long been silent; and no doubt it has been said of him (as it was by a Church dignitary of Father Dolling at his death): "We shan't be worried any more by *him* now about the righting of social abuses." Laws against which Newman declaimed are not altered yet, and we are a long way from those far–reaching reforms he advocated. But the words he wrote are not dead. They are in our midst to– day, and they stir depths to–day in the hearts of his countrymen in suggestions towards social reformation; towards the righting of wrongs just as glaring to–day as they were a century ago. Questions which can never be put superficially aside, by men who, like Newman, cannot endure to leave a social wrong unredressed, if they can by any searching find the remedy.

CHAPTER XVIII. FRANCIS NEWMAN AND HIS RELIGION

More than one person has said to me in connection with this memoir: "If the whole of Frank Newman's heterodox religious opinions be not given, the book will lose half its point."

To my mind there are quite two, if not more, sides to this question. My strongest argument, however, in favour of only dealing briefly with them is this: It is quite true that Agnosticism more or less held its sway over him during the years between 1834 and 1879. I am quite aware of how tremendous a slice that is of a man's life. But it is not an overwhelming testimony when one comes to look at it not from the worldly point of view.

There are periods in which Time—as Time—seems almost beside the mark. "A thousand years in Thy sight are but as yesterday." When the Israelites had once achieved their journey through the wilderness—nay, even through the earlier time of tyranny amongst the Egyptians–I suppose the actual years seemed as a dream *when one awaketh*.

I myself have known forty years pass, for someone afflicted with a terrible mental disability, as a watch in the night, once light pierced through the clouds of the long–darkened mental vision. Time, as sex, is purely temporary. In this present world we cannot do without either, but when Time itself passes for good, the old implements which were necessary to make the clock go round will pass likewise.

So, in Newman's case, when that tremendous slice in a man's life—forty- five years—was overpast, he sloughed off the old garments of Agnosticism, and came back to the Christian faith professed by him in early childhood so conscientiously—and, indeed, up to the year after his missionary journey, 1834.

This fact influences me largely in the matter of dealing only briefly with the time–as regards his religious professions—which lies between these two dates, and for these reasons, which I hope to prove, carry considerable weight.

The first is that people are mistaken in considering that it was his religious opinions which made Newman great. The real valour of his life was shown in the splendid aspects of Social Reform which he showed to the world; the way of the New Citizenship, of the New Patriotism, which he was for ever preaching and writing about. He was the Perseus of To–day whose wholehearted efforts were spent in freeing the Andromedas from their antiquated bonds and fetters; whose good sword was ever pointed at the throats of the dragons which lift their ugly heads against freedom— against reforms of all sorts; the dragons who take so long in dying.

But there are many who will regret bitterly that a man who served his generation so splendidly as he did in these matters should ever have written a book such as the *Phases of Faith*; for though it is undeniably clever, yet it is not convincing; and very much of it is very painful reading for those who do not care to wander out of the way in the wilderness of religious speculation and doubt.

Newman declares in this book that he did not give up Christianity; yet he gave up all that made Christianity Christianity. He said in it that he was looking for a "religion which shall combine the tenderness, humility, and disinterestedness that are the glories of the purest Christianity, with that activity of intellect and untiring pursuit of truth." [Footnote: He said once he wished for a religion which should combine the best out of all religions in the world.]

When he mentions that, in his time, "of young men at Oxford not one in five seemed to have any convictions at all," he seems to imply that it was on account of the desire for a new religion; whereas it was far more traceable to the after–effects of Calvinism and Puritanism, which have stuck, as spiritual limpets, to England's religious rocks ever since they first reached them. They are certainly looser in their hold than was the case formerly, but they are there still.

Phases of Faith was published in 1850. But the year before a book of far more religious suggestiveness had come out, though that too was a book of opposition to the accepted forms of religion, *The Soul: its Sorrows and Aspirations*.

Regarded as a work postulating a new spiritual point of view, it was vague and unsatisfying. It was without form and void. It desired that most unsatisfying thing, a religion with no dogmas:—those stakes which preserve the ground on which grow the flowers of religious truth, from those who come but to spoil and destroy.

Yet, with all its lack of convincing power, and those parts of it which are, like *Phases of Faith*, painful reading and profitless—to Christians—there are here and again striking passages such as this, whose beauty cannot fail to appeal to us: "None can enter the kingdom of Heaven without becoming a little child. But behind and after this there is a mystery revealed to but few; namely, if the Soul is to go on into higher spiritual blessedness, it must become a *woman*. Yes, however manly thou be among men, it must learn to love being dependent; must lean on God, not solely from distress and alarm, but because it does not like independence or loneliness.... God is *not* a stern Judge; exacting every tittle of some law from us.... He does not act towards us (spiritually) by generalities ... but His perfection consists in dealing with each case by itself as if there were no other...." And again: "The Bible is a blessed book if we do not stifle the Holy Spirit within us."

The second reason why I touch on these religious opinions (before mentioned) but briefly, is because of my own *strong impression* since I have been writing this memoir, that in that next chapter of existence upon which Newman has now entered, he may not impossibly be nearer the Light, the religious truth, which here he so earnestly sought, but mistakenly; and in his regret for his own phases of religious unfaith, now cast aside, may not wish them to be recapitulated anew. There is a certain pathetic sentence of his, in a letter in later life, which seems to give a certain amount of confirmation to this idea: "It is a sad thing to have printed erroneous fact. I have three or four times contradicted and renounced the passage ... *but I cannot reach those whom I have misled*."

I have mentioned before that Francis Newman returned to his earlier faith in Christianity a few years before his death.

It remains, therefore, to give the proofs which have been put into my hands regarding this fact.

Two of his very greatest friends, Anna Swanwick and Dr. Martineau, received from his own hands the knowledge that he wished it to be known that he died a Christian. I shall give a quotation from one of Newman's last letters to the former, from Miss Bruce's *Memoir of Recollections of Anna Swanwick*. In almost illegible writing, he says:—

"If I live through this year, I hope to effect, by aid of a friend's eyes, a third ... edition of my *Paul of Tarsus*, with grateful acknowledgment that, in spite of a few details, I more and more come round to the substance of the views of my honoured friend, James Martineau. Also I close by my now sufficient definition of a Christian—'one, who in heart, and steadily, is a disciple of Jesus in upholding the prayer called the Lord's Prayer as the highest and purest in any known national religion.' I think J. M. will approve this."

I should also like to add Miss Bruce's own words in this connection:—

"He" (Newman) "was drawn back at the end of his long life by the sweet reasonableness and loving sympathy of his friend Anna Swanwick, and the teaching of Dr. Martineau."

Also these words from a letter written by Anna Swanwick: "It is delightful to me to think how, when the veil shall have fallen from the eyes of our friend" (F. W. Newman), "he will love and venerate Him in Whose footsteps he is unconsciously treading." Yet I must add here that in a letter from Newman to Anna Swanwick (to which I had access) in 1897, there is no definite statement of his belief in Immortality. "If God gives me immortality, I am content. If it pleases Him to annihilate me, it is well. Let Him do with me as seemeth to Him good."

As regards Dr. Martineau's statement, I quote now from a letter received by me from Mr. William Tallack, who gave me particulars of a letter written in 1903, by Mr. W. Garrett Horder, on a meeting he had with Dr. Martineau:—

"Not more than three or four years before his death I was sitting in an omnibus at Oxford Circus, when Dr. Martineau, accompanied by his daughter, got in and took seats by my side. After I had confessed my pleasure at seeing him, he said, 'I think you ought to know that the other day I had a letter from Frank Newman saying that, when he died, he wished it to be known that he died in the Christian faith.'"

To my mind these strong assertions that Newman wished it known that he "died a Christian," which he wrote to two of his closest friends, speak for themselves.

There was also another, Rev. J. Temperley Grey, who visited Newman constantly in his last illness, and who said of his final conversion these words, in the "In Memoriam" address he gave at Newman's funeral:—

"Of late his" (Newman's) "attitude towards Christ had undergone a great change. He confessed to me only very recently that for years he had held on to Christianity by the skirts of S. Paul; 'but now,' he said, 'Paul is less and less, and Christ is more and more.' He made this statement with an emphasis and an emotion which conveyed the impression that he wished it to be regarded as a final testimony."

To those of us who are Christians these are strong words, showing clearly where, in his last illness and failing strength, he had turned for final help.

Some have called Francis Newman an atheist. But he was no atheist. A theist for many years he was: but it was because he was unable to reconcile certain historical difficulties, or to get rid of certain earlier Calvinistic tendencies, or to accept certain dogmas which seemed to him impossible of acceptation, and in this last respect he is certainly not alone.

Mr. Temperley Grey's testimony to Newman as a fellow townsman, during his last days at Weston−super−Mare (he died 6th Oct., 1897), shows him to us as a man who *acted* to his fellow men, and women, as a Christian should, although he did not, till near the end, *believe* as one.

"Without depreciating in the least his illustrious brother, it may truly be said that while the one was a saint in the cloister, the other was a saint in the very thick of life's battle. [Footnote: "Henry Newman... stood for a spiritual Tory; while Francis Newman was a spiritual Radical" (*Morning Leader*, October, 1897).] ... I would speak of him rather as the neighbour and townsman who moved to and fro among us ... and whom, distrusting at first, we ultimately reverenced and loved for his nobility of character, his simplicity of life, his tenderness of conscience, his devoutness of spirit, and his generosity of heart.

"Theologically we were far apart, but we were entirely with him in his enthusiasm for righteousness, his sympathy with downtrodden and oppressed peoples.... We were with him also in his untiring efforts to secure for women their rightful place in the shaping of our national life, and in his splendid protests against the tortures inflicted in the name of science on the poor, helpless animals, our dumb brothers. To hear the old man eloquently discourse upon these themes was to be morally uplifted.... Those of us who were admitted into the inner circle of his friends were profoundly impressed by his devoutness. He lived as in the Presence of God, and his prayers in the home, so simple, so trustful, so reverential, were always a means of grace, a real refreshment.

* * * * *

"He was a true philanthropist. He championed the cause of the oppressed everywhere.... A room in his house was set apart as a guest–chamber for persons needing a change to the seaside, but whose circumstances barred the way; and not a few were fresh equipped for the work and battle of life, as a result of his thoughtful hospitality.... Francis Newman stood by himself in his greatness, his goodness, his simplicity, and we shall not find his like again.... Above all, our friend was a truth seeker. This was the ruling passion of his life."

Mrs. Temperley Grey tells me that it was always Newman's first wife's great hope that her husband should be the means, through his ministrations during the last part of Newman's life, of leading him back to his original faith. Mrs. Newman used deeply to regret Newman's lack of definite belief, but always said when the subject was raised, "Cannot they understand that my husband is under a cloud—a mist, as it were?" Both the brothers, the Cardinal and Francis Newman, through the greater part of their lives had been restlessly searching for truth—for certainty—in their faith. Calvinism had been the black cloud under which they had both been brought up. If the *obiter dictum* of a celebrated Cardinal in the Roman Church be correct: "Give *me* the child till he is seven years old, and he will be a Jesuit all his life," then indeed it shows the tremendous power of habit, for it was only through much tribulation, through passionate inward wrestlings with those terrible tenets, and through many searchings of heart, that either brother made his way out of its toils at length. The Cardinal sought above all things Truth, through authority; no one will forget those soul–stirring words of his in his *Apologia pro Vita Sua* in which he speaks of the great peace that at last quieted his doubts and fears when he was received into the Roman Church. To many of us Authority *is* the life–buoy which

242

supports us "o'er crag and torrent till the night is gone"; but Francis Newman could not believe in it. "Authority is the bane," he would say, "of religion." He must see with his intellectual eyes, to be saved. He must see and touch Truth for himself; his intellectual self must be convinced, or he must stand outside the creeds he knew—a questioner still.

But he was honest and open in his aloofness. Did it mean loss of a distinguished brilliant worldly career (as it did at Oxford in 1830)? Well, then the career *must* be lost, for he could not bring himself to sign to doctrines which he did not believe. Did it mean unpopularity, that he held certain views on Social Reform? Well, rather than compromise, rather than temporize, he *would* stand out alone rather than yield an iota of what he held to be the true Progressive Aims for People and Land. Only—and this was a flaw, and no small one either—he often wrote his religious opinions so openly as to pain his readers. In many of his letters which I have read there are expressions relating to the religious dogmas held by his correspondents which are bluntly, unrestrainedly, bitterly used. It is true that often, at the close of a letter, there follows a hope that he had not hurt his friends' feelings; but that he must, at all costs, be open as to his own beliefs. But that apology only came as an after–thought, as it were as an attempt to dress the wound which he himself had made, and is quite unable to do away with the impression produced by the written word. *Litera scripta manet.*

In writing on "The National Church" thirty–three years after he had refused to sign the Thirty–nine Articles, he said, with emphasis, "Truthfulness of the *individual* man is essential to moral worth; but for this very reason the *system* of the Church must be lax in order to allow truthfulness to individuals." This is curious reasoning, and subversive of the idea of Unity. Still, as no one can deny that as Life implies Progression, so as regards the Churches, the inspired words that they should be "led into all truth" surely allow for progression also into higher regions of knowledge and methods of teaching. To allow for this spirit of progression Newman held that a State Church should not be tied down to fixed conditions. "No general Church system will go so far as the foremost minds.... All the moderate and wisest historians of the Anglican Church have extolled its foundations. They have judged that, take it as a whole, the Reformation went as far as the collective nation was then able to go." That it "was necessary to reform it in the sixteenth century in order to harmonize it with the higher intelligence of the best minds, so far as could be done without making it useless to the inferior minds." All this has a certain truth, but when all is said, the fact forces itself upon one that after all it is a matter for debate whether the Reformation was a "progressive" movement at all: whether it did not in reality delay progression. For it is well known to–day that it was really managed by the machinations of one of the most selfish and unprincipled of kings [Footnote: Whose conduct at this time largely hinged on the refusal of the Pope to grant him his wished–for divorce from Katherine.]—who was only progressive in the matter of wives—and by his ministers, who were, many of them, men of vile characters and greed. As to motive, it is very patent to–day what *that* was. It was that of the man who covets his neighbour's goods, i.e. the lands and moneys of the monasteries and churches, and who whitewashes his sin when his desire is satisfied. There is besides sufficient proof to–day that the great bulk of the unrepresented nation did *not* regard this act of wholesale robbery as "lawful and necessary," nor that it "harmonized" the Church "with the higher intelligence of the best minds."

To the end of his life (from his Oxford days to his death), of course, Newman was never greatly in sympathy with the Anglican Church. He did not, even at the end, own himself bound by her dogmas or obedient to her conditions. To go further into the question is, I think, not desirable here. It is enough to say that though *he was outside the visible Church*, yet he was, in life and spirit, "not far off". As was said of Stanley, "he believed more than he knew." His "life was in the right," though his doubts and rationalism led him into unbeliefs, which only at the close of his long life he renounced. And he had a far deeper longing for religious truth than have many conventional Churchmen.

CHAPTER XIX. LAST YEARS, CHARACTERISTICS, AND SOME LETTERS RELATING TO THE *EARLY LIFE OF THE CARDINAL*

It will be remembered that Francis Newman retired from his official duties at University College in 1863, with the title Emeritus Professor. As most of us are aware, this word "Emeritus" was originally given to Roman soldiers who had served out their term and been discharged, on the understanding of being given a settled sum of money which was practically the equivalent of our English half–pay. The term is now used to designate a professor who has been "honourably relieved" of his office, either because of physical disability or on account of a term of long service fulfilled. It is, in effect, a retiring pension.

Memoir and Letters of Francis W. Newman

As will have been seen by letters from Newman which precede this chapter, he retired from the office of Professor, but in no sense from his work of writing, studying, and lecturing. The enormous number of books published will testify to this. His five volumes of *Miscellanies*, his *Reminiscences of Two Exiles, Europe of the Near Future*, translation of the *Odes of Horace*, [Footnote: Which did not meet with the approval of Matthew Arnold.] *Handbook and Dictionary of Modern Arabic, Kabail Vocabulary, Libyan Vocabulary, Text of the Iguvine Inscriptions, Christian Commonwealth, History of the Hebrew Monarchy, Hebrew Theism, Early Life of Cardinal Newman, Anglo–Saxon Abolition of Negro Slavery*, not to mention many others, alone show how writing largely filled his days and occupied his mind.

Besides all this work, however, he was for ever interesting himself in any cause or society which applied to him for help, or seemed in any way to need a champion. Indeed, as Mr. Hornblower Gill says of him, "Scholar, translator, mathematician, historian, political economist, political philosopher, moralist, theologian, philanthropist, he was the most copious and various writer of his time."

For a great many years before he died Newman lived at Weston–super–Mare. But two years before his death, in October, 1897, when he was ninety–two years of age, he found himself, partly owing to senile decay and partly owing to a bad fall he had had in the spring of the year, and also to loss of eyesight, unable to take part in public affairs any longer, nor yet to write as he had been used to do.

The unpublished article on "Land Nationalization" (which is printed in this volume) came into the hands of Mr. William Jameson (to whose kindness I am indebted for it) in 1886, at which time he was Hon. Secretary of the Land Nationalization Society, and Francis Newman, Vice–President.

Mr. Jameson, at the time of sending me the article, wrote me a letter from which I shall here quote those parts relating to his friendship with Newman. He says, speaking of their first meeting: "There was an instant fellowship that endears his memory to me. I was then about thirty–five, and he past eighty. There was a quiet dignity in his manner, but no suggestion of *old age*."

One little anecdote may be of interest.

"We left a rather stormy committee meeting together, over which Professor Newman had presided. The *storm* was due to one member who had a grievance against some others. Speaking of the pity of this, Professor Newman said to me, 'You know how very strongly my brother and myself differ in opinion; yet this has never created the *slightest personal discord....*'"

Several years later. Professor Newman wrote Mr. Jameson a letter (on finding out that he was suffering from overwork and the fear of subsequent breakdown), saying these strong words of sympathy: "I charge you to give it up. Save yourself for the years to come." He went on to say that a friend of his own had kept working on for some cherished cause at the cost of much mental pressure, and had ended his days in a lunatic asylum. Mr. Jameson adds that Newman's words of counsel have often and often rung in his ears since they were first said to him, and he attributes to the fact that he obeyed them, his having been saved from a physical breakdown.

"Save yourself for the years to come" is a counsel which we, who are workers, are so often in danger of forgetting. Except in extreme youth, most men and women live far more in the present and in the past than they do in the future which lies before them, so largely to be carved into shape by their Present.

In April, 1887, Sir Samuel Walker Griffith, G.C.M.G., Chief Justice of Queensland since 1893, Secretary for Public Instruction, Attorney–General from 1874–8, 1890–3, Premier of Queensland from 1883–8, and 1890–3, was over in England, and Francis Newman was to have been introduced by Mrs. Bucknall (mother of Mrs. Bainsmith, the distinguished sculptor [Footnote: Mrs. Georgina Bainsmith, F.N.B.A., member of the Royal Society of Arts, and of the Honorary Council of the North British Academy.] to whom I am indebted for the photo in this book of her bust of Francis Newman, which now stands in University College, London) to Sir Samuel, at the latter's own special desire. Unfortunately, Newman was unable to go with Mrs. Bucknall to Sir Samuel Griffith's house, and this is his letter (kindly lent me, with Sir Samuel Griffith's reply, by Mrs. Bucknall).

"Dear Mrs. Bucknall,

"Since you tell me that time presses, I have no way but to give up to you my private copy of (*my*) Christian Commonwealth, which I now send you. Very sorry I am that I could not accompany you on Sunday to Sir Samuel Griffith's, but learning from you how graciously such a visitor from the Antipodes expressed his desire to meet me, I am really sorry that I was not able in person to attest my deep reverence and admiration as well as affection for Mrs. Butler, and my conviction that only moral and spiritual influences can quell the demon of impurity, while the *despair* which tries to keep it within limits by moderation and indulging it, is a folly and an infatuation, especially when coupled with police licenses and police espionage. Our ladies since 1869 have learned to detest the despotic police and the despotic doctor with an intensity which time ever increases.

"They must conquer at last: the sole question is,—after how much more moral damage to young men and women, and how much mental agony to our Christian martyrs.

"Our young men happily are joining this crusade. Alas, for those who mean to be Christian, and do not know the elements of Christian sentiment. [Footnote: See "Marriage Laws" (1867), "State Provision for Vice" (1869), and "Remedies for the Great Social Evil" (1869), in Vol. III of F. W. Newman's *Miscellanies*.]

"I look to you to apologize for me to Sir S. G, for offering to him a book written by me... one which my pen has defaced....

"Most truly yours,

"F. W. Newman. "Weston–s.–M., *19th April*, 1887."

This is Sir Samuel Griffith's answer:—

"Brown's Hotel, "Dover Street, W., "*21st April*, 1887.

"Dear Mrs. Bucknall,

"Accept my best thanks for Professor Newman's writings on the *Christian Commonwealth* and the *New Crusade*. I really feel ashamed to deprive you of the latter, and Professor Newman of the former, but it would be most ungracious of me to refuse to accept them.

"Pray assure him that the value of the copy of the *Christian Commonwealth* is to be much enhanced by the fact that it bears his autograph notes, and that I feel deeply honoured by the terms in which he has been good enough to express himself in his note to you, which I have read with great interest and which I enclose. I shall always regret that I had not the honour and pleasure of meeting him at Weston, but my time was too short....

"Believe me, "Yours very faithfully,

"S. W. Griffith."

Mr. and Mrs. Frederick Pennington were great friends of Newman's, and he often stayed with them from time to time. By the kindness of Mrs. Pennington I am able to quote from some letters written by him in 1881–90, and one much earlier, in 1875, in which he laments the death of Mrs. Blackburn. Mrs. Blackburn was a sister of Mr. Pennington's, and one of the most munificent of contributors to the United Kingdom Alliance in its early days, who (I am told by Mrs. Pennington) often denied herself many luxuries in order to be able to make her contributions larger. She describes her as one of the best women she had ever known.

Newman, in his letter to Mr. Pennington in 1875, says of Mrs. Blackburn:—

"I have known her ever since Michaelmas 1869, when the revelation was first made to us of the Contagious Diseases Act; and at the Congress of Social Science at Bristol she was pleased to receive my hospitality. My esteem for her was great and ever increasing...."

He goes on to say that his dread of cold and chills makes him fear a long journey, "though it is mortifying to me not to meet you and Mrs. Pennington, and many other earnest friends of this very important cause."

In 1881 Gladstone was Prime Minister, and stayed in office for five years. For almost the whole of this time the country was hardly ever at peace. The Transvaal rebellion was started in 1880 and later our own troops were defeated by the insurrectionists; whereupon the Government promptly surrendered the Transvaal.

About this time Newman writes to Mrs. Pennington:

Memoir and Letters of Francis W. Newman

"*I am not a member of Cambridge University, nor indeed of Oxford University since 1830. If I had kept my name on the book, I should have paid L6 a year, if I remember; that is, L300 in these fifty years; and as I never took my M.A. degree (because of the 39 Articles), I should even then have no vote.*

"I now act on the fixed rule *not to take any long journey in the winter months*, except from real duty. Experience guides me, and I refuse even pressure from very friendly quarters.... I am melancholy about this Cabinet and Mr. Gladstone, and ashamed to be an Englishman. All comes to me like a domestic calamity. And Parliament is so overworked that *English* misrule cannot be corrected. I look on *Ministers in the House* as nearly our worst nuisance. But I must not begin on our defective and evil institutions...."

Then in 1890 the letters begin more and more to show a change in his handwriting. He no longer wrote in his original firm, clear style, but in a crabbed, cramped manner. His words now were often difficult to decipher, and the letters of the words very shaky and undecided, bearing witness very plainly of the trembling hand of Age. After mentioning the immense number of letters which he had to answer, and how the trouble of replying was almost beyond his strength, he says, "The sister–like affection of my honoured friend Anna Swanwick has ... again and again won me to London;... but the place seems never to agree with me. Partly the whirl by night and day, I suppose, is my bane; still more, the endless meeting of fresh and fresh small talk, with the fatigue of *listening*, and the impression on my brain of miscellaneous memories when I ought to sleep. In Oxford, from like causes, I became as it were 'daft,' and from forgetfulness of the right words could not complete an English sentence. A like affection came on me in London last summer, and I had to break away suddenly, to the disappointment of friends, because my own sense of *idiotcy* was unbearable. Rest and sleep sufficed to restore me when I reached home. The inability to get out the right word, if (for instance) *suddenly* asked 'to what station I am going,' is enough to make me seem insane or half asleep.... I am increasingly aware that my *brain* is my weakest part.... On the whole I am healthy, and agile in all movement as are few men of my age (two doctors fancy that *all* men of eighty–five have pulses as *disorderly* as mine!)...."

[Illustration: CARDINAL NEWMAN FROM AN OIL PAINTING BY MISS DEANE, OF BATH. PHOTO BY MESSRS. WEBSTER, CLAPHAM COMMON]

As regards the work on the *Early Life of the Cardinal*, which was published at this time, he says:—

"I am (*under a sense of duty*) writing concerning the late Cardinal quite a different side of his character from that which for fifty years the public have heard. I knew him as eminently generous as to money, but so fanatical as to embarrass judgment of his character. Another weakness I confess and *lament*. I can write large. I begin everything with resolution so to write. But as soon as I think only of the substance, and forget the manner, my writing so dwindles that I can hardly read it myself. I suppose that weakness of the fingers is the cause. I see how deficient they are of flesh."

In September, 1890, he wrote the following letters to Rev. J. K. Tucker, Rector of Pettaugh, Suffolk, who was an old friend of Newman's, and to Mr. John Henry Tucker, [Footnote: Which have been kindly lent me by Mr. John Warren.] from which I make quotations:—

"Ever since my brother's death (Cardinal J. H. N.) I am overwhelmed with letters, and now am writing more and longer every day than my fingers can well manage, for publishers eager for my MS."

And again in October of the same year:—

"I am about to send to my publishers my *painful* contribution to the life of the late Cardinal, my brother. I am conscientiously bound to write it, because in his *fifty* years' absence from the sight of the public a new generation has grown up ignorant of the facts, and the attempt is already begun to puff them off for their beauty of style..,. My age being eighty– five, I know the truths, and must tell them. I shall be howled at as *unbrotherly*. My immediate business now is to write to numbers of correspondents of whom you are one, whom I have necessarily neglected while engaged in the most anxious work I have ever undertaken...."

As regards this book to which he alludes, his *Early Life of Cardinal Newman*, everyone feels that in some sense it belittles the writer. For there was no real need of any sort that he should have written it. From one brother to another, such an "early history" was, from some points of view, a disloyalty—and a disloyalty not altogether free from embittered personal feeling.

Was there no personal feeling roused in the lives of the two men? For the younger was practically overshadowed by the elder. It was the elder one to whom the world kotow–ed. It was the elder who——though the younger was so strikingly intellectual, and so strong a social reformer in many ways— carried the world's laurels, and who was finally given the "splendid funeral" to which Francis Newman takes exception. And there was another reason too, which I believe exercised a strong sway over his feelings to his brother in early youth, and brought into play, though perhaps unrecognized by himself, the quality of emulation, followed by keen disappointment, when failure, as regarded that incident, fell to his share. Be that as it may, it is impossible to justify Francis Newman's writing thus of his brother, in the "early history" to which I refer. Not even his keen desire for truth, which some declare to have been his motive power in the matter, accounted for it.

"I should vastly have preferred entire oblivion of him" (of the Cardinal), "and his writings of the first forty years, but that is impossible. In the cause of Protestants and Protestantism, I feel bound to write, however painful to myself, as simply as if my topic were an old Greek or Latin one." Later on he says, "I have *tried* to cherish for him a sort of *filial* sentiment," but "we seemed never to have an interest nor a wish in common." [Footnote: J. H. Newman once in speaking of his brother, said, "Much as we love each other, neither would like to be mistaken for the other." A sentence which seems to contain more meanings than one!] Perhaps no words could more absolutely convey the lack of sympathy between the brothers, than do these. "I have *tried* to cherish for him a sort of filial sentiment!" showing as it does, only too evidently, that there was no spontaneity of affection between them. The only voice that called each to each was that of old childish association and duty. Francis Newman could not be accused of seeking personal distinction or fame for itself; witness his giving up a very promising career at home in order to go on his missionary journey to Syria. Witness also his open denunciation of many existing State abuses. Witness his unceasing crusades against the stronger party (whatever it might be), which, in his opinion, oppressed and wronged the weaker section of the community, unable of themselves to obtain justice and a hearing at the court of English public opinion.

All the more, then, is it difficult to explain away sentences such as these, which seem to proceed from such an absolutely different personality than was Frank Newman's; and yet the man who reads his memoirs of his brother finds them almost on every page, and cannot understand their presence there.

"The existing generation has seen him" (he is alluding to the Cardinal), "through a mist; and if my simple statement anywhere clears away that mist, they may almost resent my truth–speaking as an impiety." As indeed they did—and do. Some of his own friends, indeed, urged him not to publish the book, but he was obdurate.

"In my rising manhood I received inestimable benefits from this (my eldest) brother.... He supported me, not out of his abundance, but when he knew not whence weekly and daily funds were to come.... Yet a most painful breach ... broke in on me in my nineteenth year and *was unhealable*." This was, of course, when Francis had been at college two years, for in those days men very often went at the age of sixteen, as he did.

But the entries of 1822 and 1823, which last would be for Francis his "nineteenth year," give no clue to the "painful breach" which "was *unhealable*"

Yet the fact that religious differences did begin between the two brothers very early in life has been proved beyond all question. Proved also is it that religious discussions were of constant occurrence between them, and that while J. H. Newman had always a strange leaning to Churchmanship, Frank Newman's religious tendencies drew him strongly towards dissent and Unitarianism.

I think the latter mentions in his *Phases of Faith* that when he first came to college he found his brother had hung up a picture of Our Lady in his younger brother's room, which he at once removed, and refused to have on the walls.

The following letter is to Rev. J. K. Tucker; in it he describes himself as a "Conscious Christian" "at the age of fourteen." But he has often described himself as holding Christianity *without* Christ:—

"I hold firmly in memory, that in Easter of 1836 I wished to conduct my *bride* to Oxford, and introduce her there to my mother and two sisters— in those Coaching days we came from Bristol and Cheltenham en route to Oxford. *I* did not plan the thought of staying a night at your father's house, in which I suppose *you and your wife* were living. No doubt the scheme was planned *by my wife* to meet *her friend*. The winter of our marriage had been one of wild snow; and the following Easter was alike untimely. I just remember the fact of your kind hospitality fifty–four and a half years ago, and the snow around us. In that visit to my mother (the last time I saw her), my young wife caught inflammation of the lungs, which I did not perceive or understand—she was so cruelly bled and cupped, that I think she never recovered it.

"It is very kind of you to keep alive in your heart the friendship of the two ladies. I perhaps ought to state that about two and a half years after the death of that wife in 1876 I married her ... friend.... Else I must have given up housekeeping, and know not into what family I could have gone. My second wife is nineteen years my junior, yet in walking, not at all my equal, but in affectionate care of me inestimable."

In June, 1892, he writes to J. H. Tucker, Esq.:—"I have not heard whether your father, like me, is favoured by life continued, but I venture to send a copy of my hymns.... To–day I have received a letter and book in *Bengali* from a believer in *Theosophy*, supposing me to be one of them! Hence, I was not too early in telling my friends that since *at the age of fourteen* I became a Conscious Christian, no unbelief has made my hymns less precious, *mutato saltem nomine*.... My change more than fifty years ago was on Historical arguments mainly."

To return to the subject of Newman's last years at Weston–super–Mare. Perhaps the most graphic descriptions of him as an old man are those contributed as "Reminiscences" by Mrs. Kingsley–Tarpey and Mrs. Bainsmith. We know him there as a man who, though hardly ever free from some discomfort or pain in those days, yet never failed in that old–world courtesy of which, alas! there is so poor a supply in the world at the present day.

We know him as a man who was always eager to help those who came to him in trouble or in any difficulty; nay, perhaps almost *too* ready to believe a cock–and–bull story of those who did not mind, for their own ends, practising on his credulity.

A lady, a relation of the Newmans', said that once on coming to stay with him and Mrs. Newman, she found a secretary in his study smelling strongly of brandy. When the secretary went out of the room, Frank Newman drew their guest aside and said, "Ah, yes, it's a sad case, poor fellow! He's getting away from the temptation of the public–houses."

But when later the secretary's rooms were searched, there were found numbers of brandy bottles hidden away, to prove that he evidently had *not* "escaped from temptation"! This lady said also that when Newman was old people not infrequently deceived him thus, and traded on his temperance views, and that he had had *two* secretaries who obtained their post on false pretences.

To conclude this chapter I should like to give one striking instance of his tender sympathy and respect for the poor and lonely. A poor charwoman had died at Weston–super–Mare who had, I believe, often worked in Newman's house. He found that she had no friends to follow her body to the grave, and so he himself, his wife and servants, walked to the funeral as mourners to show her a last respect. It is the Idea represented by his act which makes it serve as an unforgettable and very uncommon illustration of a championship of those unlucky ones who have few or none to champion them.

Could any act speak clearer of the unfailing respect and reverence for women which distinguished Francis Newman through life? Though all others should see the lonely funeral, there should be but the one Good Samaritan who crossed over the road of ordinary, usual, Conventionalities to show by his act that he recognized that class and position count for nothing before the fact of the Universal Brotherhood of Humanity and Religion.

CHAPTER XX. TOULMIN SMITH: AUTHOR, ANTIQUARIAN STUDENT, AND POLITICAL REFORMER

Among the names of those who have done most, by untiring, laborious search among old parish registers, etc., and dusty old records, to bring to light interesting social ordinances, details of ancient parish government, and gems of Norse literature and archaeological research, there have been none in the last century who have by patient work attained more knowledge of their country's inner history than Mr. Toulmin Smith.

His name is indeed familiar to everyone as the greatest living authority on "English Gilds." That book alone, by itself, is an invaluable gift to the nation. By that alone has he done so signal a service to his countrymen that no gratitude could repay it.

It is true that, owing to ill–health, Mr. Toulmin Smith unavoidably left it unfinished at his death, but there is sufficient fulness of information in it as it is, to make it worth more than an infinity of other finished books of to–day.

As Father Gasquet says in his *Parish Life in Medieval England*, of the universality of these "gilds" in this country: "Every account of a medieval parish must necessarily include some description of the work of fraternities and guilds.... Their existence dates from the earliest times." Mr. Toulmin Smith, indeed, says, "English Guilds are older than any kings of England.... They were associations of those living in the same neighbourhood, who remembered that they had, as neighbours, common obligations." But it was not only because of his *English Gilds* that he is remembered. In 1854, when he was thirty–eight years of age, he published another very important volume, *The Parish: its Obligations and Powers, its Officers and their Duties*. This was also a book towards the making of which had gone many long years of the most incessant, careful research in old documents. It was one of those rare literary buildings, each stone of which was laid with infinite exactitude and care. There is too much "jerry–building" to–day, both in houses and books.

To Mr. Toulmin Smith some of the shallow books of to–day would represent literary "pariahs." He would bar the very superficial method in which they were put together.

In *The Parish* and in many a pamphlet he set his face steadily against centralization. "The ruling passion, the guide of his life, the dream of his youth, the glory of his manhood and his later years, was the intelligent freedom of the people, based on 'the ancient ways.'" [Footnote: *Toulmin Smith, 1816 to 1869*, by the late Samuel Timmins, Esq., of Birmingham. From this pamphlet I have gained much information of his life.]

It is not difficult to understand how the friendship between Toulmin Smith and Frank Newman began. For the decentralization of the nation, better forms of local self–government, were also, each of them, a dream of the latter's, which he longed eagerly to see realized. There was another keen common interest between them. Both ardently desired the freedom of Hungary. Both wrote strongly in favour of it. Both warmly welcomed the exiled patriot, Louis Kossuth, when he came to England to collect funds for the revolutionary movement of his country. But long before Englishmen had made themselves *au fait* with the subject of the Hungarian revolt, Toulmin Smith had, in his literary studies, understood the why and wherefore of the quarrel, and had, by his words, roused his country to the true recognition of how urgent was the whole question between Austria and Hungary. It must not be forgotten, too, that all his labours amongst the tangled undergrowths of the literary land were undertaken in the leisure time he could spare from his profession. For he was barrister–at–law of Lincoln's Inn, and he was also a landowner in Birmingham (his native city), of property which had belonged to his ancestors in succession for five hundred years. He had made himself a proficient in the Icelandic, Danish, Norse languages, and was learned in the ancient history and politics of Denmark, Norway, Sweden, Iceland, and Scandinavia. [Footnote: I quote from the pamphlet on *Toulmin Smith*, referred to before.]

Mr. Timmins tells us that "while he maintained his own convictions with energy and power, he had a kindly regard for all who differed from him, a large appreciation of genuine humour, and he was in private life one of the most courteous, kindly, and genial of men. While he honoured the past and the memory of his fathers, he was no blind adherent of a falling cause, no obstinate opponent of the needful changes of the age.... Amid all the worry of a London lawyer's life, when far away in the United States and stricken down by 'grievous illness,' almost his last written words, 'I *long* to return to Birmingham,' express the passion of his life."

The friendship between Toulmin Smith and Newman probably began in 1849, in connection with the formation of the Hungarian Committee. This I am told by Miss Toulmin Smith, to whose kindness I am indebted for permission to use the following letters.

She believes that her father was introduced to Newman by Mr. John Edward Taylor (of Norwich). She says she has a keen memory of Francis Newman coming to her father's house at Highgate at that time, with Pulszky and other Hungarians, all eager in the "efforts for reform and constitutional freedom and local government." But later on, she adds, many difficulties arose, and "about 1852 something connected with Louis Kossuth" (and the Hungarian movement) "caused a coolness" between the friends, and their correspondence seems to have come to an end after September in that year. Newman, owing to his University College engagements probably, I think retired from his position on the Committee in October, 1849.

Francis Newman to Toulmin Smith.

"University College, Gower Street, "*8th Jan.*, 1850.

"My dear Sir,

"I rejoice in your ward–mote exertions, and I beg you will not think that I am indifferent to them."

[This refers to "a series of meetings during the winter of 1849–50 in one of the Wards of the City of London; part of a movement endeavouring to rouse the citizens to a sense of civic local duties."] [Footnote: I am quoting from notes *re* these letters, kindly supplied by Miss Toulmin Smith.]

"On Wednesday I have to attend a meeting of our Professors here which will interfere with the Wardmote.... I exceedingly want presence of mind, if there is any tumult, so as to remember quickly enough what is to be said. Against a mob I could *act* with firmness, but I could not speak with promptitude. Moreover, I suffer physically from the air of a crowded room, and never go to *hear* a speech when there is a chance of my being able to *read* it."

The next letter I quote from is dated from Church Street, Old Eastbourne, August, 1850. It begins with questions of canvassing at University College, and goes on to touch on the subject about which he and his correspondent were at one: local land reform:—

"I have been here less than a week, but was at first unsettled, and my servant did not know whither to send my letters. It is fine air, rather bleak downs" (this is an unappreciative criticism of those exquisitely rounded outlines), "but with sunny days very pleasant and healthy.

"I am glad to hear of your Bristol excursion. If one could convert some sheriff of a county, I should like to see the thing tested in some practical form, i.e. to assemble every month a Parliament of County Freeholders to do some real work—as, if roads, or public lands, or docks, etc., were to be dealt with; or to protest against a Private Bill in Parliament, and claim to have the settling of it.

"I wish you knew Tom Taylor. He is an able man, desiring Reform, and is on the Public Health Board in some legal capacity. He heartily wishes to develop the local powers, and will not admit that they are practically undermining them. He fully assented to all I said in theory, but thought I misconceived what they were actually doing.

"Believe me, sincerely yours,

"F. W. Newman."

Tom Taylor, journalist and playwriter, was born 1817 in Sunderland. For two years he was Professor of the English language and literature at University College. He was called to the Bar of Inner Temple in 1845. He acted as Secretary to the Board of Health and Local Government Act Office. After the year 1846 he devoted himself chiefly to playwriting, and in 1874 was editing *Punch*.

The following letter is dated September, 1850:—

* * * * *

"It is not Tom Taylor only who honestly believes the Sanitary Board to be engaged in teaching Central and Local Powers to *co−operate*, and to be anxious to leave *bona fide* power of the most important kind to the localities. Only a few days ago a friend of mine (a physician) was proving to me this very point in them. We who are not lawyers do not understand points rapidly enough (or cannot remember them) to see where a great principle is violated.

"I do not care about the Sanitary Board *per se* ... but what I think you are most wanted to do is to show that, however much the Parliamentary franchise needs reform, yet a *greater* need is that of limiting the functions of Parliament, and giving them to County Assemblies or Town Motes.

"That word *Mote* is almost obsolete! May not the fact itself be a text to you? The modern substitute, 'meeting,' has no taxing powers, no legal officers, no constitutional power any more than a mob.... The sands of the Whigs run fast out, and it is high time for the Radicals to have a creed. Do you find any Chartists listen to you? If you cannot convert a Sheriff, I should be as well pleased with a hundred Chartists, for they learn from one another by contagion."

In this year there was put forward a project for a society to make more local government possible. This was later carried out under the name of the "Anti−Centralization Union."

In November, 1850, decentralization was again to the fore in the minds of Newman and Toulmin Smith, as is shown here; and what the former says he puts very trenchantly, forcibly:—

"7 Park Village East, "R.P., *Oct. 16th*, 1850.

"My dear Smith,

＊ ＊ ＊ ＊ ＊

"I can speak with much freedom and energy (but no *wit*) on a subject on which I have information and feel interested: but I cannot make an after– dinner speech of compliment, nor talk on a subject which I do not feel I have very maturely considered.... In regard to *local government*, I think you would disarm the fears or scruples of many excellent and wise persons if you made prominent that you do not wish to return to the Middle Ages, or disown that progress of society which has knit England into a single State. I think it high time to make an outcry against a system of infinite legislation, in which we are subjected to laws too numerous for anyone to be acquainted with; yet I doubt whether we shall get a hearing with the most influential minds unless we make it clear that we fully understand that the progress of society forbids our returning to the simplicity of law which the good Saxons had under Alfred and his successors. The gap is vast, and there is *no danger whatever* of our becoming too simple; yet this fanatical aim will be so surely imputed to us (in days when such men as Lord John Manners in Politics and the Puseyites in Church are afloat) that it is not needless to disown it even to candid and strong–headed hearers.

"I am asking Froude to dine with me on Tuesday, the 29th instant, at 6 o'clock, to meet you and *some other friends* whom I want to bring together: as I believe he will then be in London....

"*Thursday, 6 o'clock.*—I have just got Froude's reply, *Yes* : so please to say Yes, too.

"In haste, sincerely yours,

"F. W. Newman."

As to the real meaning of the word "Democracy" Newman deals with it thus:—

"*What is* Democracy?... Show that if one town governs itself by universal suffrage, that *is* Democracy, so long as the people really exercise interest in their public concerns; but that if a whole country, as France, elects an Assembly, that is *not* Democracy, but Empire delegated to an Oligarchy, because the people at large cannot understand, follow, and control public measures.

"I do not mean to dictate this, or any one mode; but I feel strongly that you must put a sharp curb on all invective *until* you have fully developed the difference between the common Radicalism and your own views. Pulszky says he is satisfied you were not *understood* at the Radley Hotel dinner. Radicals are almost as slow as Tories to admit a new thought.

"I should also like to have the question brought out: 'What has been, historically, the Service performed by Monarchy and Centralization?' The answer is: 'It has formed nations into larger masses, and lessened or destroyed *border war*.' The inference is, that the great and peculiar function of the Central Government is, in fact, what the American Congress does, viz. to maintain peace at home between the several States, and make the country *One* in resisting hostile attack. To do more than this, should be rather exceptive, and confined to subordinate matters, else Centralization becomes mischievous...."

And again, later in the year, in answer to a letter from Mr. Toulmin Smith:—

"What I said of 'Democracy' was meant as *argumentum ad hominem* to that side, not as intending to identify myself with it, but I see the danger you speak of. Query: Would 'popular government' do? Even Conservatives wish for a Commonwealth and for *Constitutional* Government. No doubt *Unity* is the true word, not Centralization; but I think this Unity without Centralization would never have been coveted by kings, so that in fact we have bought the advantage of Unity at the expense of submitting to (more or less of) Centralization."

Twelve years later, John Ruskin put forth a method which cannot fail to commend itself to every reasonable mind; a method which, if treated from the decentralization point of view, seems to offer good solution to the crux of English pauperism, at any rate, if dealt with under the aegis of *Local* government. That "*bona fide power of the most important kind to the localities*" *as Newman said, should be conceded; that the "Government schools" of which Ruskin speaks should, in each place, be directly under Local Control.*

The passage to which I am alluding is from *Unto this Last*:—

"Any man, or woman, or boy, or girl out of employment should be at once received at the nearest Government School" (training schools, at which trades, etc., should be taught) "and set to such work as it appeared, on trial, they were fit for, at a fixed rate of wages determinable every year; that being found incapable of work through ignorance, they should be taught; or being found incapable of work through sickness, should be tended; but that being found objecting to work, they should be set, under compulsion of the strictest nature, to the more painful and degrading (?) forms of necessary toil; especially to that in mines, and other places of danger (such danger being, however, diminished to the utmost by careful regulation and discipline), and the due wages of such work retained, cost of compulsion first abstracted, to be at the workman's command so soon as he has come to sounder mind respecting the laws of employment."

LETTERS TO MRS. KINGSLEY

"Weston–super–Mare, "*4th Nov.*, 1877.

"Dear Mrs. Kingsley,

"I hurried home from Manchester to meet an expected widow friend here, who has just left me. Somehow or other she and her little girl engrossed me much, and made me neglect my intended warm thanks for your very kind letters, and for your phrases even of affection, to which, be assured, I am not inattentive or apathetic, though I imperfectly know how to respond to that which I do not seem to have duly earned.

"Your children were as kind and attentive to me as you could have been yourself; but I much regret not to have met you and Mr. Kingsley, to whom I beg you to give my kind regards, and believe that it is always a pleasure to meet you, and that I am necessarily proud of having made so *fruitful* a convert ... though our severe ones will remind me that you do not wholly abstain from fish!

"Believe me, yours heartily,

"Francis W. Newman.

"I am bringing out a *dreadful* pamphlet!"

"28 Cumberland Terrace, "Regent's Park, London, "*25th May*, 1878.

"Dear Mrs. Kingsley,

"Concerning the controversy about increase of population, I forgot to add what I think has moral weight, that the theory which makes men bewail every increase on the ground that *at length* the earth will be overfilled would be in argument just as powerful if the size of the earth were increased to that of Jupiter, or to that of the sun. It simply deduces from the axiom / *fact* that any finite area whatsoever will at length be overfilled by a constant unchecked increase—a reason why we should actively check the increase NOW and HERE—a deduction wholly void of good sense.

"Again, I did not mention what reduces John Mill's school to something worse than negative error, the certainty that their doctrine will not be obeyed by any but those whom we would desire to have the peopling of the earth, viz. the people of most intellect. If the highly intelligent and conscientious obey John Mill, we evidently must look forward to the peopling of every land by the most backward and least intelligent part of the nation.... Malthus was shocked by the system of encouraging very early marriage and large families for the mere sake of getting men as food for gunpowder: but if people marry (say young men at 27 or 28, not at 17 or 18) he denounces as unnatural and unimaginable that society or law should frown upon a family as being too numerous. In every moral aspect of the case, John Mill is opposed to Malthus, and his followers have no right to call themselves Malthusians. I feel confident that human population would waste *if* every man adopted the doctrine *either* of John Mill *or* of certain American theorists....

"With best regards to all yours, "I am, yours most sincerely,

"F. W. Newman."

"15 Arundel Crescent, "Weston−super−Mare, "*12th Feb.*, 1880.

"Dear Mrs. Kingsley,

"Your kind letter, yesterday received, gives me great concern. I never wept through simple grief, but once in my life through grief at ingratitude; and I think I never felt so painful a pang in my heart. I can well imagine that a sense of another's ingratitude may terribly overthrow anyone's health. I believe my dear sister, whose death you so kindly mention, suffered *in part* from excess of anxiety through being made executrix to her husband's will, involving great perplexity, but *also* from the fraud of an old and trusted clerk. Her husband had several small strokes of paralysis, and for two and a half years before his death probably had not his mind always perfect. He delegated many confidential writings and documents to the clerk, who with his wife was much respected by the whole family. After his death his accounts were inexplicable. Three of his sons worked hard at them for weeks together, and at last discovered frauds, by which the clerk had not only embezzled money—how much they know not, but counted above the thousand—and had depreciated the property in selling it by representing it as having been for years a declining business: this was to hide his pilferings. When charged with it, the man *became raving mad*. Lawyers knew not how to recover property from a maniac who could not defend himself: and my sister was in such grief for the man's wife, that she knew not whether to wish to recover a farthing. How the matter stood she either did not know or did not like to tell me—to the last; but the mysterious disease which ate away her strength, I in my private mind ascribe to anxiety from this affair and her sudden and strange responsibility as trustee for ladies.

"This dear sister was the fondest object of my boyish affections; and through life she was the self—sacrificing, devoted character which from earliest years she displayed. Five sons, one daughter, and two daughters— in—law were present at her death, all fervent in love and duty. Her husband was one of ten children, and all that family were singularly united. Her only daughter will now live with two of her aunts, who have been almost at her side since birth. My sister was so long in a very precarious state that I did not expect her to survive the winter of 1878– 9, and at last death came as a relief and release.

"It has always troubled me that I have so little power to promote the industrial interests of friends. When I was a professor in London I used to be entreated to find pupils for tutors (when I had not half as many pupils as I desired for myself) and to recommend others to publishers and editors, when I could neither get a publisher to risk a shilling on what I wrote, nor more than one editor to accept an article from me. Now, I would most gladly recommend ————; but it is well to say frankly that no one ever asks me, nor do I *at all* know who wants anything, nor can I guess in what direction to inquire. But be sure I shall not forget, if the occasion opens.

"I yesterday heard awful tidings of widespread murrain in the sheep of these parts (Somerset and Monmouth and all between) ascribed to last summer's wet. One farmer (as a specimen) has lost 1000 sheep; the hotel– keepers are bidden to *beware of mutton.* This I have from an associate of our society.

"Indoors I am happy; but I am so gloomy for the prospects of the country that I do not like to talk about them. Kind regards to Mr. Kingsley.

"I am, most truly yours,

"F. W. Newman."

"Weston–s.–M., *19th Oct.*, 1880.

"Dear Mrs. Kingsley,

"Behold me (in imagination, as I really am) still at home on our great vegetarian day.

"I warmly thank you for your kind letter, and was purposing to write, but in heaps of letters could not find yours with the new address, which I have now entered in my book.

"I have finally resolved not to bustle about so late in the year, and have resigned my place as President in consequence. But it is reported to me that the Executive will prefer to exempt me from attendance in this month....

"Public affairs make me very melancholy. Mr. Gladstone is not to blame for the state of Ireland; but both in Afghanistan with India and in South Africa, I think he has allowed his colleagues to neutralize his public professions, and has made compromises most calamitous.

"The ministry seems to me not worthy of the Parliament. I do not doubt that the plutocracy in the next ten or even five years will have a heavy and deserved fall, but with how much convulsion and suffering in Ireland, in India, and in South Africa, all inflicting miseries on us—you will live to see: I fear it cannot be small, and that our institutions, called Fundamental, will be very gravely shaken.

"I honour your Piscarian position, and with our society would recognize it; but the discovery that you all eat fish forbids me to glory that I have converted a family to our Rules! With kind regards to Mr. Kingsley and the rest, I am,

"Your sincere friend,

"F. W. Newman."

"Weston, "*26th April*, 1883.

"Dear Mrs. Kingsley,

"... I am apparently assuming the position of one who (like the Pope) makes an ALLOCUTION to all *who will listen*. Each of us may imitate him. I have given away eighty copies to make my allocution known. I suppose I ought to have sent one to you, but circulation is hard work. Alas, it costs a shilling! Can you get it put into any Manchester Library? (Trubner my publisher.) It is called *A Christian Commonwealth* and is as much against our unjust wars as a Quaker could desire.

"In haste, ever yours,

"F. W. Newman." "Kind regards to all yours."

"Weston–super–Mare, *9th April*, 1884.

"My dear Friend,

"... My dismay and disgust at the proceedings of a ministry, of which Mr. Gladstone must bear the *full responsibility*—which indeed he accepts by defending all its atrocious proceedings—have disinclined me to write, more than I must, on any but private or literary topics....

"A new struggle is made by this unscrupulous ministry to retain the execrable C.D. Acts.

"I am sorry that the Bishops have again turned the scale in the unrighteous retention of the law against a man's marriage to his deceased wife's sister. When do the Bishops rally against sanguinary injustice and dire oppression? "I have just had two hundred and fifty copies struck off of the enclosed leaflet, which aims to suggest to the haters of unjust war, especially Quakers, in what direction they ought to work, viz. to lay the foundation of an *entirely new* political party. No candidate for a vote could complain that he was humiliated by being required to profess himself a VOTARY OF JUSTICE.

"I throw these leaflets in this and that direction as *feelers*. Of course more can be printed when wanted....

"With best regards, "I am, yours,

"F. W. Newman."

"15 Arundel Crescent, Weston–super–Mare, "*3rd Jan. , 1887.*

"Dear Friend,

"You need not think me dead yet; but you easily might, so estranged am I to Manchester.

"Yet I at least have life enough to be able to wish all welfare and blessing to you and yours in this New Year. The accumulation of letters has always thwarted me when I have tried to find your last letter.... I seem to remember that you then told me of the marriage of your eldest daughter and of the literary efforts of another. Since then we have had the overthrow in the W.K. of the Safe–Harlot–Providing Law, and indeed it must have been as early as 1885; and the episode of Mr. Stead and his prosecution was later! A great moral change has been wrought (for the better, I say) in our ladies by that wickedness of our ruling classes with the aid of wicked medical theories provoking indignant protest. To drag printed matter into daylight is no doubt very offensive; but without sweeping it away no sound health is to be expected. The ladies, I fancy, will now, more *perseveringly* than men, keep in activity the Purity Society. And if some of them seem a little *too* active—I ask, how *can* this odious system of sin, crime, and cruelty be crushed without hot enthusiasm? And where was enthusiasm hot without partial error? Fire burns!

"This reminds me of my sending you (at your request) a load of anti–vaccination literature, and I am wondering whether you were able to turn it to service. THAT monstrous iniquity *must* come down; but the medical schools and *your Irishmen* block out our movement.

"I wonder how you and Mr. Kingsley look on Mr. Gladstone. I never condemned his *measure*, though I have always (for years back) declined to aid a Parliament for all Ireland and *still more* the expulsion of Irish deputies from the English Parliament.... But I did not intend here to enter Irish politics further than to indicate that while I am anti–Gladstonian, I cry 'Ireland for the Irish,' 'India for the Indians,' 'Egypt for the Egyptians,"—*come what may* to the English 'Empire'! [But I have never read in history of any empire being ruined or harmed by Justice, Mercy, or Purity.]

"I suppose I must say, 'Alas!' that the older I become [81 last June] the more painfully my creed outgrows the limits of that which the mass of my nation, and those whose co–operation I most covet, account *sacred*. I dare not (unasked) send to friends what I print, yet I uphold the *sacred moralities* of Jew and Christian [Hindoo and Moslem] with all my heart. Two mottos, or say *three*, suffice me:—

"The Lord reigneth.

"The righteous Lord loveth righteousness.

"The Lord requireth Justice, Mercy, and Sobriety of thought, not ceremony or creed.

"Accept for all of you my warm wishes. "Your Vegetarian friend of old,

"F. W. Newman."

[No date. Probably *1st March*, 1888.]

"My dear Friend,

"What a violent winter it has been in very many places! Nor is it all over. After the awful 'blizzard' in New York, and its minor horrors elsewhere, and the many fatal avalanches, I see this morning fresh inundations in Hungary from sudden melting of snow. The sudden chill which smote your husband was but a mild type, it seems, of the death fatal to so many. Other deaths from cold, reported to us, have reminded us of your great and sudden loss; yet what had I to say to you? I have thought that the echo from your son in Calcutta may have made your grief break out afresh.... I trust that time, which has not yet at all had softening powers, has not added any fresh bitterness on a fuller realization....

"Affectionately yours,

"F. W. Newman."

"Alas! my dear friend, that your generous son Leonard had not more experience how vain is a man's swimming power against the current of an *ordinary* river. I have known this in the Tigris, in the Nile, and even in the Thames, though the bathing men in several places called me a first– rate swimmer. Longfellow in 'Hiawatha' has touching and powerful lines on *disasters never coming singly*, but as vultures accumulating round a huge carcass.

"Wisdom comes too late for the individual; yet it is not useless for *others* to inquire after causes. Did your husband pride himself on not wearing a specially thick coat in winter and *roughing* it as do some vegetarians?... I rather believe that man is a tropical animal, hairless, made for a climate warmer than ours, and needing much aid from clothing.

"Ever yours,

"F. W. Newman. "Herewith I return your interesting scraps. "*21st March*, 1888."

Extract from a letter, 7th Jan., 1889.

"More and more I believe, that as our clearest DUTY is in *this* world, it is wholesome that our most eager interest (*if unselfish*) should be in this world and not (with Count Tolstoi) so full of eagerness for immortality, that it is an effort with him to refrain from suicide! I *accept with grateful* submission whatever of after–life the Supreme Lord gives—or does not give. My desire cannot affect His actions, and in fact I *never* have been able to work myself into *any* desire for a future so undefined and unimaginable. This will show how ill I deserve a little of (shall I say) praise or compliment in your last.

"With kind salutes to your daughters, "I am, your sincere friend,

"F. W. Newman."

"The Firs, West Cliff Gardens, "Bournemouth, "*17th Aug.*, 1889.

"My dear Friend,

"How extraordinary you must have thought my silence, after your kind letter from this place. Perhaps you imputed it to illness. That is not true. Yet it may be called half true: for illness of my wife is one topic, and increased *weakness* makes me slower in the smallest matters—such as handling a book, or duly buttoning a shirt or coat: while I have been dealing with proof–sheets from always two printers, sometimes four. My day is cut short at each end—for in the colder months I cannot sit at my desk until my fire is lighted, and my eyes are wearied before evening candlelight. Meanwhile my unwilling correspondence has rather increased than lessened....

"I am achieving a long hoped for work, in which of course I have to pay the printers—i.e. to leave in some connective available form whatever miscellaneous important printing I have ever published, ethico–political, theological, economical, historical, aesthetic, critical, mathematical: indeed, the mathematical is all new, not reprint.

"I take as vivid an interest in all that concerns public welfare, of England, Ireland, and foreign countries, and hope I ever shall. More than ever I see that our best work for God is to work for God's creatures, not excluding gentle brutes.

"Is it possible that you are even now *here*? That would be very good news.

"Your lazy friend, with much apology,

"F. W. Newman."

"Northam, near Bideford, "*19th May*, 1890.

"My dear Friend,

"Your two letters were indeed doubly welcome, and brought me virtual pardon for two neglects, of which the worst was, the keeping locked up (and still in prison!) the letters which you bade me to return...

"The *chief* want of Cornwall, I was told by an old resident, is *soil*; the rock is too near the surface. Herein art will do much in a few generations. Attica and Palestine—stony soils—bore plentiful pine fruit. Our Channel Islands utter the same thing. In England the *landlord* is the effectual starver of the soil. Bishop Stubbs, a first–rate authority on agriculture, explains the immense excess of crops raised acre by acre under *peasant* culture, 'because the farmers' land is labour–starved.'"

* * * * *

"*15th July*, 1891.

"... The state of Ireland under existing factions would much have discomposed your patriotic husband. As for me, who cannot pretend Irish patriotism, things now look better.... But the aspect on the whole is to me far more encouraging than alarming. The reign of false aristocracy is fast declining; the rising powers everywhere ask for *justice* between orders and (as never before) between the two sexes, and the power of women is about to signalize itself in most valuable directions—for the benefit of *both* sexes, and for the first time to claim nationally that moral and Christian Right shall be the aim of Law.

"But I confess if we wish to attract ancient nations to Christianity, we have first to reconsider our creed fundamentally, a terrible summons to Protestants as well as Catholics....

"I have not with me *your last*, and I hope I do not evade any question.

"With best wishes to you and all yours, "I am, your earnest friend,

"F. W. Newman."

"*27th Nov.*, 1891.

"My dear Mrs. Kingsley,

"So many of my juniors die, that my friends when they do not hear of me may well fancy that I am decrepit and declining. That is not true; only my muscular strength is less. I cannot walk so far nor work so much, but no vital organ seems to fail; nor can I write so much or so long....

"The longer I live, the more hopeful and more interesting I find the whole world. In spite of crime, folly, and misery, the massive nations seem to improve. The good—i.e. our sounder party—become wiser and stronger, as well as in proportion more numerous. Our worst misrule has been in Ireland and in India. The crisis in Ireland seems to me turned for the better. Misrule in India is met not by insurrection, but by constitutional and loyal, widely demanded Reform, such as, I feel convinced, the enlarged franchise in England will support too warmly for the old routine to resist. All the churches are seeking *moral* reform.... Reforms lately too great to think of, we now calmly contemplate as certainties of a near future. Lord Herschell, an ex–Chancellor, pronounces that the legislative power of the House of Lords is an evil unbearable. Scotland and Wales are ready to demand abolition of the State Church. The English party called Liberal (I think miscalled) desire the same, and within the last ten years I come to think, rightly. Other reforms, too numerous to detail, cannot be trifled with or the nation be blinded. While I wonder at all this, I see that Scandinavia and Germany, even Belgium and France, are moving for *moral* objects, and also against war.

"Is there not plenty in all this to draw forth hope, joy, and thankfulness, and in every conviction, that amidst all our tumult the Lord reigneth? I rejoice that I have lived to see this day, and expect to rejoice more while I live.

"How you have fared this year I seem not to know, but believe that you have my earnest good wishes for you and yours.

"I am, yours most truly,

"F. W. Newman."

"Bournemouth (undated).

"My dear Friend,

"Your letter of July 12th from Margate has reached me here, to which place I came because my wife five years ago gained such health here, and all the year and past autumn she has never felt sure of health at home. I cannot think she manages herself rightly, yet she believes, with no small reason, that I am not a safe traveller without her; yet of the two *I* seem the stronger. She is better here, perhaps, because she is more in the outer air. I must add, I too have recovered from my fall, and am fairly well, though I do not pretend to be strong yet (as the French would say), *Que voulez vous?* when I am past 88.... I am glad to learn about your children. I have good hope concerning the coming future, though the foes of progress call us faddists because we think *national morality* paramount to vicious routine. May but the Good prevail!

"... I now argue *for* Fish–food as not to be forbidden or frowned on, but do not lessen my esteem of our Manchester V. E. M. Society, nor lessen my contribution to it, though they can only receive me as an outsider.

"I turn a vegetarian argument against them on the Fish question, but I have no time now for it.

"I am bringing out another volume on Paul of Tarsus, which, when complete, I hope to send you.

"With warm salutes, I am yours,

"Francis Wm. Newman. "My wife desires her kind thought to be named."

"*1st Nov.*, 1892.

"My dear Madam,

"I have not time nor strength to search out your last kind letter, which perhaps informed me when your two sons from India were expected and when they were to leave you....

"I do fairly well, if I potter on in my old solid routine. My 88th year makes pretension to *strength*; but when so many moans are heard about *neuralgia*, not to say influenza, I feel myself much favoured by the total absence of pain, except merely what is incidental to a thin body with some sharp bones. In rising from bed I am aware of small discomforts, which I shake off on standing upright, and similarly after sitting in one posture. I have not enough suffering to claim pity. I can wish the same to all my friends, especially to my wife.

"To my judgment the world ... is in an entirely novel state, which forebodes a wholly new future, and requires new thoughts, new policy in our rulers, *with much higher* MORALITY if grave overthrow is to be averted.

"The United States of America *ought* to be our leader in chief, but mainly through ... the dreadful colour war that is year by year waxing worse. The only thing clear to me is, that their *home* calamity must for a long while hinder their giving aid to the world. The policy in Russia is so fatal, and its result presages an overturn of the scale of the France of 1793. This makes all foresight impossible, except that every State is safest which least violates the laws of universal morality. That England can avoid great retribution seems to me scarcely probable. But as soon as morality is allowed to speak loud in high places, I believe our main dangers will quickly disappear. The prospect cannot be defined, but is to me of intense interest. Britain seems to me immensely superior to its own ruling classes in goodness, and the good is sure *at length to prevail*, to the benefit also of your Ireland.

"With kindest best wishes, I am, "Most truly yours,

"F. W. Newman."

CHAPTER XXI. LANDOWNERS AND WAGE RECEIVERS BY FRANCIS W. NEWMAN CONTRIBUTED BY MR. WILLIAM JAMIESON

[Presumably written in 1886, when Newman was Vice–President of the "Land Nationalization Society." It was kindly sent me by Mr. William Jamieson, who was Hon. Sec. to the above Society at the time. I wish to express here my sense of gratitude to him for much help and information regarding his own work with Newman in 1886.]

The tendency of English industry for a long time back has been to exalt the land_lord, or chief man in any locality, into land *owner* (a phrase implying that no one but he has legal right in the land), and to convert a larger and larger fraction of the nation into wage receivers, liable to be cast out of work either at the simple will, or by the imprudence or misfortune of their paymaster. In order to analyse the natural results of this juncture, we must follow the method received in Political Economy, of taking an imaginary case, far simpler than any which is actually met in human life, so as to make all the conditions of the problem known to us by hypotheses. Let us suppose an island, secluded commercially from the rest of the world, and peopled by a vast working lower class under three small ruling castes. The island is physically divisible into three parts: *first*, marshy coast land, abounding with shrubs, canes, rushes of many kinds, from which human garments of various sorts can be made; *secondly* rolling land, eminently suitable for the cultivation of grain, and of certain fruit trees and roots on which the whole population live; *thirdly*, the mountain land, on which are timber trees and copses affording firewood; also quarries of stone, gravel pits, lime rocks, and mines of copper and iron. Of the marshy coast land, the *second* lordly caste is acknowledged to be absolute owner; the first or highest caste owns the rolling land, which is the arable and cultivated portion; and the *third* caste owns the mountain land and its products. From the first comes the food of the native, from the second comes the clothing, from the third the houses. It is possible that gravel, lime, and stone can be found in rolling land, and that fruit trees either exist or if planted would bear fruit in the marsh land, some even in the mountains; but the ruling castes follow ancient custom, and the working caste has no right to innovate. They work *under* and *for* their masters, and receive wages *in kind* —that is, as an equivalent for their work, a definite but liberal supply of the three necessary articles—food, clothes, and house accommodation. Money does not exist, nor tame animals in our island. To add sharpness to our imaginary case, and to make argument intelligible, we must assign definite numbers to the working population; but from whatever numbers we start, the argument and the practical result will be the same. Let us suppose the first caste to employ *ten thousand* cultivators; the second caste to employ *three thousand* knitters and plaiters; the third caste *one thousand* masons, miners, and carpenters. Each of these castes furnishes to the workman such rude tools as are necessary, but these remain the property of the masters, not of the workmen.

The soil and climate being favourable, and the habits of the people simple, a few hours of work suffice; and like many barbarians, they have been accustomed to much idle time, which they employ in sport; moreover, by the connivance or good of the superior caste, they have been accustomed to pick or steal largely the leaves of an intoxicating grass, and the masters to whom the whole produce of their labour belongs, have large superfluity after paying their wages; hereby the lordlings easily feed domestic servants and exhibit themselves in gay clothing with superior dwellings.

But the tendency of the workers to drunkenness shocks a certain religious preacher, who traces the vice to idleness and sport. He goes about the island urging upon them a higher morality. They widely receive him as a divine messenger, and under his exhortation they become more industrious and more conscientious in their work; not only working more hours, and curtailing their sport, but in every hour using more diligence. In consequence, the masters are enriched by stores somewhat embarrassing. Grain comes in, more than they want: their barns begin to overflow. Garments are too many for the warehouses. Huge piles of timber block up the yards, besides masses of stones, and heaps of other superfluous material. Before long, the masters conclude that their simplest course for checking supply is by lessening the number of the workmen. The increased diligence of the people (we may suppose) has made the work of three men on an average as efficient in all tasks as were *five* men previously. Thus sixty do the work of a hundred; and the masters discover that what had been the normal average produce will be maintained, if they dismiss forty out of every hundred dependents. Not only so; but retaining their usual surplus, which we may call their rent, at the old level, they will be able to raise the wages to these workmen whom they still keep, since instead of a hundred they will have only sixty now to feed and clothe; and only for these do they feel morally responsible. Forthwith they actually dismiss forty out of every hundred. Each landowner cares for his own workmen as by a sort of social duty; but for those who are discharged he feels no responsibility. In the average result the landowners who had had a hundred workmen, but now only sixty, take as increased rent the food and clothes of ten, and use it to add ten servants to their domestic retinue, but add to the wage of the sixty whom they keep at work, the food and clothes previously received by thirty of the forty whom they have dismissed. Thus they raise wages by one half—that is, they pay in the proportion of one hundred and fifty instead of one hundred.

The labourers, clothworkers, and builders who are dismissed (the remaining thirty out of every hundred) being without work and without houses, are at once in a state of beggary. Only by betaking themselves to some *new industry* will they be able to get a livelihood, and it rests with them to devise their new industries. Meanwhile they can only subsist on charity, which is doled out to them chiefly by the fellow feeling of those of their class who are still in work. The increased wages of these enable them to be liberal; in fact, the increase has on an average been just what the discarded men previously earned.

A parliament of the higher classes is in due course assembled, and a member came (?) to the distress of so many men out of work. But a distinguished literary writer, member of a Politico–Economical Club ... eases the consciences of the higher castes by pointing out that in fact the island is much increased in prosperity. Rents had, no doubt, risen, but only as one mark of prosperity, for their increase was in a much smaller percentage than that of the rise of wages. These had increased by the very remarkable ratio of 50 per cent. It was true that many men were out of work. That was to be regretted; but it was a *passing phenomenon.* They would before long find work somewhere or somehow.

The discarded workmen hitherto had had no great variety in their tasks, and were always set to work by others without exercise of their own inventive powers. Yet out of a large number of men there are always many of good talents, some of original genius. The idea of many new forms of industry springs up. Oil for food has been hitherto raised from the olive tree; now an ingenious man would extract oil from several shrubs or trees, and make candles, or else oil for lamps. A second wishes to plait carpet socks, sandals, and umbrellas. A third would make boats, with ropes, and oars, and sails. A fourth would add wheelbarrows and casks to the baskets already in use. A fifth has noticed wild ponies on the mountains, and desires to catch them and make needful harness. A sixth would plant fruit trees in gardens, and not take the chance of wild fruit. But on every such plan they are at once checkmated: first, because all these natural products are accounted the absolute property of the upper castes, and must be bought; next, most of their new schemes need a yard or a garden and right of access by a road, and workshops, beside a dwelling–house. But the land, as well as the raw produce, is inaccessible to them; yet on them, hungry and destitute, is laid the task of originating the new trades. Can this seizure of the land and its natural products as the private property of a limited number of families be morally justified? In its origin was it attained by violence and robbery? Else, has it grown up by gradual and cunning perversion of law? These three questions point at the principle of landowning. Another question rises: Is it good for a nation for *the great majority* to retain life only on condition that there is someone ready to pay wages for their work and able to discard them? In the imaginary case thus drawn the increased industry of the workers which produced superfluity is the beginning (to them) of change for the worse. Their spontaneous industry causes overproduction, and leads to the dismissal of many workmen. Our economists treat every increase of productiveness as an unalloyed good. It is good, provided that men are not kept idle by it. Evidently there is no national gain from sixty men doing the work of a hundred, if thereby forty men are tossed into unwilling idleness, and must live on charity, some of the forty losing all habits of

276

industry, and perhaps becoming criminal. This is a national loss.

Further, our hypothesis that the men voluntarily become more industrious may be called an extreme and unlikely case. For that very reason it has been here adopted. The ordinary causes give us *a fortiori* argument, because they are ever in action. *Skill* naturally increases among men employed continuously on any work. In a settled, industrious nation small improvements accumulate. In modern Europe the cultivation of mechanics and chemistry conduces to a steady improvement in tools, a cheapening also of tools, and introduction of such more complex tools as we call "machines," by dint of all which human work constantly becomes more effective, so that fewer and fewer workmen are needed for *the same amount* of produce. Thus the normal and natural order of things, wherever *the wage–system exists* tends to dispense with some, or many, of the workmen. This is a clear gain if the men thus displaced *are instantly taken up for some other service.* But this seldom can happen; often their old skill is made useless, and before they can learn a new trade they become demoralized, and many perish. The loss of their industrial position is a grievance and a national mischief which our "Economists" are prone to undervalue, and pass unnoticed.

Let us contrast the case of men who work not for a master, not for wages, but for themselves; holding their own little homestead, from which they cannot be driven out. Such is the case of back–settlers in the Far West of the United States. Each perhaps carries out with him a box of stout clothes, some agricultural tools and important seeds, and either *squats* on a bit of wild land, or by a very easy payment buys possession of the Federal Government. This bit of land the settler counts *his own.* With the aid of friendly neighbours he builds the rude log–hut. The felling of the trees needed to construct it makes an opening for small culture. In a very few years he raises more food than his family needs. If the season and the roads favour, he sends his superfluous barrels of corn and fruit eastward, and recovers an equivalent. But what happens if wide distance part him from civilized towns, if the roads are swampy and not made by art, and the conveyance of food be too onerous to remunerate him? All his neighbours being in like case, there is a local Overproduction of food; yet not one of the little community is thereby made a pauper. No one is able to expel them from their rude homes, or forbid their cultivation. They are not made outcasts or idlers. Simply they are kept poorer, than with access to a market they would have been; but they lessen their production of food, and either with the females of the family work at clothing, or execute carpentering. In many ways they can use their time to produce articles which they could have bought in a better finished state had the market of the East been open to them. The present writer was informed by an Englishman who in the American Civil War had penetrated very far West, that he had seen with his own eyes a colonist *burning wheat as fuel*, because he had it in so great excess. Probably he had plenty of green maize for his horses and pigs.

Whenever a man retains a house of his own, and has neither rent to pay nor any excessive taxation, if only he have a moderate plot of land for workshop and garden, he is not made destitute, though he do not directly raise food for his household, but works at some domestic manufacture. Our "Spitalfields" poor who fought a long battle with the hand–loom against the loom driven by steam power, might not have been at length utterly ruined if they had had freehold houses and some small garden in a healthy country. If the system of huge factories had had to compete with domestic manufacture conducted by private families living in small freeholds, it is possible that the battle might simply have driven the independent workers either to buy small steam engines for their aid, or what now is more obvious, to hire power from some company, as from a Gas Company or Water Company, which had it in superfluity. Such, in the opinion of some far– sighted men, may very possibly be even now the solution of our difficulty.

At present the Trade Unions gravely mistake the end for which they ought to strive. They mischievously unite two objects. First, they are Benefit Societies. The funds of a Benefit Society ought to be forbidden by law to be spent in warring against capitalists; this enables the directors, or a majority of them, to confiscate the whole contributions of any member who disapproves of the war.

Next, the main effort to raise the status of the workmen is ill–directed towards raising or sustaining the *rate* of wages, else towards dictating concerning the management. This effort is ill–directed, first, because it is liable to aim at an impossibility—i.e. to extort from a master a wage so high that he prefers not to light his engine fires; next, because to raise the *rate* of wages does not secure continuous work, and idle days neither tend to sobriety nor give pay. Strikes which inflict vast loss upon the workers cause loss to the masters also, and make them less able to pay high wages. But beyond all these, if the Unions were wise, they would struggle against the system of wage–earning, wherever it is new and needless; that is, as far as possible, strive to recover the system of domestic manufacture. For certain new and peculiar industries undoubtedly combine, and large capital is essential; even in them the effort ought to be towards uniting, *as far as possible*, the interests of each workman, and of the company, the opposite of which is in general

278

the Union policy. But for every old trade independent work is physically possible, under the condition that the workman have a fixed homestead. To effect this ought to be the main effort of the Unions.

In the thirty–two years between the battle of Waterloo and the Irish famine, the farmers and manufacturers were like two buckets of a well; when one was up, the other was down. But now, both at once are down. The causes are clearly separate.

Our manufacturers when allowed to accept payments from abroad In wheat and sugar and foods and all raw produce, Immensely increased their foreign sales; and during the Cotton Famine, capital was largely invested in building new cotton mills, as if we were to supply all the world.

But the European Continent more and more chooses to compete with us, and from more causes than one deprive our merchants of their customers. Between us and our rivals more of the *same sort* is produced than the existing markets can take: this is again Overproduction. Hence stagnation in our manufacturing districts. Meanwhile, in near thirty years of manufacturing prosperity after 1847, the increased riches of these towns enriched the farmers and enabled the landlords to raise rents in England, and in consequence, by dint of landlord power, rent rose in the whole United Kingdom. At the same time, Englishmen found too little encouragement to invest their savings on English soil, and preferred to invest many millions on foreign railways and on foreign loans; and the payment of their dividends is made largely by imported foreign food. Their investments at first were an advantage to our manufacturers, while they sent out railway plant and carriages and locomotives. Now foreigners compete with us even as to these, and the imported food competes with the farmers. Thus a double failure convulses us.

How much better, if instead of quarrelling for distant markets (and *it is said* conquering Burmah in the hope of advantage to our merchants) we had *a native population of small cultivators*, prosperous enough to be valuable as well as steady customers to our manufacturing towns, and gradually (in the course of several generations) another population of country folk, substituting domestic manufactures for those of factories with wage earners!

CHAPTER XXII. THE RIGHT AND DUTY OF EVERY STATE TO ENFORCE SOBRIETY ON ITS CITIZENS BY F. W. NEWMAN, M.R.A.S. PUBLISHED IN 1882 IN PAMPHLET FORM

No human community can be so small as not to involve duties from each member to the rest; duties to which a sound human mind is requisite. Neither an idiot nor a madman can be a normal citizen. The former ranks as in permanent childhood; the latter, being generally dangerous, must be classed with criminals. A dehumanized brain impairs a citizen's rights because it unmans him,—disabling him from duty, even making him dangerous. In India, such a one now and then runs amuck, stabbing every one whom he meets: in England, he beats and tramples down those nearest to him,—those whom he is most bound to protect. A human community cannot be constituted out of men and brutes, nor ought civilized men to be forced to carry arms or armour for self–defence. For all these reasons, to be drunk is in itself an offence against the community, prior to any statute forbidding it, prior to any misdemeanour superinduced by it. In the State it is both a right and a duty to enforce (as far as its means reach) sobriety on every citizen, rich or poor, in private or in public; and with a view to this, to use such methods as will best prevent, discourage, or deter from intoxication.

When a national religion totally forbids the use of intoxicating drugs, vigilance in the State is less needful: public opinion, or even public show of disgust and violence, effectively stifles the evil. But if the national religion does not forbid the use, but solely enjoins moderation (a word which everyone interprets for himself), a far heavier task falls on the State, whose right and duty nevertheless in this matter several causes have concurred to obscure, not least in England and Scotland. Out of the teachings of Rome, our forefathers very ill learned the rights of the State or the distinction of Morals from Religion. Although even men not highly educated must have known that Moral truth is far older than any special system of Religious beliefs, yet in the popular idea morals have no other basis than religion. Hence, the demand for freedom of conscience against any oppressive State policy (besides the vices of Courts and Courtiers) led to a vehement jealousy of State power even in moral concerns. Many generous minds feared, that to concede to the State a right of enforcing morality, covertly allowed religious persecution. *Who* first uttered the formula—"The only duty of the State is, to protect persons and property"—is unknown to the present writer; but certainly fifty, forty, even thirty years ago, this principle was widely accepted by radical politicians and active–minded dissenters. The late Dr. Arnold of Rugby regarded this denial of the State's moral character as a widespread, untractable and mischievous delusion.

After long torpor the prohibition of Lotteries showed that Parliament was waking to its moral duties. Little by little, the mass of the middle– classes and the gentry imbibed nobler views of human life, and have discovered, that of all the powers which make a nation immoral the State is the most influential. One day of licensed debauch undoes the work of the Clergy on fifty–two Sundays. No wonder that in the past the State collectively has been our worst corrupter: but to open this whole question space does not here allow. A long struggle has gone on, to implore public men not to connive at drunkenness—a national pest which for more than a century was greeted with merriment though politically avowed to be criminal. None dare now to laugh at it, except the depraved men who laugh at bribery, and use drunkenness as a trump–card at elections, and, if in office, rejoice on the vast revenue sucked by the Exchequer out of the vice and misery of the people. Earnest religionists of every creed have happily rallied to a common conviction, that the State has grievously failed of its duty and must now turn over a new leaf. Our worst opponents are men who cannot be reckoned in any religious body, men who find nothing so sacred as Liberty to buy and sell and indulge appetite; generally eccentric "Liberals," who are in many respects too good not to esteem, and too intellectual to despise.

One of these some years ago opened attack on me in a private letter, which summed up the arguments decisive with this class of "advanced Liberals"; in whose hatred of *Over Legislation* I heartily share. He taunted me for thinking that the State ought to concern itself about the drinks of citizens more than about their dress; saying that I could not hold the State to have a control of public morals without, in logical consistency, admitting the right of Parliament to forbid dancing and card–playing; or to command my attendance at any Church worship, or to fine and imprison me for heresy. The double confusion here involved is wonderful from an educated man, and lowers his reputation for good sense. Religion is a topic on which eminent persons and foremost nations widely differ: concerning Moral Duty there is more agreement in mankind than perhaps on anything that is beyond the five senses. To argue that in claiming of the State an enforcement of duties cardinal to citizenship, we admit its right to dictate in religion, is a pestilent anachronism; it confounds Morals with Religion just as did the ancient world, Pagan and Hebrew. Again, the test of soundness in Morals is found in the agreement of the human race. There is no nation, no elementary tribe of men, so ignorant or so besotted, as not to condemn drunkenness as immoral and utterly evil. In justifying penalties against a vice condemned by all mankind, we justify (forsooth!) the punishing of amusements thought harmless by a great majority everywhere. Such an assertion is not the less silly, even in the mouth of a disciple of John Stuart Mill. Of course we all know that Law cannot be made against every misuse of time, or of energy, or of money. There is certainly no danger whatever that a modern Parliament, elected from very different circles and representing widely different elements, will ever adopt as its measure of sound morals the special opinions of any historical sect, however virtuous and wise.

Neither of an individual nor of a community does *the highest interest* consist in Liberty, but in soundness of morals; without which Liberty only means licence to be vicious; licence to ruin oneself, and diffuse misery to others. To a man not proof against the omnipresent drinkshop, high wages are a curse; days called holy and short hours of work do but more quickly engulf him in ruin. But he pulls others too down in his fall. That nearly every Vice tends to waste, and preeminently intoxication by liquors or drugs, certain Economists are strangely slow to learn. Moreover, nearly every widespread vice makes wealth and life less enjoyable to the whole community. Confining remark to the vice of drunkards, it suffices to point in brief to the enormous extension which it gives to Violent Crime, to Orphanhood, to Pauperism, to Prostitution, to disease in Children, and to Insanity. Hence comes an enormous expense for Police and Criminal Courts, for Jails and Jail-officers, for Magistrates and Judges, for Insane Asylums, and Poor Rates. Hence also endless suffering to the victims of crime and to the families of criminals, and a grave lessening of happiness to innocent persons by the ribaldry of drunkards planted at their side, with fear lest their children be corrupted; fear also of personal outrage. Our daily comfort largely depends on homely virtue in our neighbours. In every great organization of industry the drunkenness of workmen is a first-rate mischief to others, crippling enterprise by increased expense and risk. From sailors fond of grog and tobacco, proceed fire in ships out at sea; and on foreign coasts, broils that disgrace England and Christendom, and lay a train which sometimes explodes in war. The drunkenness of a captain has before now stranded a noble ship. On a railroad, access of the engine driver to drink is a prime danger; and shall we say that there is no danger in Parliament legislating when half asleep with wine, and hereby open to the intrigue of any scheming clique, who may wish to fasten suddenly on the nation fraudulent or wicked law? Wisely does the American Congress forbid to its members wine in its own dining-room, because those who have to make sacred law are bound to deliberate and vote with clear heads. Evil law is of all tyrannies the most hateful, and makes a State contemptible to its own citizens—thus preparing Revolution.

English Statesmen have yet to learn Yankee wisdom; but no one who is, or hopes to be, in high office dares to speak lightly of drunkenness. The celebrated Committee of 1834 advised Parliament to reverse its course, with a view to the ultimate *extinction* of the trade in ardent spirits. The advice was disgracefully spurned; yet neither the legislature nor the executive has ever dared to deny that drunkenness is a civil offence. Our opponents plead only for the *use*, not for the *abuse* of intoxicating drink.

No doubt, teetotallers maintain that all use of such liquors for drink is an abuse. The avowals of Dr. William Gull, who calls our view extreme, beside those of Sir Henry Thompson and Dr. Benjamin Richardson, seem to justify the extreme view: so do the Parisian experiments of 1860–1. Yet it is not necessary to go so far *in a political argument*. I desire to obtain common ground with such men as my friend Mr. P. A. Taylor, M.P. for Leicester, and waive our difference with him as to *moderate use*. Let us admit (that is, temporarily) that as Prussic Acid is fatal in ever so small a draught, yet is safe as well as delicious in extract of almonds and in custard flavoured by bay–leaf, so alcohol is harmless, not only in Plum Pudding and Tipsy Cake, but also in one tumbler of Table Beer and one wineglass of pure Claret. Let us further concede that the propensity of very many to excess makes out no case for State–interference against the man whose use of the dangerous drink is so sparing, that no one can discover any ill effect of it on *him*. Nevertheless, irrefutable reasons remain, why we should claim new legislation, and a transference of control over the trade from the magistrates who do not suffer from it to the local public who do.

First of all, let me speak of undeniable excess. At one time perhaps it was punished by exposure in the pillory or stocks; but for a long time past, the penalty (when not aggravated by other offences) has been at most a pecuniary fine: five shillings used often to be inflicted. A "gentleman" who could pay, was let off: a more destitute man might fare worse. Inevitably, the vices of the eighteenth century affected national opinion. The wealthier classes were so addicted to wine, that to be "as drunk as a lord" became a current phrase. From highest to lowest the drunkard was an object more of merriment than of pity, and scarcely at all of censure, unless he were a soldier or sailor on duty. When a host intoxicated his guests, it was called hospitality; to refuse the proffered glass was in many a club an offence to good company. Peers and Members of Parliament, officers of Army and Navy, Clergymen and Fellows of Colleges—nay, some Royal Princes—loved wine, often too much. Who then could be earnest and eager to punish poorer men for love of strong beer? The preaching of Whitefield and Wesley began the awakening of the nation. A very able Spaniard despondingly said of his country: "A profligate individual may be converted, but a debased nation never"; and the recovery no doubt is arduous, when the national taste has been depraved and vicious customs have fixed themselves in society. Even now, few indeed are able to rejoice in the punishment of mere drunkenness; for, the only penalty imagined is a pecuniary fine, which never can prevent repetition nor deter others; when most severe, it does but aggravate suffering to an innocent wife and children. To be "drunk *and disorderly*" is now the general imputation before a magistrate. Unless molestation of others can be charged, the drunkard is very seldom made to feel the hand of the law. Hereby many persons seem to believe (as apparently does one bishop) that, as a part of English *liberty*, every one has a *right* to be drunk. While we complain that authorities are negligent and connive at vice, after accepting and assuming the duty to prevent it; the *sellers* of the drink are open to a severer charge. A man too poor to keep a servant is glad to get a wife to serve him. She is to him housemaid and cook and nurse of his children. For all these functions she has a clear right to full wages, besides careful nurture during motherly weakness. The husband manifestly is bound to supply to his wife *more* than all she might have earned in serving others, before he spends a sixpence on his own needless indulgences: and the publican knows it; knows, sometimes in definite certainty, always in broad suspicion, that he is receiving money which does not in right belong to his customer. Of course he cannot be convicted by law; but in a moral estimate he is comparable to a lottery–keeper who accepts from shopmen money which he suspects is taken from their master's till, or to a receiver of goods which he ought to suspect to be stolen. Such is the immoral aspect of traders, who now claim "compensation," if the twelve– month licences granted to them as privilege, for no merit of their own, be, *in the interest of public morality*, terminated at the end of the twelve months. *In the interest and at the will of landlord magistrates* such traders have borne extinction meekly, over a very wide rural area. What made them *then* so meek and unpretending? Apparently because against powerful Peers and Squires impudence was not elicited in them by the encouragement of a John Bright and a Gladstone.

How then ought the State to deal with a drunkard? Obviously by the most merciful, kind, and effective of all punishments—by forbidding to him the fatal liquor. How much better than asylums for drunkards! asylums which make a job for medical men, take the drunkard away from his family and business, without anything to guarantee that on his release from prison he will have a Will strong enough to resist the old temptation. Such asylums please medical philanthropy; nor is any animosity displayed against them in Parliament. How can we account for the fact, that M.P.'s who strongly oppose interference with the existing shops, and avow as much distress and grief at drunkenness as is possible to any teetotaller, have never proposed to withhold the baneful drink from a convicted drunkard? Did it never come into their heads? Had they never heard of it? This would convict them of ignorance disgraceful in an M.P., still more so in a Minister. Perhaps someone charitably suggests: "They think the prohibition never could be enforced." To this pretence General Neal Dow makes reply: "What we Yankees have done, you English certainly can do, WHENEVER YOU HAVE THE WILL." Nothing is easier, when anyone has been convicted of drunkenness, than to send official notice to all licensed shops (say, within five miles) forbidding them to supply him, under penalty of forfeiting their licences. At the same time it should be a misdemeanour in anyone else to supply him gratuitously. (It would be pedantic here to suggest after how long probation, and under what conditions, this stigma should be effaceable.)

The misery which husband can inflict on wife, or wife on husband, by drunkenness, has led many Yankees further, and—to our shame—we have as yet refused to learn from them. If a wife (with certain legal formalities) forbid the drinkshops to supply her husband, this should be of the same avail, as if the husband were convicted of drunkenness before a magistrate. Of course a husband ought to have the same right against a wife, and either parent against a son or daughter under age. Such an enactment, as it seems to me, ought to be *at once* passed, as a law for all the Queen's realms, not as matter for local option. Passed over the heads of existing magistrates, it would remain valid over whatever authority may succeed them.

This is no place to dwell on any details of horrors inflicted on the country by the present imbecile control. Of course, it is far better than the *free trade* in drink, towards which Liverpool twenty years back took a long stride, with results most wretched and justly repented of. How deadly is now the propensity of the country, will sufficiently appear from an experience of the late Sir Titus Salt in his little kingdom of Saltaire.

For a single year he made trial of granting to four select shops a licence to supply *table beer* in bottles, delivered at the houses in quantity proportioned to the number of inmates;—a more severe limitation than any previously heard of. Yet in the course of some months evil grew up and multiplied. Something stronger than table beer (apparently) had been substituted. The liquor was smuggled into the works. Disobedience and disorders arose; and at length a deputation of his own men complained to him that their *women* at home were getting too much of the drink. At the year's end he cancelled the licences, and to the general content and benefit restored absolute prohibition. Nothing short of this extinguishes the unnatural taste. Female drunkenness is a new vice, at least in any but the most debased of the sex: yet alas! courtly physicians now tell us that it has invaded the boudoirs of great ladies. Such has been the mischief of Confectioners' and Grocers' Licences.

Unsatisfactory as has been the control of the drink trade by the magistrates, their neglect has never been resented in higher quarters, ever since, by gift of the Excise, Parliament made the Exchequer a sleeping partner in the gains of the Drink Trade. The Queen's Exchequer has hence a revenue of about thirty–three millions a year, of which probably two–thirds, say twenty–two millions, is from excess: a formidable sum as hush–money. No earnest reformer expects the leopard to change his spots. A transference of power is claimed, chiefly under the title of Local Option. To give the power to town councils has been proved wholly insufficient in Scotland; though the Right Hon. John Bright seems obstinately to shut eyes and ears to the fact.

Again and again in crowded meetings the Resolution has been affirmed: "The people who suffer by the trade ought to have a veto against it."—Those who seem resolved to oppose every scheme which seeks to break down and restrict this horrible vice, tauntingly reply, that this measure would ensure its continuance in its worst centres. They do but show their own unwisdom herein. The Publicans know far better, and they avow, there is nothing they so much dread as local option. In Maine itself, a State frightfully drunken in the first half of the century, the opponents of Neal Dow in the State Legislature scornfully allowed him to carry a Bill which gave to each parish *Permission* to accept his measure as law. They expected that the drunkards would outvote it: but to their discomfiture found that the drunkards were glad of his law, and nailed it firm. Let all sound–hearted Englishmen trust our suffering population to use their own remedy. Under Local Option we now embrace two systems which have been already discussed in Parliament—that of Sir Wilfrid Lawson, and that upon the outlines of Mr. Joseph Cowen's Bill.

Personally I yield to Sir Wilfrid Lawson the highest honour. Beyond all other men he is the hero in this long battle. If I account his Bill defective, he will not blame me: for in its original form, which he would be glad to carry, it closely resembled the Maine Law, and superseded the Magistrates. He has simplified it by making it only a half–measure. After Parliament has been teazed by the drink question for more than twenty–five years (one might almost say, ever since 1834), after candidates at every election have been made anxious by it, we must calculate that all public men will desire to make a *final* settlement and get rid of the topic in Parliament. But Sir Wilfrid's Bill, whatever its other merits (and I think them great), will not set Parliament free. For so soon as any district adopts his permission to stop the Drink Trade, an outcry must arise from local medical men and chemists and varnishers, demanding new shops for their needs: and intense jealousy will follow, lest the new sellers, though called chemists or grocers or oilmen, presently become purveyors of drink; hence a fresh struggle must continue in our overworked Legislature concerning the new and necessary regulations. Sir Wilfrid's half–measure supersedes neither the Magistrates nor the Parliament, though for two hundred years the Nation has suffered through the laxity of both. Surely we chiefly need real Provincial Legislatures, and, until we get *them*, Local Folk Motes and *Local Elective Boards* are our best substitutes.

This is the other and the complete measure: yet something remains to be said on it. The great evil is, that by reason of competition, a trade cannot live, except by pushing its sales. The Americans have wisely seen that the necessary *sales* must be effected by Agents publicly appointed, with a fixed salary and nothing to gain by an increase of sales. Such Agents must receive public instructions. This was, in fact, Sir Wilfrid's original scheme, only that it forbad absolutely the selling wine or beer for drink, *unless by medical order*; and the last condition would involve in Parliament endless contention. It is simpler, and I think far better, to give to an Elective Board a general free discretion. Parliament *might* indeed dictate that sales should go on through a public officer only.

I, for one, should rejoice in this. But the most eager teetotaller will not hope that in the present generation any English Parliament will be *more* severe against a wine–loving gentry, and more dictatorial to medical men, than is the law of Maine. If therefore it did command that sales should be *without gain*, it certainly would not allow an entire prohibition of selling alcohol as beverage to be imposed on the Agent for sale. It is not so in Maine; and this fact occasioned Mr. Plimsoll's stupendous blunder, who declared in Parliament that the Maine Law was a dead letter in Maine itself. The fact on which he built this outrageously false assertion was that when Mr. Plimsoll asked for Whiskey, the Agent instantly sold it to him without a moment's hesitation. But why? "Because he knew that Mr. Plimsoll was an English M.P. and a teetotaller."